THE CAT HERBAL

By the same author

FAIRY SPELLS: Seeing and Communicating with the Fairies

The Cat Herbal

Simple Green Remedies for Your Cat

Claire Nahmad

Illustrated by Clare Jeapes
with decorations by Martyne Raven

SOUVENIR PRESS

First published 1999 by
Souvenir Press Ltd,
43 Great Russell Street, London WC1B 3PA

ISBN 0 285 63509 3

Typeset by Rowland Phototypesetting Ltd,
Bury St Edmunds, Suffolk

Printed in Great Britain by
Creative Print and Design Group (Wales), Ebbw Vale

This book is dedicated to my sister,
Lindy Nahmad, to her feline
companions Salvador and Siesta, and to
all the cats that came before, especially
Smokey, Fluff, Tom, Sam, She, Ginger,
Sally and Suki, and not forgetting T.C.
and Benny.

Acknowledgements

My great influences in herbalism have been, first and foremost, the illustrious Maria Treben, whose book *Health through God's Pharmacy* (available through G. Baldwin & Co., see Useful Addresses) is a testament to the healing powers of herbs, and which in my opinion no home should be without; David Conway, the Welsh herbalist, whose delightful little herbal *The Magic of Herbs* I highly recommend; Juliette de Baïracli Levy, whose spirited and pioneering book *The Complete Herbal Handbook for the Dog and Cat* should be compulsory reading for all pet-owners; Dr Pitcairn, whose book *Dr Pitcairn's Complete Guide to Natural Health for Dogs and Cats* (with Susan Hubble Pitcairn) is also essential reading; the trio of noble and benevolent doctors, Dr Bach (*The Work of Dr Edward Bach, An Introduction and Guide to the 38 Flower Remedies*), Dr D. C. Jarvis (*Folk Medicine—the Honey and Cider Vinegar Way to Health*), and the venerable Dr Fox of Sheffield (*The Working Man's Family Botanic Guide to Health*), whose shades I salute. I would also like to thank my editor, Tessa Harrow, for her help and guidance; and, finally, my mother, for ensuring that my garden did not revert to a wilderness whilst I worked on *The Cat Herbal*.

Contents

Note to Readers

The aim of this book is to provide information on the uses of herbal remedies in the treatment of various feline diseases and injuries. Although every care has been taken to ensure that the advice is accurate and practical, it is not intended to be a guide to diagnosis. Where your cat's health is concerned—and in particular a serious problem of any kind—it must be stressed that there is no substitute for seeking advice from a qualified veterinary surgeon at the earliest available opportunity. All persistent symptoms, of whatever nature, may have underlying causes that need, and should not be treated without, professional elucidation and evaluation and subsequent monitoring.

It is therefore very important, if you are considering trying herbal remedies to treat your cat, that you consult your veterinary surgeon first, and if the cat is already being treated with prescribed medication, do not stop it.

If your cat has been seriously injured and may require emergency surgery, do not give anything by mouth; a few drops only of Bach Rescue Remedy, placed on the tongue, are all that can be allowed in case the cat needs to be given an immediate anaesthetic.

The Publisher makes no representation, express or implied, with regard to the accuracy of the information contained in this book, and legal responsibility or liability cannot be accepted by the Author or the Publisher for any errors or omissions that may be made or for any loss, damage, injury or problems suffered or in any way arising from following the advice offered in these pages.

Introduction

There is no doubt that human civilisation, especially within the last two hundred years, has inflicted upon the cat, that wild-natured, inscrutable, resilient animal, a loathsome host of miserable diseases which are continuing to burgeon. At one time, perfect health, very rarely impaired or encroached upon, was the common birthright of animals living out their natural lives in the wilderness. Even when human beings began to domesticate them, in our ancient past, this birthright of sound health was not as endangered as it is today. There existed superbly skilled cat doctors, working largely with herbs, true craftsmen and women of their art, who knew how to alleviate feline suffering and effect a full recovery. These cat doctors existed in ancient Egypt and many other parts of the ancient world.

Today, we have our own animal doctors, the veterinary surgeons. We, as owners or human companions of the cat, could not do without these thoroughly trained experts. But a philosophy is in force today, often among the international body of veterinary surgeons as among almost all establishments, that sneers at nature, that considers humanity superior to her provisions, guidance, inspiration, example, and especially her parameters. This philosophy advocates the use of artificial, chemical medicines that seem to express the essence of our own mentality whilst we have developed as a planetary society down the years. These medicines all too often dominate the system and forbid the proper functioning of the animal's own natural resilience and healing propensities; they savagely and speedily suppress the problematic factors causing the disease or condition, and the result is often that the virus or bacteria return in a new form, much strengthened and armed for a fatal encounter with a system weakened, vulnerable and unable to offer proper resistance.

Of course, I am not denigrating veterinary surgeons in any way whatsoever. I have the greatest respect for them as highly-trained specialists to whom we can entrust the care of our sick animal friends for diagnosis and advice. It is simply that I advocate the use of herbs as a holistic, natural method of dealing with illness and disease, a method that is in organic harmony with the body and the environment. Many vets nowadays are interested in and sympathetic to herbal remedies, and make use of them in their own practice.

Some people feel that herbs and cats don't go together. They see cats as entirely carnivorous and believe therefore that herbal medicines are just as unnatural for the cat as chemical medicines. This is a perfectly understandable point of view, but it is in fact a myth. Wild cats are their own wise herbalists, and they consume a variety of herbs, flowers and grasses, leaves and tree-barks, when they live in their natural state. They also consume the intestines of their prey, which are very often herbivores—even rats and mice eat grains and berries. In the wild, their prey would most often be rabbits, birds and young deer, from the stomachs of which they would consume ingested seeds, fruits and vegetation; and so cats, by nature, make use of herbs, and are kept healthy by them, when human beings do not intervene in their lives.

Because of our cruel, thoughtless and greedy treatment of the animal kingdom throughout history, I feel we owe our animal brethren an unconscionable debt, perhaps especially to cats, as the feline has suffered more at our hands than any other animal (except, of course, those countless millions who suffer miseries and indignity through modern farming methods, or, even worse, the desperate, lonely and agonised laboratory animals, whose fate is too dreadful to contemplate). It was common practice at one time in our western civilisation to torture and abuse cats, and even now, when they have attained such widespread popularity that they are generally treated with the affection and respect they deserve, our pollution of the environment and our ignorance of their needs has caused us unconsciously to afflict them with many a distressing disease that they would never have contracted if they lived roaming free in the wild.

It is my sincere hope that this book will help all human carers and companions of the feline to pay back a small part of the debt we owe, by returning to them their health and vitality through proper feeding and the therapeutic use of herbs. Moreover, I hope you will catch my enthusiasm for herbs and the wonders and marvels of their spirit-endowed cosmic forces, that factor X which we do not fully comprehend at present, but which one day we will, without at all removing from them their inherent mystery and the intimation that they are bestowed by divine benison. All the herbs in this book are helpful to humans as well as to cats. If you want to use them for yourself as well as your cat, as I hope you will, simply increase the *amount* taken ten times, and put in one heaped, rather than one rounded, teaspoonful of herb per cup.

I am connected to the famous Welsh herbal doctors known as Meddygion Myddfai by my Welsh grandfather, Levi Edwards, whose family were herbalists, and to an English herbal tradition by my grandmother, a natural Yorkshire 'wisewoman' who also used healing herbs. In his book *The Magic of Herbs* (an excellent little herbal and one of my favourites), David Conway tells the story of Nelferch, a nymph of a lake called Llyn-y-Fan Fach in the Black Mountain in Wales, who left her home to marry a widower's son, Gwyn. He fell in love with her when he saw her whilst watching his cattle one day, and persuaded her to marry him, after his third attempt, by finally offering her semi-baked bread. She left him after some years, as is always the case in such stories, because he broke the conditions imposed on him when Nelferch's promise of marriage was given. In this instance, he struck her three times, although only trivially or playfully on each occasion. They made their sorrowful farewells, and Nelferch returned to the depths of the Black Mountain lake. She only ever emerged once more, appearing to her eldest son, Rhiwallon, to prophesy that he and all his male descendants would become herbal physicians, and to this effect she presented him with a sack of herbs and a series

of teachings on how to use them. Her advice was recorded
in a thirteenth-century manual inscribed in Welsh which contains almost one thousand herbal recipes. My grandfather
Levi brought his herbal knowledge to his family from his
own father, and although I have few historical details, I like
to think that his medical botany derived directly from this
Celtic source, even if, as I am the one to have inherited it, it
would make Nelferch's prophecy slightly off-focus! Whatever
the truth is, it is certain that many of the herbal recipes in
this book are drawn from an ancient Celtic source, and that
faery women and the inland waters they inhabit are potent
healing symbols in the Celtic cosmology. In this context, it
is interesting to remember that the Celtic mother-goddess,
Ceridwen, spirit of the rising moon and the stars, was
attended by a train of white cats who carried out her orders
on earth. Ceridwen had a great cauldron which she used to
brew up her healing magic with herbs and flowers, so it would
seem apposite that her herbal tradition (for all the faery
women of Wales were associated with Ceridwen and her
magic cauldron) should be used for the health and healing
of cats.

It only remains to say—with apologies to Dr Fox, the
respected nineteenth-century herbal physician of Sheffield, for
appropriating and adulterating his quote—that I hope this
book will ensure there is help at hand for even the most
seemingly hopeless cases of feline suffering.

> That cats may live in health and joy
> And all their varied powers employ,
> And die by weight of years.

Chapter One

Keeping Your Cat Healthy

'Let food be your medicine, and let medicine be your food'. Such was the motto of the ancient Greek doctor Hippocrates. You can keep your cat healthy and long-lived by providing it with food that will nourish and revitalise it, banish toxins and bestow longevity. Unfortunately the commercial brands of cat food will not give these results if they are not generously supplemented.

First, it is essential that your cat is not given an all-meat diet. This taxes the kidneys heavily and causes poor bone formation. I would advise that two days of the week, four days apart, are kept completely meat-free. A wide selection of fresh, non-meat substances should be given, chosen from those listed below. On one of the days, fast the cat from noon until the morning of the next day, keeping it on liquids only, and giving it laxative herbs late in the evening.

MEATS

Give poultry, rabbit, fresh fish (not too much, or else the cat will develop thiamine deficiency), liver (again, feed restricted amounts because vitamin A poisoning will result from over-provision), lamb and breast of mutton. Meaty bones are very good for cats, but they should be provided immediately or shortly after meals so that the stomach is cushioned against them. **Never** offer cooked bones; they become brittle and splinter into dangerous shards. If you follow these two simple rules, your cat will derive healthful benefits from chewing on bones, and will come to no harm.

OTHER PROTEIN FOODS

Replace meats frequently, and supplement your cat's diet freely, with non-meat protein foods such as cheese (in limited measures as it is very fatty and the body stores toxins in fat, which can build up quickly, with negative results for the cat's health), eggs (give the yolks raw; egg-white must *always* be offered well-cooked), mashed potatoes (most useful for combining with fresh, finely chopped herbs), brown rice (a highly nutritious food), cottage cheese (a cheese much lower in fat than the hard varieties, so plenty can be given), yogurt (excellent for the stomach—I have found that animals generally develop a taste for strawberry yogurt, a doubly beneficial food, as all the edible berries are prime health tonics), wholemeal bread and a variety of grains such as barley, rye, oats and corn (maize). I have found it better not to feed animals too much wheat, as an overabundance makes them lethargic and causes stomach problems. Bran should be given in minute doses to compensate for the roughage lost to the cat when skin and hair are not available for them to eat along with their meat, as it would be in the wild. Don't give more than a sprinkling (added to meat feeds) as it can be an irritant to the stomach. However, you can feed tinned corn freely. I dislike tinned products for both humans and felines, but corn or maize, together with pineapple, are perhaps the only two foods that do not lose a significant amount of their vitamin content during canned storage. Most cats love corn, and it is rich in vitamins and protein. Feed oats in flakes—don't cook them, but soak them overnight in milk. Rye can be given as crispbreads. Barley is given as flour (see below).

Nuts are an excellent source of protein, vitamins and minerals, but they have to be ground and made into flour before being offered as a safe and palatable food. Walnuts, peanuts (only uncooked—never roasted) and almonds are best for cats. Stir about a teaspoonful a day, three days a week, into the early morning cereal feed. Barley flour can be used in the same way. Never use pine kernels which, although highly nutritious for dogs, are harmful to cats, as pine oil is toxic to them. Desiccated coconut is a good tonic for cats, and should be added to cereals, one teaspoonful three days a week. Slices of raw mushroom are also appreciated.

ROOT VEGETABLES

All root vegetables are good for cats, but feed no more than a heaped teaspoonful at a time, very finely minced, as otherwise they will be unable to digest it. Remember to scrub, or at least to scald, carrots before grating, because of the liver fluke, a parasite that attacks the liver and can be difficult to banish.

GREENS

It is most important for a cat's health that it should be given a 'side portion' of greens with every meal. These can be cooked vegetables (sprouts, green beans, asparagus, etc.) lightly boiled and mashed (particularly into potatoes, which can be served with a little sea salt and butter, or mixed directly into the meat), or finely shredded salad vegetables, treated similarly. Sometimes the cat will eat them as they are, if the minced greens are combined with sweetcorn, or a teaspoonful of desiccated coconut is sprinkled over them.

FRUIT

Cats generally like to chomp on slices of apple or pear; they will often eat berries with relish (see Fruit Jelly, p. 18), and they enjoy slices of melon or juicy peaches. See what your cat likes best, and pander to its preferences. If its stomach is a little upset after eating fruit, feed it with a spoonful of barley water, barley flour, slippery elm gruel or arrowroot jelly. This hardly ever fails to eliminate the problem.

HERBS

Many of these are mentioned in the text; however, you will help to keep your cat in optimum health if you take care to feed the following, chopped very fine and given as herb salads (cats cannot digest cellulose properly, so all green matter has to be snipped or chopped until it is well minced): dandelion (stems and leaves); clover; feverfew; wild garlic; fennel; nasturtium; mallow; watercress; mint; parsley; catmint; couchgrass; chickweed; speedwell; borage; balm; comfrey; sage; raspberry leaves; blackcurrant leaves; sorrel; lime leaves; elm leaves; and St John's wort.

WATER

Provide fresh drinking water at all times. I prefer to use spring water, which is free of the chemical processes and disinfectants of the water companies (true, it does contain an infinitesimal amount of arsenic, but I still find it preferable!). I also like to add a few drops of apple cider vinegar to the drinking bowl, which ought to be ceramic, not metal or plastic. Barley water (see p. 20 for the recipe) can also be added to the drinking water. However, if your cat obviously doesn't approve of these additions, leave the water unadulterated; it is probably wiser to make additions to it only every other day.

MILK

Be careful of giving too much milk, because it can upset the entire digestive system of an adult cat. Some cats significantly lack the enzyme lactase, which is needed to digest the milk starch lactose, and the result is malabsorption of the small intestines (the cat cannot assimilate its food properly) with accompanying diarrhoea and abdominal pain. Milk also forms an unhealthy mucus in the stomach, which nurtures worm infestations. This does not mean that milk should be considered a banned or useless food; on the contrary, it is good for cats, but only in small doses. I would recommend no more than one saucerful every other day (three a week in all), and if your cat has difficulty even with this restricted amount, leave it out of the diet altogether. There are some preparations available on the market nowadays that are lactose free. They might be worth a try, so ask your vet for details. Otherwise, feed your cat fresh milk, not the powdered or long-life adulterations, as it is by far the healthiest.

TONIC FOODS

The following foods all have a tonic effect, which will dispel mental and physical lethargy and malaise, and help to keep your cat in optimum condition. Balance is the key to good health, so don't be tempted to go overboard and give too much, or the therapeutic virtues of these power foods will be lessened. Feed some regularly in the stated doses, where indicated. Others can be given a few times a week, or every now and then as a treat.

Honey

This food was considered to be the ambrosia of the gods, and in fact it is a miraculous substance. It contains within it every mineral and every vitamin needed to sustain life, in the exact tiny amounts which the animal body requires each day. It is a natural sedative, yet it gives energy and renews vitality. It calms, strengthens, nourishes and purifies, because amongst its other virtues it is also an antiseptic. It protects the stomach and rests the entire system, because it has been predigested in the stomach of the honey bee—an animal which is viewed as a mystical priest of the garden and the wilderness in ancient folklore, humming anthems of praise as it visits its earthly temple, composed of flower shrines. Honey heals and restores. It is a manifestation of the healing life-force of the sun. Hippocrates esteemed this substance above any other. When he died, bees swarmed and clustered on his grave, and it was said that the honey which these bees gave was imbued with magical healing properties of wondrous power and divine potency.

Many similar stories are told of bees in folklore ancient and modern—bees which cluster on their keeper's grave if that person possessed saintly virtues. Three or four years ago, my local television station ran a news story about bees which swarmed around the house of their keeper after she had died and had been laid out inside, awaiting burial. There were television pictures of the bees swarming, hovering and reswarming above her front door.

Honey drops (small balls of solid honey) can be given, either plain or combined with shredded herbs (very finely minced), a few drops of apple cider vinegar (see below), or with either of these and rolled in barley, nut, or slippery elm bark flour (simple cornflour will do, just to make them less sticky). Give plentifully in illness, and one or two a day (depending on the size and age of the cat) on a regular basis. Push them gently down the throat (see Giving Pills p. 21).

Apple Cider Vinegar

Another of nature's miracle foods, this vinegar conveys the healthful properties of the apple in concentrated form. It provides potassium in an acid base, which is how it is best assimilated by the body (potassium is vital for the functioning of all the major organs). It rids the body of rheumatism and arthritis, especially when taken in conjunction with honey, sterilises the digestive tract, and seeks out and destroys harmful bacteria and morbid deposits in the system. It eliminates unhealthy acids from the kidneys, peps up the stomach, guards against heart problems and calms the nerves. Give one teaspoonful per day (always diluted!), either in spring-water and honey, combined with honey drops (a few neat drops are mixed into them) sprinkled over food (meat and vegetables only—don't put into milk or cereals) or in the drinking water. A combination of these methods is best. Always buy *apple* cider vinegar, rather than just cider vinegar, as the latter is often a product of only the cores and the skin. Boots the chemists sell a vinegar that is made from whole, organically grown apples.

Parsley

This is truly a tonic herb for cats, and it should be included in their diet every day. Chop or snip very finely, and mix into the meat. If your cat hates it, make a tisane by pouring boiling water (in this case about one-quarter of a cup) over a palmful of the herb, letting it infuse for one minute, and then using it to pour over the food, or to give by dropper if there is no other way.

Stinging Nettles

This is another invaluable tonic, which can be added to a meat stew (use the new, tender tops and let them simmer for five minutes—they can be put inside cat-sized dumplings made with cornflour, too), or used to make an infusion which can be poured over the meat, into the drinking water (don't let it stand for more than 12 hours, though—it does go off quite quickly, certainly within 24 hours in hot weather) or other cereals if it is sweetened with honey. Cats seem to find the taste quite pleasant.

Catnip

There have been dire warnings over the past few years concerning the sinister nature of this herb. Cat owners have been told to beware of giving too much, as it has a hallucinogenic effect on cats. It is not right to rubbish other people's experiences and conclusions, so do please bear the warning in mind; but I have to say that catnip is one of nature's most beneficial herbs, for humans as well as cats, and that I have never known its effect on felines to be anything but benign. My advice is to give it every few days as a treat, or, better still, to grow a patch in the garden, if possible, and to allow the cat free access. Catnip has certainly never adversely influenced the behaviour of my cats, but if you do notice peculiar behavioural changes, then of course immediately begin to limit the cat's consumption.

Valerian

A little fresh valerian is a definite pick-me-up for an exhausted, depressed or recuperating cat. Here I *would* advise

caution in feeding, because a little goes a long way! Sometimes cats don't eat it, but simply give themselves a rub with
it. Put a small amount in the food, very finely minced, or
sprinkle it over cereals. Dried valerian is beneficial too. Tie
together a few sprigs of it, dried or fresh, and place in the
cat's bed to help recuperation after illness, or to cheer a
lethargic cat that is depressed after a physical or emotional
trauma. Its nervine properties are similar to those of catnip,
only stronger, especially in the roots.

Couchgrass
Allow your cat access to couchgrass, because it is a strong
dissolvent and cleanser, and contains many minerals and
trace elements necessary to the feline. Gather it and snip it
very finely if your cat is an indoor cat. You will find it growing
wild on wasteland in cities, or even growing at the edge of
pavements and walls, in fact wherever nature can take a hold.
Take care not to gather this coarse, wiry grass (it is a bladed
grass that can slice into flesh quite nastily if pulled up care-
lessly) along verges that are bombarded with exhaust fumes
or contaminated by dogs. Give a heaped teaspoonful three
or four times a week. Most cats will eat it happily, but if
your cat is an exception, a standard tisane will be a great
health benefit. Give five dropperfuls night and morning, four
times a week.

Kelp
Both Juliette de Baïracli Levy (*The Complete Herbal Handbook for the Dog and Cat*) and the American doctor D.C.
Jarvis pioneered the inclusion of seaweed in the diet of animals and humans. All the minerals and nutrients from the
land continually wash into the sea, occupying as it does the
lowest portion of the planet's surface. Glaciers, rivers and
the ever-moving winds transport and discharge particles
which course downwards to the sea. Whilst the land is eroded
and impoverished, the sea swells and grows rich. As Dr Jarvis
points out, the oceans are the catch-basin of the land. Therefore, by consuming food from the sea, we can replace those
nutrients lost to us from the land. Giving your cat fish from

the sea would be one way of doing this; but with seas so heavily contaminated these days, it would seem wiser to choose kelp as a regular addition to the diet. It is a cleanser, and unless the pollutants are overwhelming, it purifies itself and its own environment. It is rich in iodine, which can be displaced in the body by too great a salt intake, by stress, by eating food grown in iodine-impoverished conditions, by chlorine-treated drinking water, and by the action of nervous stress on the body cells. Lack of iodine produces such nervous stress, so the problem becomes a vicious circle. Iodine is needed to sharpen the intelligence and the reactions, to give calm and poise to the mentality and the nervous system, to renew the energy circuits of the body and to eliminate unwanted fat, which is a dumping-ground for toxins. Only a few drops of iodine are present in the entire human body (obviously less in the feline), and yet its presence balances the health of the whole organism.

Administer one-quarter of a five-grain kelp tablet to your cat per day. It has to be given with a meal; and as cats dislike the taste, it is necessary to disguise the crushed quarter-tablet in a strong-tasting food, such as hard cheese (white cheeses are better for cats—they find the yellow kind difficult to digest). A little piece can be given as a treat before a meal, with the quarter-tablet, compact or powdered, concealed within it.

Dried Fruits

These can be given, thoroughly diced and mixed with a little oatmeal, cream and honey. Most cats will usually be enthusiastic about this meal. Give it twice a week, and use only enough cream to moisten and combine the fruits and oatmeal. Dates, figs, apricots, raisins, sultanas, currants, in fact any kind of dried fruit, can be given. Don't give more than a good teaspoonful of the fruits, and add the oatmeal in the same measure. Make sure that the cat drinks plenty on the days that you serve dried fruit, because it soaks up fluids from the stomach wall, and can cause aching and bloating if the stomach becomes dehydrated.

Turmeric
This powerful healer, so honoured in India's Ayurvedic medicine, aids the digestion, sees off infections, inhibits tumours (especially in animals), prevents dysentery and arthritis, attacks intestinal parasites, protects the liver, gall bladder and heart, and eases congestion. See if your cat will tolerate it sprinkled sparingly over meat (less than one-eighth of a teaspoonful, twice a day, once or twice a week). If the cat refuses to be a curry connoisseur, give the same dose in a little warm, semi-skimmed milk.

Ginger
Ginger is warming and disinfectant, and contains many healing virtues. 'Every good quality is contained in ginger' is an old Indian saying. Use a pinch in warm milk, on cereals, or in the honey drops you feed to your cat.

Garlic
Garlic is a healing wonder, a powerful antibiotic and anti-protozoan (it kills microbials and other parasites in the blood and in the system generally). Grate a small clove over the meat daily, disguise it in cheese or wrap it in honey drops. Never give more than about half a teaspoonful a day, and never all at once. Miraculous as it may be, it can be an irritant to the stomach in incorrect doses.

Barley Water
This is a most soothing and healing preparation. See p. 20 for the recipe and correct dosage.

Brown Wholegrain Rice and Lentils
This is a power food, rich in energy and nutrition. It can be provided once or twice a week.

Fruit Jelly
This is composed of a selection of fresh berries. See p. 18 for the recipe and the appropriate amount to feed.

Yogurt
This food is restorative and demulcent, and can be given in small doses several times a week. Sometimes cats will accept fruit yogurts, but if not, whip up plain yogurt with a small amount of cream and honey. This should make it go down very well.

Yeast
Give a small pinch every now and again on food and cereals. Yeast is a power healer, but too much can cause fermentation where it should not take place.

Oils
Sesame, corn and sunflower are the three edible oils that are good for cats. Give a small teaspoonful mixed well into a rice or lentil dish, or half the amount in meat feeds, several times a week.

Linseed Tea
This preparation is very therapeutic for cats. Pour a pint of boiling water onto half a tablespoonful of linseed and a teaspoonful of liquorice root, seal the vessel, allow to stand in a warm place for five hours, then strain and refrigerate. *Always* warm before administering. Pour half a tablespoonful onto the meat feed from time to time, mix it into a potato or rice dish, or give it by dropper as a tisane. The tea will keep fresh for a week in the refrigerator.

Herbs
Dandelion, wild garlic, clover, watercress and feverfew are all tonic herbs to serve as finely minced greens. Give about a teaspoonful at a time. (See Chapter Five for a description of their respective properties.)

If you have to use dry feed, please consider combining it with parsley water, nettle water, linseed tea or a tisane prepared from the small-flowered willowherb, as dried foods cause the urine to become concentrated and stagnant. This promotes the development of cystitis, a common and painful condition in cats which can also adversely affect the kidneys.

*   *   *

Finally. Some people, knowing my pro-vegetarian stance, have questioned my recommendation of a fish and meat diet for cats. I do share the mystical belief (voiced in the Bible and championed by many philosophers and prophets through the ages) that all living beings on earth will one day thrive on an unadulterated vegetarian diet. I am not a specialist in animal nutrition, so I cannot advise here on the intricacies of an adequate vegetarian diet; but I do very much approve of the idea, and I would heartily recommend Juliette de Baïracli Levy's booklet on the subject, *Healthy Vegetarian Dogs and Cats*.

Chapter Two

Nursing Your Cat at Home

When your cat is ill, it needs peace and quiet in a warm, clean, well-ventilated room free from draughts. Provide a snug bed with bedding that can be changed regularly. Make sure that the bed is large enough for the cat to lie stretched out if it wishes; if its body temperature is lower than normal (keep a check) you will need to provide a hot water bottle, but supply it very warm rather than scalding hot, as they can cause burns. To doubly insure against this, wrap the bottle in a thin towel before placing it near the patient. Litter trays must also be provided, and changed every day, as the cat must not be allowed out of doors until it has completely recovered. It is a good idea, though, to sit outside and nurse it for a while in the sun and fresh air, although this is not advisable if the weather is cold. Unless it is a very warm, sunny day, put a blanket round your cat whilst you are nursing it. For the duration of its illness, young children and other animals should not be allowed to disturb the patient. In the evening, keep electric lights rather dimmer than usual, and use lamps rather than ceiling lights. A bright overhead light is distressing to a sick cat.

FEEDING

Fasting an ailing cat is almost always good for it. Wild animals fast naturally when they are ill. Their instinct tells them not to eat because all the limited energies of the body must be unified in fighting the disease or condition which afflicts it. There are none spare for the complicated process of digestion and elimination. Food should not be given unless the patient readily accepts it. It is *vital*, however, to provide plenty of fluid. You will be giving your cat the necessary herbal tisanes and infusions, of course, and feeding it honey and apple cider vinegar in spring water, as advised in the text (the usual dose is half a tablespoonful of apple cider vinegar and one large heaped teaspoonful of honey per half-cup of water); but also make fresh water available, and give a little milk if the cat will take it. Never give cold liquids, especially to a sick cat. Herbal tisanes can be given very warm, whilst other liquids are best given no cooler than tepid.

INVALID DIET

Dr Fox's Invalid Jelly

Beat up the yolk of an egg in a bowl, add six tablespoonfuls of mashed potato, mix well, add a little boiling water until the whole is converted into a jelly, and mix again. Add a little warm milk and honey, and give a few teaspoonfuls as a semi-liquid feed every four hours.

Fruit Jelly

All the berry fruits are good healers. Take one-quarter of a pint of cranberries, blackcurrants, blackberries, raspberries, gooseberries and strawberries, if available (i.e. fill a cup with an assortment of these fruits), add two tablespoonfuls of spring water and simmer very gently for fifteen minutes. Add half a tablespoonful of honey, mix well, and give one teaspoonful night and morning.

Beef Tea
Dice half a pound of beef, put the pieces in a basin with half a tablespoonful of butter, two cloves, two small onions and a teaspoonful of salt. Put into the oven on a medium heat for fifteen minutes and stir well until it produces a thin gravy; add a pint of water, let it simmer very gently for twenty minutes, skimming off every particle of fat; when done, pass through a sieve. Take up a tablespoon by dropper, and give it to the patient every six hours.

Rice, Parsley and Cheese Gruel
Cook the rice in the usual way, using milk and water; then combine it with mashed potato, add a handful of parsley, *very* finely chopped, mix all together well, and add enough milk to make it runny. Then stir in enough cottage cheese to form a pasty consistency. Give two teaspoonfuls every three hours.

Oatmeal Gruel
Take a tablespoonful of the meal, mix with a little salt and stir it slowly in a pint of gently simmering water for five to seven minutes. Skim, and add enough plain yogurt to make it runny. Feed three teaspoonfuls every four hours.

Sago Gruel
Stir two tablespoonfuls of pearl sago into a pint of water, and add a little salt; boil for about fifteen minutes, until converted into a thick jelly. Sweeten and thin with honey. Give three teaspoonfuls every four hours.

Herbal Honey Drops
Small balls of solid honey, mixed with the shredded relevant herbs and a few drops of neat apple cider vinegar, should be pushed gently down the throat. Give one or two every three hours.

Slippery Elm Gruel
Beat a tablespoonful of powdered elm bark into paste with water, adding a little salt, and stir into a pint of yogurt thinned with milk, just beginning to boil; take the yogurt

from the heat, and continue stirring for two or three minutes, until the elm is dissolved. It can be sweetened with honey. Give two teaspoonfuls every four hours.

Tapioca Jelly
Soak the tapioca for three or four hours in water; spread it on a broad dish, pour additional water over it to cover one inch in depth; simmer over a slow heat until the jelly is formed. It can also be made with milk or yogurt, and sweetened with honey, for extra nourishment.

Arrowroot Jelly
This is made by mixing half a teaspoonful of arrowroot with half a cupful of boiling water; season with nutmeg and honey, and give two teaspoonfuls every four hours.

Jellied Pearl Barley
Take smallest China rice and pearl barley, of each two table-spoonfuls; isinglass and hartshorn shavings, of each one tablespoonful; boil in three pints of water until it is reduced to one pint; when cold, a jelly is formed. Mix a heaped teaspoonful of this jelly into a broth of beef tea and stinging nettle tops, and give three tablespoonfuls night and morning.

Barley Water
Boil two ounces of pearl barley for a few minutes in a little water (two heaped tablespoonfuls); strain, add four pints of boiling water; boil down to two pints, add honey and grape juice until the whole measures two and a half pints. Give six dropperfuls every three hours.

*   *   *

Choose a few of these recipes, and feed to the patient accordingly. If you choose more than four, halve the stated dose. Don't give any solids if the cat is on a complete fast (most of the preparations given above can be fed in virtual liquid form), but as it recovers make thick gruels of some of the recipes and give them as an intermediate stage between liquids and a normal diet. The herbal honey drops should be given even when the cat is on a complete fast, as honey is such a marvellous healer and restorative.

SPOONFEEDING

Some cats will cooperate without coercion. If yours won't, take it firmly by the scruff of the neck, twist your wrist so that the head tilts backwards and the mouth falls open. Give the liquid in drops from the bowl of the spoon, making sure that the cat swallows after every quarter of a teaspoonful to avoid choking.

GIVING PILLS

If the cat is docile and cooperative, it is simply a case of sitting it on a table, grasping the head from above at the corners of the mouth where the jaws meet, tipping the head back and, with your right hand, opening the mouth by pushing on the lower jaw with your forefinger and pulling down (use your nail rather than the soft tip of your finger in case you get bitten!). Push the pill very quickly right to the back of the mouth, over the mound of the tongue. Then close the cat's mouth and gently stroke and massage its throat until it swallows by reflex action. Herbal pills are always soft pills (unless you buy commercial brands which are compacted), which makes life a little easier for the cat.

ADMINISTERING MEDICINES BY DROPPER

Follow the directions given for spoonfeeding. The dropper should be emptied in two squirts, half a dropperful at a time, one before the cat first swallows and one directly afterwards. The procedure is brisk. Where washings of the throat have to be given by the herbal tisanes (as in tonsillitis, for instance), the solution has to be given in half dropperfuls to obtain the washing effect, which means emptying the dropper one-quarter of its measure at a time into the mouth.

Some cats hate being given medicine. They salivate

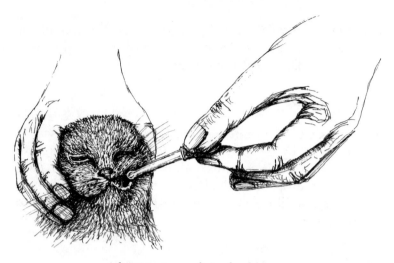

Administering medicine by dropper.

profusely, and the tisane is ejected with the overflowing sal-iva. By tilting the head firmly and emptying the dropper right onto the back of the tongue, most of the medicine will go down. However, see below for methods of dealing with complete non-cooperation.

THE INTRANSIGENT CAT

When your cat puts up a mighty resistance to treatment, the only way to transfer medicine or other necessary liquids from the spoon or dropper into the cat, or to administer pills, is to wrap a large towel or blanket firmly twice around the cat's body, so that it is swaddled like a papoose with its head sticking out at the top. This neatly puts paid to all resistance, although you may need to enlist help to give the medicine or pills, as the patient will certainly not keep its mouth open for you. Speak reassuringly to the cat during the procedure and be as gentle as possible, which might allay its probable suspicion that you have suddenly decided to murder it. Here are two other methods which have been proved to work when faced with a thoroughly intransigent cat (although I cannot offer any guarantees). The first is to talk to the cat when it is calm and not stressed in any way (i.e. when you are not trying to administer medication). Speak to it intelligently, and explain clearly and precisely why it needs to take the medicine, how the medicine will help it, and the dire consequences that will result if the medicine continues to be refused. Don't assume an authoritarian or condemnatory tone, just chat as it were in confidence, and do this whenever you have the opportunity. Language is not meaning itself, it is simply the vehicle of meaning and communication. The second method is to instruct your astral body to visit the cat's astral body as you both sleep, and to explain simply and earnestly how important it is that the cat cooperates. This may sound very strange, but there is an overwhelming amount of evidence for the existence of such an astral body, and no evidence against it. The trick is to programme your sleeping self to do as your waking self bids. One way to do this is to supplicate your guardian angel. Ask out loud that you may be helped to achieve your objective (tell the angel in clear and definite language what your objective is) and repeat this three times before falling asleep. You will probably not be able to give this method much credibility at the moment, but if you follow the instructions as I have given them, and your cat gradually begins to offer less resistance to your nursing efforts, you may change your mind! A third method is simply to ask the angels to help the cat to cooperate with its medication, particularly the great Angel of the Animals or Bast, the Egyptian cat goddess. I have found it most helpful to sincerely petition St Francis to help in the matter. When we are faced with seemingly insoluble problems, the way forward always seems to be to trust in a higher power and let go at the confused and limited earthly level. Then help comes to us, and the impossible knot falls away.

ENEMAS

It is little known how effective enemas can be in cases of serious disease. Dr Fox, a much esteemed nineteenth-century medical botanist who lived and practised in Sheffield, said of enemas:

they are invaluable agents where the powers of life are so much impaired that a rational fear is entertained as regards the administration of cathartics by mouth. We can speak from our own experience, and with confidence say that we have seen diseases of the most malignant character relieved, and in some instances cured, where medicines in any other form were inadmissible, such as tetanus, vomiting, inflammation of the bowels, colic, fits, fevers, diarrhoea, dysentery and putrid sore throats where the patient was unable to swallow. Injections composed of bayberry, cayenne and lobelia are useful in cases of suspended animation.

Dr Pitcairn (author of *Dr Pitcairn's Complete Guide to Natural Health for Dogs and Cats*) also speaks highly of the therapeutic value of enemas. The dose for an adult cat is one teacupful of solution. It is injected, part by part, into the anus with a syringe. It is gradually and gently done, and the infusion used is always comfortably warm. These enemas cause no distress or discomfort to the cat if undertaken properly. Use a small bulb rectal syringe and work steadily and slowly, keeping the cat's hindquarters raised throughout the procedure. Have a plastic bowl on hand for the bowel evacuation that the enema will induce. If it does not happen, up to half a pint of solution may be injected. It is helpful to have assistance on hand to soothe the cat and hold it in position.

ELIZABETHAN COLLAR

These are invaluable for prevention of interference with compresses and poultices, or when the cat must not scratch or groom itself. Simply cut out three-quarters of a circle of cardboard, fit it like a cone around your cat's neck and join the ends together with sticky tape.

STEAM BATHS AND INHALATIONS

Put the cat in an open-mesh carrying cage and suspend it firmly above a bowl on the floor. Pour very hot water into the bowl

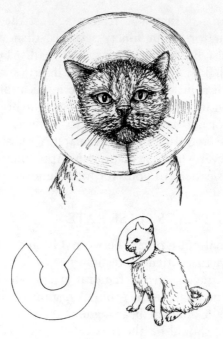

How to make and fit an Elizabethan collar.

(from the kettle, just off the boil) and put in the therapeutic oil or the herbal infusion relevant to the cat's condition (eucalyptus oil or Friar's Balsam (just a little) is good for respiratory problems). A heavy towel should be thrown over the top of the cage, large enough to drape over and cover all sides, to prevent the vapours from escaping. Ideally, the cat should be three and half feet above the steaming water, but take care that the initial vapour is not scalding as it rises. Stay with the cat to make sure that it does not detach the cage from its suspension and land in the boiling water! Allow about ten minutes before finishing the steam bath.

TAKING A CAT'S TEMPERATURE

Ask a friend to hold the cat in place by grasping its scruff. Talk to it and stroke it as you slide a stubby-ended thermometer gently into the anus until about one inch or two centimetres of it is inside the cat. Move the thermometer carefully until you can feel that it is resting against the wall of the rectum. Wait for about ninety seconds, then withdraw it, clean it whilst holding it steady, and read. Make sure the mercury is shaken down firmly before insertion. Dipping the instrument in a little corn oil before application will make the operation more comfortable for the patient.

A cat's normal temperature varies between 38.6°C and 39°C (101°F and 102°F). If the mercury shows a reading above this level, your cat is feverish. Apply herbal remedies and take the patient to your vet for diagnosis.

CHECKING A CAT'S PULSE RATE

A cat's normal pulse rate is between 110 and 140 beats per minute when the patient is resting. Check it by putting the tips of your fingers on the femoral artery which is located deep inside the thigh, in the groin. A healthy cat has a strong, regular pulse. Count the beats against the seconds hand of a watch. There should be about two beats per second.

MOVING A SICK OR INJURED CAT

Put a sheet under the cat and transport it as if in a hammock. Restrict movement of its body as much as possible. Take it to a warm, quiet place where you can begin nursing it, and put a blanket round it. Make up a hot water bottle, but ensure the water is very warm, not boiling, and place it near the cat, only not too close in case the cat should come in contact with it and suffer burns and blisters (overheating can worsen shock). Let the cat lie flat, without raising its head, so that it is in no danger of being choked by blood, saliva or vomit. Don't give anything by mouth, as the vet may need to administer anaesthetic. A few drops of **Dr Bach's Rescue Remedy** may be put onto the tongue. If the cat is in shock without injury, or you cannot contact a vet for some reason, follow the instructions for Shock, p. 132.

ARTIFICIAL RESPIRATION

You may need to resuscitate the cat. Check that the airway is clear, then put your lips close to the cat's nostrils and emit a steady stream of air directly into them for three seconds. Stop for the count of two seconds, then repeat. The second method is to lay both palms on the cat's chest over the ribcage and depress briskly to force out air from the lungs. Don't press too hard, or you may damage the ribs, or cause the cat to vomit and choke itself. Release the pressure immediately so that the chest expands and the lungs fill with air. Wait for five seconds, then repeat the procedure until the cat regains breath.

HYGIENE

Keep the cat, its bed and bedding, its toilet tray (you may well need to employ more than one) and its environment scrupulously clean during its illness. Use a **dodecine** preparation (read the label), which is safest for cats. Other types of disinfectant can harm them.

Chapter Three

Preparing and Administering Herbs

GATHERING HERBS

Gather your herbs in a basket; a wide, flat one is better than a deep small one. Never use plastic bags, as herbs wilt and turn black and slimy very quickly inside them. Metal containers are also harmful to them.

When an illness is severe, it is important to use fresh herbs to treat it. Once gathered, the sooner they are brewing in the pot and administered to the patient, the better. If you find it impractical to seek out the herbs in the wild so that they come fresh to the pot every day, gather enough to last a few days. Lay them out in your basket, taking care not to crush them. At home, let them lie flat on clean paper or cloth, lightly covered with kitchen paper, in a cool, shaded place. In cases where the illness to be treated is in an advanced stage, fresh herbs daily, administered very frequently, are often the only method of effecting a complete recovery. When the ailment is not so serious or life-threatening, dried herbs may be given.

When you gather from the wild, you must know your herbs so well that there cannot be any mistake in identification. It is not always easy to learn from books. Find an expert who will befriend you and enlighten your perplexities. If you are earnest in your endeavours, especially when you intend to help others, either animal or human, the right help will come. Faith is the key. When you sincerely wish to use the herbs of the earth for healing, health and happiness, you are reaching out to the Goddess, and she cannot help but hear you. Remember that you will find quite a number of the herbs described in this book readily available at your nearest garden centre. The staff will also order items for you. Supermarkets sell several varieties rooted in containers, which can be transplanted into the garden, or into windowsill plant pots.

Fresh herbs may be gathered from the earliest stirrings of spring until the end of November. There are some, like rosemary, which you can gather virtually all year round. When you collect herbs for drying, there are times and seasons to be observed so that the plants you pick will be especially rich in their cosmos-endowed properties. Herbs absorb qualities from sunlight, moonlight and the light of the stars. The electromagnetic vibrations of the planets influence them, as do the winds, the rain, the dew, the earth in which they are rooted, and the spiritual energy of the cosmic beings (fairies, nature spirits and angels) who nurture them. All of these dynamics have to be taken into consideration by the herb-gatherer, although it is a simple matter to do so.

Roots are best extracted in the early spring or during the autumn. Leaves may be collected before and during the time of flowering. Flowers should be taken just as the herb's flowering season begins. Fruits should be gathered as they are beginning to ripen fully.

It is better to cut herbs, for drying or otherwise, on a fine sunny day, in the morning when the dew has gone, or at noon, when the volatile oils are most active. If you cannot gather at these times, be assured that the plants are still valuable, even though their healing properties are not quite so marked or vigorous. In all circumstances, take only strong and healthy plants which are not infested with blight or pests. Pick what you need carefully, taking the new shoots from the middle of the plant so that it is not harmed. Never pull up a plant unless you need its roots, and then only when you have found a large group. Talk to the plant in your heart. It is a living being, and it will respond to you. Your heart-communication will activate the subtle cosmic forces so that they are attuned to you, and eager to help you in your endeavours. You must convey to the plant that you need the blessing of its leaves, stems and flowers for your healing work, or, if they are for you, for your sickness.

ASKING THE FAIRIES

You can ask the fairies to help you with your herb gathering. The traditional method is to wash your feet, forehead and hands in ritual purification before setting out. Ask the fairies to guide you to the location of the herbs you need, and then to influence you to select those which contain the most concentrated life-force. Always pass the first plant by, and take only what you need (for that day or for the week). Bless the herb as you take it, and thank it for giving of itself to make you, or your cat companion, whole. Try to gather in a waxing moon on either a Sunday or a Monday (of course, it's not always possible to follow these directives). Never forget to thank the fairies. In this way, you will procure their goodwill and blessing, and they will augment your acts of herb-healing with their own subtle life-energy.

Take care not to gather herbs which grow along busy road-sides where they are continually saturated in toxic fumes, and be wary of the banks of heavily polluted rivers or water-ways, or of industrial sites and busy railway embankments. If fields are sprayed with pesticides and fertilisers which are inorganic, don't stray close to their edges when gathering, and avoid using plants growing among the crop.

DRYING

Vigorous washing of herbs immediately begins to flush away their properties, so only gather clean plants. Wash them briefly under a gentle flow of water, give them a good shake, and spread them out in thin layers on cloth or clean paper (kitchen paper is best, it can be dried out over radiators and reused after it has soaked up the initial dampness, but *never* use newspaper). They must be dried quickly in warm, airy, shaded rooms. If the cloth or paper underneath the herbs becomes very damp after you have laid out freshly washed herbs on it, it must be changed, or it will cause the herbs to become mouldy. Of course, if your herbs are entirely clean and from uncontaminated areas, there is no need to wash them.

Dry roots and bark (or thick-stemmed herbs) in a warm oven, keeping the temperature even and low – not more than 35°C (95°F). Roots and bark, of course, have to be washed and cleaned well before drying. Test your herbs for dryness by bending them. If they are brittle and snap, they are ready to be put into green glass jars (to keep off the sun) or, if you have only plain glass, put them into a cupboard. Do not keep them forever. When spring comes, clear them out and gather a fresh harvest. Herbs lose their virtues over time.

OILS

Take two ounces (50g) or a good handful of the herb you have chosen, and either traditionally crush and pound it to refinement, using a mortar and pestle, or, more simply, use a blender. Now take eight fluid ounces (16 tablespoonfuls) of corn oil or almond oil (any vegetable oil will do, but I find that olive oil goes rancid very quickly) and one good tablespoonful of apple cider vinegar. Put your pounded herbs in a glass jar, pour in the oil and the vinegar, and leave in a warm place, somewhere in the sun or by a stove or radiator, for two weeks. The jar must be sealed and well shaken daily. Strain the mixture through muslin or gauze, squeeze the residue of oil out of the herbs and add it to your compound (i.e. the strained mixture) and store in a green glass jar (or in a cupboard—see above). Throw the herbs away and start all over again, adding fresh herbs to your infant oil until its fragrance is sharp and pleasing. These oils can be used to give your cat aromatherapy, or for healing and massage, as described in the text. Remember that catnip and valerian oil act as tonics for cats.

TISANES

The general rule is one rounded medium-size teaspoonful per half-cup of water if the herb is dried – **see pp. 33 and 231 for precise measurements.** For fresh herbs, one heaped teaspoonful is the correct measure (to allow for the water content not present in the dried herbs). Some herbs have to be used more sparingly (rue, lobelia and wormwood, for example). Half a teaspoonful is generally sufficient, although if an illness or worm infestation is very severe, one level teaspoonful may be used. When making up a mixed tisane, it is a good idea to measure half a rounded or heaped teaspoonful to one-quarter of a cup of water so as to avoid making huge quantities that you will never use when treating your cat. Tisanes can be kept in the refrigerator for a week, but if the illness is severe, they should really be prepared fresh every day. If you do have to refrigerate a tisane, always warm it before offering it to your cat.

Making the tisane is simple. Just snip the fresh herbs to the required quantity, or take the correct measure of the dried material, put in the teapot (your own special herb teapot which must never be used for any other purpose than brewing herbal teas and which should always be pottery, earthenware or china, *never* metal or any other substance); boil the kettle and pour the required amount of water into a glass measuring jug, then pour immediately over the herbs in the pot. Leave to brew for 30 seconds, certainly no more than one minute (I prefer half a minute). If you are using dried herbs, infuse for a little longer, but no more than two minutes. The tea should be a sparkling lime colour, or a pale lemon, never cloudy or muddy in appearance. However, stinging nettle tisane does go dark very quickly, turning from its original pleasant light green to almost black. This is nothing to worry about. As long as the tisane smells fresh, it is safe to use. Administer the tisane immediately (you can run the filled dropper under the cold tap for a moment to bring the tisane down to blood heat). The sooner the herb is in the pot, poured out and strained as a tisane, and in the patient, the better.

Where I have indicated that a certain ingredient of a mixed

tisane is 2 parts, 4 parts, etc., this simply means that the measure of the designated herb is to be used two or four times over, or as many times as are directed in the text. So if, for example, you come across a recipe recommending 2 parts camomile, 4 parts stinging nettle, 1 part catnip, 1 part elder, you would make up the tisane by adding two rounded or heaped teaspoonfuls (depending on whether the herb is dried or fresh—see above) of camomile, four of stinging nettle, and just one each of catnip and elder, as the measures for these last two ingredients are standard (standard = one part, or one rounded or heaped teaspoonful). **Important: always use half a cup of boiling water per teaspoonful of dried or fresh herb.** For example, for this particular recipe, you would use four cupfuls of water, because the recipe consists of eight herbal 'parts'. **Take note: half a cupful is a quarter of a pint or 150ml. When administering herbal medicines to your cat, use a large, 'fat' dropper from a 20ml medicine bottle (available at any chemist) if the patient is fully grown; the 'thin' type of dropper from 20ml bottles if aged between ten weeks and six months; for a kitten younger than ten weeks, give herbal medicine in the 'thin' dropper from 10ml bottles; and if less than two weeks old, give only half a dropperful to each dropperful recommended in the text, from the 'thin' 10ml droppers.**

DECOCTIONS

Sometimes a herbal decoction is preferable to a tisane, especially when using roots. Put them in the required amount of water (standard measures apply), bring to the boil, take off the heat and allow to soak for 20 minutes. Mash the roots underwater with a wooden spoon, strain, allow to cool to blood heat, and administer. (Roots have to be grated or chopped before being infused.)

INFUSIONS

An infusion is simply a tisane that is allowed to brew for 5 to 20 minutes rather than the half a minute generally advised throughout the text. Many herbalists, ancient and modern, prefer the infusion. Where I have given old herbal recipes (especially those of Dr Fox, the botanical physician from Sheffield), long-brewed infusions are the order of the day. These recipes are certainly effective; but I have always worked with the lighter tisanes, brewed for half a minute, which, I find, give excellent results. Whilst I can vouch for Dr Fox's concoctions, my own experiments have led me to conclude that the longer-brewed tisanes are not so effective, except very occasionally under certain circumstances. I have outlined these occasions in the text. For external use (such as a mallow foot-bath, for instance) the infusion is almost always more effectual than a tisane.

Cold Infusions
Some herbs (mallow, mistletoe and dandelion roots, for example) need to be infused in cold water. In this case, put the herbs in the required amount of cold water overnight, mash the herbs with a wooden spoon in the morning, strain, warm until tepid, and administer.

JUICES

Squeeze out the juice from the fresh herb with your fingers, or crush the herb with a rolling pin. If you have a juice extractor, even better. Let the expressed juice drop into little tinted glass medicine bottles and seal or stopper them well. They will keep for a week in the refrigerator, but make up a fresh supply after this period of time. (Ideally, they should be prepared daily.) The juice can be given as medicinal drops, diluted in a little spring water, or applied direct to the flesh or the corner of the eyeball, as required (see the A–Z for directions).

TINCTURES

Take three tablespoonfuls of the required herb, let it lightly fill a vessel, and pour over it two pints (about a litre) of apple cider vinegar (the vinegar must be apple cider vinegar, that is, a vinegar won from the whole apple, not just the skin and cores, as are the constituents of plain cider vinegar). Seal well, and put to stand in a very warm spot for three weeks (ten days will do, if you need the tincture urgently), giving the bottle a vigorous shake twice a day. Ensure that the apple cider vinegar entirely covers the top layer of the herbs.

After the allotted time, strain away the herbs; if the tincture is to be taken by mouth, use only the clear liquid, *not* the sediment. The wet herbs can be used to make compost for your garden or plantpot herbs (they make a wonderful mulch). If the tincture is to be used only as a rub or a lotion, the herbs can be wrung out into the compound itself (it will make it a little cloudy, but is harmless if not consumed). If it is to be applied to sore, broken or sensitive skin (e.g. prolapses) or to the eyes, use whisky instead of vinegar; otherwise dilute very well. Keep the bottled tincture away from sunlight once the process is completed.

OINTMENT

Warm petroleum jelly in a pot on the stove (ceramic potato pots are good vessels for this procedure) or simmer lightly in a microwave oven, stirring in a little honey and a pinch of salt. Pound four handfuls of the required chopped herb in your mortar and pestle (or in your blender!) gradually adding the herbs to the jelly as you go (you will need a big jar of jelly to accommodate all the herbs). Then warm through again, put into pots, and leave to gel. This method particularly lends itself to the use of charms as the ointment is being concocted.

Fresh Ointment

Crush the stems, leaves and flowers of the chosen herb, or put them in the blender. Spread a clean piece of cloth with the resultant pulp, and put straight onto the appropriate area of the body, binding round with a bandage to keep in place. A strip of polythene covered by a further bandage will prevent the ointment poultice from becoming uncomfortably wet. Keep on for as long as possible (but not more than ten hours),

A herbal poultice.

when, after an interval of two hours, the process is repeated. Bandages should never be tight.

HERBAL POULTICES

Boil up two pints of water in a pot. When it begins to bubble, hang a sieve over it (the bottom must not reach the water) full of the required herb, either fresh or dried, and cover. Let the water simmer for 10–15 minutes, then remove the herbs and spread them on cheesecloth, if possible, or any light, thin material. This cloth is bound straight onto the affected area so that the herbs come into direct contact with the skin. Cover with a woollen cloth (a scarf serves nicely) and bind on firmly but *not* too tightly with bandage, making a two-thirds overlap every turn. Secure the bandage with a safety-pin (the large, extra-safe ones that are used for babies' nappies). If the poult-ice is to be put on to a limb, wind the bandage down to envelop the foot so that the secured end doesn't dig into the flesh and cut off the blood supply. The poultice must be kept warm, so every half-hour nurse the cat and hold a comfortably warm (not hot) water bottle against the poultice for five minutes or so. Don't leave the poultice on for any longer than two hours, except at night when, if it can be made comfortable enough, it can be left in place for eight hours.

HERBAL BATHS

Use one small bucketful of fresh herbs, or half the amount of dried herbs. Let them soak overnight in cold water, warm

Giving a herbal bath.

and strain the next day and pour into the bath. Keep the bath warm, and let the cat sit in it for 15 minutes (try trickling warm water down the patient's spine to keep it calm). Rub the worst of the water off with towels, and then let the cat dry thoroughly by constantly wrapping it in fresh, dry, warmed towels. Finish off with a hairdryer. It is a good idea to use a baby bath, and to put a rubber mat in the bottom. If the cat is very agitated, give it a small plastic crate to cling on to whilst the bath is underway. Sometimes, only the hind-quarters of the cat need be submerged (see the A–Z for details). Lavender and catnip oil can be added to the bath, to calm the cat's nerves.

STEAM BATHS

See pp. 24–5 for instructions.

COMPRESSES

A piece of cotton wool, big enough to accommodate the affected area, is moistened with the appropriate herbal tincture, juice, ointment, oil or infusion, and is laid on the afflicted region. If Swedish bitters is used, it is best to rub a little marigold, agrimony or cleavers ointment, or some lavender or St John's wort oil, onto the area first, to prevent itching and dryness (see SWEDISH BITTERS, p. 193). The compress is then bandaged in the same way as a poultice (see above). Never bandage tightly. **Important: compresses must be kept warm.**

HERBAL VINEGARS

These are highly beneficial for cats, and should be applied where indicated in the A–Z.

Horseradish Vinegar

Shred horseradish and place it in a bottle. Apple cider vinegar is poured over it until well covered. Leave to stand in a warm room for 14 days. Use straight out of the bottle, without straining. The best way is to let it soak onto cotton wool balls or kitchen paper, to avoid the sediment.

Raspberry Vinegar

Good for FELINE RESPIRATORY DISEASE (Upper and Lower) and other feline (and human!) complaints, this vinegar is well worth taking the small amount of time and trouble necessary to prepare. To one pint of apple cider vinegar, add one pint of bruised, ripe raspberries; let them stand in a warm room for two days, and after straining them, put in three-quarters of a pound of honey (15 tablespoonfuls). Boil the compound, and remove the scum as it rises. The longer it boils, the thicker it will be. When cold, put into small tinted bottles, cork and seal and store them in a dry place.

HERBAL PILLS

Finely mince all the measures of herbs that your cat needs to take for the day, or for a few days (a week at the most), bind the mass together with honey, roll the whole in corn, barley, or oat flour and divide into small balls that you can administer as pills. Roll again in slippery elm flour or cornflour, and store in the refrigerator. Of course, pills can be made up individually to be sure of measurements (about one-third of a teaspoonful of minced herb can go into a pill for a big cat, less for a small cat). This is necessary when administering the more potent herbs as fresh greens (wormwood and rue, for example).

Please note: for all hot herbal preparations, be sure to keep the teapot or other vessel firmly sealed whilst infusion takes place, otherwise valuable properties are lost via the steam.

I would like to add a word or two about herbal-healing charms. I make use of them whilst gathering, preparing and administering herbs. This is an ancient tradition and, I believe, very beneficial to the outcome of the application of herbal medicine. The charms are a form of blessing or prayer, and our heritage of materialism should not be allowed to prevent you from using these charms and runes if you feel comfortable doing so. For me, they are an essential component of the healing process. You can read more about this ancient art of rune-healing in Chapter Ten.

Chapter Four

A–Z of Cat Ailments and Their Herbal Remedies

ABDOMEN

Cancer
Yarrow, the herb of mercy, can sometimes bring about a cure for this merciless disease so much on the increase today. Great dedication to the patient is required, because the tisane must be administered very frequently. It is particularly important to gather the herb in bright sunshine so that the curative properties of its volatile oils are at their highest potency. Prepare a standard **tisane** and feed it to the patient hourly throughout the day and evening. Give as much of two dropperfuls as the patient can comfortably take. If the cat is very sick, it is usually the case that one drop can be ingested every fifteen minutes. Once in the morning and once in the evening, mix half a teaspoonful of honey into the warm **tisane.** If very loose bowel movements occur, reduce to one daily dose. Minimise the patient's food allowance, and feed a combination of the **tonic foods** listed on pp. 9–16. Persist and have faith. Even in the most serious cases this disease has been successfully combated. The wise carer will know when the

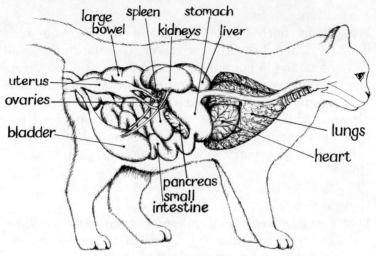

The main organs of the cat (female).

cat's suffering is too great to justify a prolonged course of treatment. Even so, marked relief and progress have often been evident after a surprisingly short time.

Whilst the **yarrow** remedy is being given, make a **compress** of **Swedish bitters** and apply it to the entire abdomen area, leaving it in place for up to two hours daily. A **horsetail poultice** should be administered in the evening and kept on overnight (if not tolerated, apply for at least two hours during the day).

Alternatives

An alternative **tisane** consists of one part **stinging nettle**, one part **yarrow** and two parts **calendula** (**marigold**), dosage the same as above. Additionally, leave one small teaspoon of **calamus roots** to soak in cold spring water overnight, strain in the morning and refrigerate in a medicine bottle. Administer half a dropperful of this decoction night and morning, warming the dropper before use. Never give more than this dosage.

In one dropperful of the tri-herb **tisane** (detailed above) dilute two drops of **Swedish bitters** and administer to the patient half an hour before the daily main meals. Give another dropperful half an hour afterwards, also containing the drops of **Swedish bitters**.

Herbal Supplements
Fresh herbs, finely minced and mixed well into your cat's daily meal, will help to fight cancer. One-third of a small clove of **garlic** (do not use more), the seed called **Job's tears** (again, use very small amounts) and the **Japanese shiitake mushroom** (lightly cooked and well-diced) are the herbal supplements to use. Never use more than one small level teaspoonful of garlic or one rounded teaspoonful of the other herbs. Also give **parsley, watercress, wild garlic** and **red clover.**

General Debility
Lady's mantle tisane is a wonderful restorative for weakness and debility of the abdomen. Give half a dropperful every two hours. If a queen suffers injuries after birth, continue the treatment for a month. If she is inclined to miscarry, begin to administer the **tisane** three weeks after she has mated. The tea will strengthen the uterus and its developing foetuses. After laparotomy (the surgical opening and closing of the abdomen) has been performed, the **tisane** provides a tonic for speedy healing and the prevention and cure of inflammation.

Swollen, see also Pyometra, p. 125

Alternatives
Yellow deadnettle, camomile, sage, feverfew and **lemon balm** are all beneficial for abdominal disorders. A **tisane** is required in each case, and its application is as above.

Herbal Supplements
Feed **fennel seed pills** and **dill seed pills**, two with each meal. The seeds must be crushed and ground. The measurements are 2g in each case. Dice a few leaves of **sweet basil** or **marjoram, parsley** or **spearmint.** Alternatively, 4g of ground ginger and 4g of ground cloves can be mixed with sufficient honey and wholemeal flour to make fourteen **pills,** one to be given each morning and evening so that they last a week. The fresh leaves of **feverfew** and **lemon balm** can also be made into **pills,** or diced finely and mixed into food.

ABORTION see Abdomen, general debility, p. 42

ABSCESS (for Dental Abscess see p. 73)

Sterilise a pair of scissors (first sterilise a clean bowl and colander by pouring boiling water into them; empty bowl, place a clean pair of scissors inside, fill it with boiling water, allow to cool for a minute, then empty the bowl with the scissors into the colander; use as soon as they are comfortable to touch). With the utmost gentleness and care, clip away any matted fur. If the area is dirty, clean with swabs of hot **stinging nettle tisane** into which one teaspoonful of apple cider vinegar has been added (two teaspoonfuls per cupful). Use a light touch, because the smallest pressure will cause pain. Apply **tincture of marigold** followed by **golden rod pulp** (stalk, leaves and flowers). Place under a pad and bandage on. Remove this in the evening and replace with a **horsetail poultice** to stay on overnight. Prepare a standard **tisane** of equal parts of **stinging nettle** and **horsetail** and administer by dropper six times a day for one month. The external treatment should be continued daily until the abscess has completely healed.

Alternatives
The powdered root of **golden seal** can be purchased from herbalists. Make four teaspoonfuls of the root powder into thirty standard **pills**, and feed one a day for a month. Administer **tincture of speedwell** by mouth, one drop every hour at first until there is marked improvement. Then give a standard **tisane** of equal parts of **speedwell, blue flag, cleavers** and **gentian** for one month. Bathe the abscess with hot **lavender tisane** (as hot as the back of your hand can stand) three times a day until the abscess has healed. **Lavender oil** will help to soothe the skin and encourage the fur to grow back quickly, and should be applied once the wound is clean and free from infection. If the abscess should 'point' (come to a head) and begin to discharge, clean away the infected matter with the hot **lavender tisane** into which one teaspoonful of apple cider vinegar has been added. Even if the abscess drains completely,

it is still necessary to administer one of the **tisanes** recommended above, so that the patient is internally cleansed. **Never squeeze an abscess,** as it is actually a capsule formed by the body to contain the infection. If this protective barrier is destroyed by squeezing, the infection is forced back into the system and cellulitis may occur (large localised swelling or badly swollen legs and feet). If this happens, the herbal treatment described above is effective (**stinging nettle** and **horsetail** should be used) but your vet must monitor the situation. A third alternative treatment for abscesses is half a dropperful of **sanicle tisane** morning and evening, and the application of a **slippery elm poultice** three times a day.

Tips
A high standard of nutrition greatly reduces the tendency to develop abscesses and will undermine their severity if they do form. Feed a combination of the **tonic foods** listed on pp. 9–16 to keep your cat healthy, and cut down on its meat intake. If an abscess patient runs a high temperature, keep it off solids and offer instead a meat and vegetable stew to which **stinging nettles** have been added (one small palmful per serving—wear gloves to measure!). The meat portion of the stew should be one-tenth of the patient's normal consumption, and can be dispensed with altogether if the fever continues. Add a few drops of vitamin C to strengthen the immune system. Regular dropperfuls of honey and apple cider vinegar diluted in spring water (one tablespoonful of vinegar and two of honey per cup) and of **sage tisane,** two daily of each, will restore a generally weak and sickly cat prone to abscesses, to prime condition.

Herbal Supplements
Feed **watercress** and **radish,** chopped very fine and combined with the main meal. The leaves and seeds of **squash** are also very beneficial. They can be ground and diced and fed as **pills,** or shredded and added to the daily meals.

ACNE

Administer six dropperfuls daily of **stinging nettle** and **horse-tail tisane** and one dropperful morning and evening of honey and apple cider vinegar (half a teaspoonful of each) and apply a **horseradish vinegar** directly onto the affected area. Dab off with a clean tissue after ten minutes.

Alternatives

The purifying, tonic effect of the **dandelion** can be given as an **infusion**, a dropperful before eating in the morning and a dropperful at lunchtime. If this remedy is used, combine it with a **stinging nettle tisane**, given by dropper, three to four times daily. Apply **marigold tincture** to the acne twice daily.

Tips

Cats tend to develop acne around the mouth, when they are less than fastidious groomers. When the acne has subsided, wash around the mouth once daily with a (comfortably) hot **tisane** of an antiseptic herb such as **golden rod, horseradish** leaves, **marigold, nasturtium, thyme** or **watercress**. This will prevent the problem from recurring.

Herbal Supplements

Feed **watercress**, finely shredded, in the daily meal. Chop fresh **dandelion roots, leaves** and **stems** and combine with meat or give as **pills**.

ACRAL LICK DERMATITIS

A bored, agitated cat tends to develop this problem. Two drops of the **Bach Flower Remedies Mimulus, Heather** and **Impatiens** in honey and apple cider vinegar diluted in spring water (half a teaspoonful each of honey and vinegar) are given by dropper twice daily. Also give a **camomile** and **golden rod tisane**. If the patient has caused sores or ulcers to appear, treat as for ACNE, ALLERGIES and ULCERS.

Tips

Try giving the cat more attention, providing a window for it to look out of, offering toys, leaving the radio on (playing classical music—some cats find rock or pop agitating) and avoiding long periods of close confinement and isolation. Hang crystals in the window to cast dancing, provocative rainbow patterns on the floor and walls. Tape down the lid on a shoebox, cut paw-sized holes in various shapes on the sides and top, and place different coloured ping pong balls inside. The cat will love trying to retrieve them. There are cat puzzlers on the market nowadays that it might also appreciate. An aquarium provides endless fascination for a cat (make sure it is firmly covered!). A bird feeder hanging by the window will also keep the cat alert and occupied.

ACTINOMYCOSIS (fungal disease)

The cat must be given a **marigold infusion** bath. If the patient cannot tolerate a full bath, then bathe the affected areas (see Herbal baths, p. 36). Make a compress for the swellings from **tincture of marigold** diluted with boiled water. **Marigold tisane** should also be given by dropper four times a day until the condition has completely disappeared.

Herbal Supplements

Give **watercress, wild garlic** and especially fresh grated **garlic;** give a clove a day (stagger the dose).

AGEING

Your cat may be with you for as long as twenty years, and from the start you can take action to ensure that it lives to a healthy old age, beyond its usual ten- to fifteen-year span, with very little loss of quality of life as time progresses. Give three drops of **Swedish bitters** (about one-quarter of a teaspoonful) night and morning in a dropperful of **stinging nettle tisane** every other day. Alternate with half a dropperful of **rosemary tisane,** and once a month, rub a **rosemary lotion** into the coat made from the **leaves** and **flowers** boiled for two minutes in water into which two drops of **rose oil** have been mixed. Use a hairdryer on the coat afterwards. After your cat has passed its ninth year, prepare a daily **tisane** of equal parts of **horsetail** and **speedwell** and administer two dropperfuls daily. Add half a level teaspoonful of honey and the same of apple cider vinegar to the morning and evening dose of **stinging nettle tisane** and **Swedish bitters** for a truly remarkable tonic against ageing. (Human companions can take it too!)

Alternatives
A very ancient Druidic recipe was collected in Anglesey by the herbalist and magician David Conway. The Druids spoke of it as the 'Draught of Immortality' and valued it as a rejuvenating tonic. It is presented here in its original form with the exception of two added ingredients, **catnip** and **couchgrass**, both of which are highly medicinal herbs and, of course, excellent for cats! Make an **infusion** from **chervil, heather, honeysuckle, red clover, vervain, couchgrass** and **catnip**. Give one teaspoonful of this potion night and morning in a dropperful of honey (half a teaspoonful) and spring water. The patient should take the tonic from new moon to full, every other month.

A tiny pinch (*very* minute) of **cayenne powder** added to the above recipe will guard against mental and physical deterioration.

Herbal Supplements
Shred two or three leaves of **lemon balm** finely and mix in well with the patient's meal.

AGGRESSION

Two of the **Dr Bach Flower Remedies, Holly** and **Impatiens**, should be given in a dropperful of honey and water, two drops of each, morning and evening. In addition, administer a **horsetail tisane** four times daily.

Tips
If the cat tries to dominate you, use the **Vine Flower Remedy** as well as the two given above. If it is aggressive because it has been frightened, so that its behaviour seems self-defensive, add **Rock Rose Remedy** instead of **Vine**.

Herbal Supplements
Feed one tip of a teaspoonful (less than one-eighth) of **kelp powder** (or crush one-eighth of one **kelp tablet**) and combine with food daily.

AIDS (feline immunodeficiency virus)

Give an **infusion** of **plantain** and **sage**, two dropperfuls three times daily. **Horsetail** and **stinging nettle tisane**, four dropperfuls daily, should also be given to the patient. Morning and evening, a **speedwell tisane** into which a single drop of **Swedish bitters** has been mixed must be administered together with a **sage vinegar rub**. (Make the **vinegar** by gathering a handful of **sage flowers** and macerating them for ten days in apple cider vinegar.) Massage this preparation well into the coat, but don't make the fur too wet. Dry off with a hairdryer afterwards. **Sage** must always be gathered in bright sunshine to obtain the full medicinal power of its volatile oils. Naturally I cannot absolutely guarantee recovery from this stubborn and malignant disease, but I do urge you to try the herbal treatment given.

Tips
If the patient is weak and sickly, fluid retention may occur. If this happens, stop all treatment except for a **horsetail tisane**, which should be given by dropper six times daily. As soon as the fluid clears, continue the full herbal programme.

Herbal Supplements
Feed the **fresh leaves** of **wild garlic** freshly chopped and combined with the daily meals (this is a *vital* and *essential* tonic). Give finely diced **Japanese shiitake mushrooms** and feed a selection of the **tonic foods** listed on pp. 9–16. Also give raw **garlic** daily, **parsley** and **watercress**. **Chickweed** is helpful, too.

ALLERGIES

For the allergic cat, regular dropperfuls of **stinging nettle tisane** are necessary. Be sure to add half a teaspoonful of honey and half a teaspoonful of apple cider vinegar to the morning and evening doses. Administer four times daily for twelve weeks. If the allergies are still present or if they return, continue the treatment.

Alternatives
A few drops of **Swedish bitters**, given in the morning and evening, will alleviate the tendency to be allergic. If the hay fever or other allergy is very bad, and accompanied by frenzied scratching, soak the cat's fur in a solution of **stinging nettle, camomile** and **lavender tisane** which has been allowed to cool to a temperature just below tepid (warm water will worsen the irritation). If the cat has a horror of being submerged (as many do!) simply sponge onto the fur from a bowl. Groom the patient well (but gently, in case of broken skin), keep it indoors and allow the coat to dry naturally.

Herbal Supplements
Saturating the system with **garlic** is most important. Feed it raw every day. Two or three leaves of **feverfew** shredded fine and mixed well in with the daily meal often help. Pulp two small chrysanthemum flowers daily and feed as **pills**.

ALOPECIA (feline endocrine alopecia—hair loss)

Wash the coat in **stinging nettle tisane**, and rub **stinging nettle tincture** into the skin where hair loss has occurred. If the skin is sore or broken, dilute the tincture.

Alternatives
A concentrated **decoction** of **walnut leaves**, massaged daily into the coat, will help in cases of hair loss. Roast sesame seeds until semi-burned, mix with petroleum jelly and smear onto the bald patches three or four times daily (when using this cure it is important to fix the patient with an Elizabethan collar (see

p. 24) to deter ingestion of the ointment). Cut a slice of fresh **ginger** or **garlic** and massage the bald patches with it until all the juice has been extracted. Repeat four times daily.

Prepare a **tisane** from **walnut leaves, mullein leaves** and **red sage** and massage daily into the coat (dry off the patient with a hairdryer). Rub **castor oil** into the coat, alternating daily with **rosemary tisane** into which a few drops of **olive oil** have been added. When using the **castor oil** treatment, apply sparingly and ensure that the patient wears an Elizabethan collar for a few hours afterwards.

Herbal Supplements
Feed a combination of the **tonic foods** listed on pp. 9–16, especially the crushed **kelp pills**.

ANAEMIA

Prepare a standard **tisane** of **stinging nettle, agrimony, parsley** and **cleavers**, and give four dropperfuls six times a day.

Herbal Supplements
Feed plenty of **wild garlic** (an infusion can be made from the **bulbs,** if the **leaves** are past their best). Also give generous portions of **parsley**. These herbs are best given in honey **pills,** as honey is very beneficial in the treatment of anaemia. Fruit jelly (see p. 18) is just as important, but use the black berries—bramble, bilberry, elderberry and (black) grape, as well as strawberry. **Peppermint** and **spearmint leaves,** chopped and put into honey **pills,** are very helpful, too. **Watercress** should be given regularly, chopped and administered in the same way; and **stinging nettle tops,** as part of a meat stew, are also a cure for anaemia.

ANAL SAC PROBLEMS

The cat has two scent glands on either side of the anus, depending in two little sacs. These can become blocked or infected. Give **stinging nettle tisane** and moisten below the anus with a few drops of **Swedish bitters** in the morning and

marigold tincture in the evening. Dilute the tincture if it is vinegar-based. Let both remain on the skin for no more than two hours, then wash gently with the **stinging nettle tisane** and apply a few dabs of **St John's wort ointment**.

Tips

If the cat is showing signs of discomfort (rubbing the anus along the floor, turning sharply, as if shocked, to look at the tail, licking frantically beneath it, or if a discharge, inflammation or swelling develops around the anus) it is possible to empty the sacs yourself. Put on latex gloves, have a supply of damp and dry tissues on hand, and perform the procedure on a hard floor surface protected with newspapers. Imagine the periphery of the anus is a clock face to find the anal sacs at the eight o'clock and four o'clock positions. You will feel them as two solid swellings about the size of a large pea. Holding a wad of disposable towels in your palm, place your finger and thumb at either side of the anal opening in the specified positions and exert a gentle inward pressure. The ejected fluid should cover the towel (don't get your face too close to the trajectory—the contents of the sacs are very foul-smelling!) If the sacs don't empty, move your fingers to position them more accurately and try again. *Never* press hard as your cat will suffer and the sacs could become damaged, which will compound the problem. If the sacs don't respond to gentle pressure, treat with herbs as described above. If the patient evinces pain when the anal area is touched, or if there is severe swelling, redness or growths, a **horsetail poultice** must be used. Apply during the day and then again overnight, and feed the patient a **horsetail tisane**, four dropperfuls daily. A **horsetail hip bath** must also be given daily (just sit the patient in a washing-bowl with its anal area well submerged—there is no need to soak the entire body). This will clear polyps and infection and is a much better solution than having the sacs removed. Although the domestic cat doesn't miss them, the operation is not straightforward. If pus, blood or a thick black substance is expressed from the sacs, the **horsetail** treatment above, together with **stinging nettle tisane**, must be commenced immediately.

Herbal Supplements
Feed the **tonic foods** listed on pp. 9–16 to prevent constipation. A **stinging nettle tisane**, cooled and given in the water
bowl regularly in the morning will help all anal and bowel
problems. Beware of 'junk' foods and avoid giving snacks of
human food.

ARTHRITIS

Give two dropperfuls of **horsetail tisane** half an hour before
feeding in the morning, and the same half an hour before the
evening meal. Also administer three times throughout the
day, four dropperfuls of **stinging nettle** and **speedwell tisane**.
Honey and apple cider vinegar in spring water should be
given, mixed with one teaspoonful of **Swedish bitters**, once
a day, and two dropperfuls of honey and apple cider vinegar
in spring water without the **bitters**, every four hours. (Two
teaspoonfuls of honey and two of vinegar per cup of water.)
For swollen, deformed joints, apply a **horsetail poultice** or
crinkly cabbage leaves (ordinary **cabbage** will do). Heat well
with an iron and apply as a **compress**. Leave on overnight
and apply a **compress of Swedish bitters** for four hours during
the day. **Comfrey tincture** should also be rubbed into the
affected joints several times a day, especially in the evening.

Alternatives
A Welsh recipe of considerable antiquity, called Physig Cryd
Cymalau and collected by David Conway, offers a cure for
arthritis and arthritic pain. Please be careful to substitute
speedwell for **comfrey** if your cat has a heart condition.
Again, I have added the cat's favourites, **couchgrass** and **catnip**, to the ingredients: **candytuft** (or **meadowsweet**), **cleavers,
comfrey, cowslip** (or **rue**), **stinging nettle, couchgrass** and
catnip. Prepare an **infusion** and give to the patient morning
and evening, three dropperfuls each time, mixed with one
teaspoonful of honey (one-third of a teaspoonful in each
dropper). A **poultice** of the same herbs can be applied overnight to swollen joints.

Tips
A cat suffering from arthritis must never be fed 'junk' food or unsuitable human food as treats. It is essential too that the protein intake is reduced by one-half. Feed the patient a combination of the **tonic foods** listed on pp. 9–16 and ensure that it takes exercise – you will have to encourage this if the cat is very arthritic. Help the patient out by giving it a **sage vinegar rub** (see information listed under AIDS, p. 48).

Herbal Supplements
Combine the patient's food with **wild garlic**, several leaves per serving, shredded very fine. Also give **watercress** and **celery**. A little pinch of **cayenne pepper** (the dose must be *very* minute) in each meal will work wonders on arthritis. If the patient dislikes it, feed it in a dropper with honey and spring water (half a teaspoonful of honey).

ASTHMA

Mix one teaspoonful of the fresh juice of **coltsfoot** into a dropperful of warm honey (half a teaspoonful) and spring water, and administer night and morning, or when the asthma is very bad. If there is a lung infection, boil one-quarter of a cup of spring water with one teaspoonful of honey and two teaspoonfuls of apple cider vinegar. Let it go just off the boil and add two teaspoonfuls of a **thyme** and **plantain tisane** (made up of equal parts). Steep for half a minute, take up by dropper (cool the filled dropper in a cup of cold water if the mixture is too hot—test a drop on your inside wrist to check) and administer it all to the patient immediately. If the condition is severe, the same medicine can be given twice more throughout the day, only after the initial dose the quantities must be halved (even the water must be reduced to one-eighth of a cup (38ml)). **Thyme** and **plantain tisane** can be given without the honey and vinegar in less severe asthma cases (four dropperfuls throughout the day).

Alternatives
Macerate two tablespoonfuls of **pansy, purple flowers** and **leaves**, in a glass bottle containing one pint of apple cider vinegar, for seven days. Shake it well once a day. At first, feed the patient two drops of this **tincture** in **horehound tisane** sweetened with honey, one dropperful three times daily (two drops of **tincture** each time), gradually increasing the dosage to five drops of the **acid pansy tincture** per dropper. (Acid tincture of **lobelia** is also effective.) Prepare a **speedwell tisane** and administer to the patient, two dropperfuls four times daily.

Herbal Supplements
Feed **garlic pills** and one-quarter of a teaspoonful of **kelp powder** (or one-quarter of a tablet) daily.

BAD BREATH see Teeth (p. 137)

BASAL CELL CARCINOMA see Tumours (p. 146)

BIRTH see Abdomen, general debility (p. 42)

BITES

Give **Swedish bitters** (one-quarter of a teaspoonful) in a **stinging nettle tisane,** one dropperful morning and evening. Place the fresh, crushed **leaves** of **plantain** on the wound after washing it with **thyme tisane** (in an emergency, apply the bruised **plantain leaves** without preliminary bathing). Clip away the fur to fully reveal the site of teeth-punctures.

Alternatives
Administer a **marigold tisane** and apply a **golden rod poultice** (the pulped **leaves, stalk** and **flowers**) directly to the wound. A **thyme** or **speedwell tisane** and a **horsetail poultice** can be substituted. A **decoction** of the **root** of **gentian** is excellent as an internal treatment, and **gentian tincture** should be applied direct to the wound.

Herbal Supplements
Feed finely shredded **wild garlic** and **watercress** until all
wounds are completely healed.

BLACKHEADS see Acne (p. 44)

BLADDER

For CYSTITIS, prepare a standard **tisane** of equal parts of
parsley and **couchgrass**. Add a small half-teaspoonful of apple
cider vinegar to each dropperful given, and administer three
dropperfuls six times daily. (Also see general notes under
Cystitis, p. 71.)

Alternatives
A **tisane** of **corn silk** (the fine webby filaments that hang
from the ears of **Indian corn,** the 'corn-on-the-cob' variety)
or **golden rod** will relieve the condition.

Tips
This condition is indicated when the tom spends longer than
usual on the litter tray or on a toilet spot in the garden, when
he appears to strain with much twitching of the tail and the
problem is clearly not constipation, or if there is constant
licking of the penis or beneath the tail. If the cat appears very
unwell and in pain, apply a **hot horsetail poultice** and take the
cat to the vet **immediately,** as a completely blocked bladder is
an emergency. If your cat needs to have an operation (perineal
urethrostomy) give a course of the **couchgrass, small-
flowered willowherb** and **golden rod tisane** (two dropperfuls
night and morning) for the duration of a month, three times
throughout the year, to prevent the problem recurring.

Herbal Supplements
Cucumber and **watercress** (as well as fresh **parsley**) help to
cure and prevent **cystitis.**
　　For Feline Urolithiasis Syndrome, or Blocked Bladder,
which only affects male cats, make a **tisane** of equal parts of
couchgrass, small-flowered willowherb and **golden rod.** Add

half a small teaspoonful to each dropperful and administer three dropperfuls four times daily. Once a day, soak the patient's hindquarters in a **horsetail bath** (as hot as is comfortable) and feed three dropperfuls of **horsetail tisane** whilst the patient soaks. Dry off with a hairdryer afterwards.

Blocked Bladder

Prevention and cure for this condition is also effected by a **tisane** prepared from the **small-flowered willowherb**, a panacea for all bladder problems. It is especially useful for **cancer of the bladder**. Prepare a standard **tisane**, to be administered morning and evening, two dropperfuls each time.

Herbal Supplements

Feed the patient **couchgrass**. If there is no access to a natural source outside, snip the fresh herb into small pieces, chop it, and feed it compacted into **pills**. It is a good idea to do this in either case, as an artificial mode of life restricts the cat's instinctive impulse to seek out and consume this important medicinal plant.

BLASTOMYCOSIS (fungal disease)

To clear up the lung infection caused by this disease, see p. 53 under Asthma. The patient must also be given a **tisane** made of equal parts of **stinging nettle, marigold, St John's wort, speedwell** and **yarrow**, two dropperfuls three times a day. Treat as advised on p. 43 if abcesses appear. An old remedy for all dermatitis conditions, whether caused by bacteria, fungus or parasites, is prepared in three steps. First, take one small teaspoonful each of **sassafras bark, sarsaparilla, gum guaiacum, queen's delight, polypody root,** and one-quarter of a teaspoonful of **cayenne.** Pulverise finely, mix well, and pass through a fine sieve. Then take half a tablespoonful of **burdock root,** one good teaspoonful of **fumitory,** and one small teaspoonful each of **bittersweet root** (American), **wood sanicle** and **cleavers,** simmer in two pints of spring water down to one, and strain. Finally, take half a tablespoonful of the powder already prepared, pour half a pint of boiling water over it, stir well, and let stand until clear. Using only the clear liquid (any sediment should be discarded) mix it with the first pint of strained infusion. Refrigerate, but warm before administering to the patient; two dropperfuls three times daily.

Herbal Supplements
Feed **couchgrass, wild garlic, garlic pills** (plenty of these), **honey pills,** and **watercress.** Vegetable matter must be shredded and mixed with food.

BLEEDING

To staunch profuse bleeding, feed the patient **horsetail tisane** by dropper and apply a **compress** of the cooled **tisane.**

Herbal Supplements
If the cat has lost a lot of blood, feed **parsley** (finely shredded) for a month to replace the lost iron.

BLEPHARITIS (inflamed eyelids)

Wash the eyes with **camomile tisane,** and apply the same as a **compress** to the eyelids. Also, see Conjunctivitis, p. 70.

Herbal Supplements
Feed finely shredded **wild garlic** and honey **pills** until the condition has disappeared.

BLEPHAROSPASM (closed eyelids, spasm of the eyelids, squinting)

Maria Treben tells of a wonderful 'Camomile witch' who healed all pains in the eye with a special **compress.** It is prepared by pouring one-quarter of a pint of boiling milk over a heaped tablespoonful of **camomile** (fresh, but dried will do). Infuse the concoction for three minutes, strain it, and use as a warm **compress** over the closed eye. This will help the patient to relax its eye muscles and will remove the cause of the pain (foreign matter in the eye, soreness from slight injury, etc.).

BLINDNESS

This condition is not the terrible hindrance to cats that it is to humans. Nevertheless, an attempt to restore the sight is worthwhile. If the problem is a detached retina (occurring especially after a blow to the head) or a porous retina, apply a **compress** of **Swedish bitters** to the closed eye twice daily, to be left in place for an hour each time. For all cases of blindness (except of course where the eye has been destroyed beyond repair), give two dropperfuls of **eyebright tisane** three times daily. Wash the eyes with **eyebright tincture** (well diluted if vinegar-based) whenever the **tisane** is administered.

BLUE EYE

This condition is an indication of severe inflammation or an increase of pressure in the eyeball. Your vet must be consulted immediately. If it is a case of inflammation, treat as for blepharitis (see p. 57). Also give a **stinging nettle tisane,** two dropperfuls three times daily. If there is injury but no infection, treat as for blepharospasm (see p. 57). If it is glaucoma or cancer, see pp. 93 or 62.

BONES

Where there is infection or growths on the bone, or where a bone fracture has not healed well, **comfrey poultices** should be applied each night until all symptoms have disappeared. The **poultice** is made from **comfrey root powder,** two teaspoonfuls mixed with two tablespoonfuls of water two minutes off the boil and one or two drops of **corn oil.** Smear this concoction onto a piece of cloth, place very warm onto the appropriate area and secure with a bandage. **Comfrey leaves** make an excellent **poultice** for dislocation and sprains. Pour boiling water over one-quarter of a cupful of **leaves,** strain immediately and apply the pulp as a **poultice. Comfrey tincture** can be used as a **compress** for the site of an imperfectly healed fracture, or where there is rheumatism and swelling of joints.

Bone Diseases
Give two dropperfuls of **yarrow tisane** four times daily, plus one dropperful morning and evening of **stinging nettle tisane** and **marigold tisane**. Use **yarrow** and **comfrey tincture** as a rub for the affected area four times a day. **Swedish bitters** should also be given as a rub morning and evening (use sparingly). If a bony growth or protrusion is discovered to be cancerous, see Tumours (p. 146).

Herbal Supplements
Fresh **stinging nettles** are a tonic for bones. They can be fed to an ailing cat in a meat and vegetable stew.

Bone in the Throat
Arrowroot jelly, slipped into the side of a choking cat's mouth, is said to help the bone to come out. A tenth-century Anglo-Saxon remedy is to say three times 'I buss the Gorgon's mouth'! If the cat is choking so violently that an emergency situation arises, turn it upside down and shake it. When the obstruction has cleared, give it a few drops of **Dr Bach's Rescue Remedy** to ease the shock of both the misadventure and its remedy. Even so, the cat is likely to remain markedly unimpressed with you for quite a while afterwards.

BOWEL MUSCLES (weak)

When muscle tone in the bowel and anus area is poor, due to age, accident or debility, bowel obstructions can occur (see Constipation, p. 70). The cat might eventually suffer from **prolapse of the rectum**. To both cure and prevent this, give the patient two dropperfuls of **lady's mantle tisane** four times daily as soon as you are aware that the anus muscle is weakening, or when prolapse has actually occurred. The **tisane** must be mixed with three drops of **shepherd's purse tincture** for the morning and evening doses (six drops only per day).

The **shepherd's purse tincture** must be rubbed well into the skin around the anal area (well diluted), into the base of the tail, between and under the back legs and all over the stomach. Do this three times a day. Where prolapse has occurred, first wash your hands and then gently bathe the anal area with **thyme tisane**. Dab dry and apply **marigold ointment**. Using a light and gentle pressure, ease the protrusion back into place until the anus looks normal again. Wash your hands and begin the herbal treatment described above at once. If the **shepherd's purse tincture** is not immediately available (it takes ten days to prepare) use **Swedish bitters** as a **compress** during the intervening time, as an emergency measure.

BRONCHITIS

Prepare a **tisane** of equal parts of **coltsfoot, plantain** and **speedwell**. Add one-quarter of a teaspoonful of honey to each dose (two dropperfuls) and give four times daily. Each of these herbs can be given individually to heal bronchitis, but for severe cases I prefer this combined recipe for its expectorant, purifying and anti-inflammatory action.

Alternatives
Lungwort tisane helps to clear bronchitis. Its furry leaves can be rubbed into the patient's chest (go underneath the forelegs as well as above). **Stinging nettle tisane** is also an excellent remedy. A **compress** can be made of the boiled, pulped leaves and applied to the chest if breathing becomes difficult or painful. Be sure to add the recommended dash of honey to all the **tisanes** for bronchitis or asthma, because of its wonderful healing effect on the respiratory tract.

Herbal Supplements
Feed **wild garlic**, finely shredded; also **stinging nettle leaves**, boiled, pulped and mixed well in with the daily meals.

BRUISING (IMPORTANT—see also Shock, p. 132)

Marigold tincture diluted in boiled water (fifteen drops to one-quarter of a cupful) and used as a **compress** will heal painful and tender bruises. If the cat has been severely bruised, it is likely to be in shock, and must be treated according to directions given under that heading (shock is serious and can kill). Leave the compresses on for two hours, or overnight.

Alternatives
Comfrey tincture, applied neat as a compress, will ease bruising (dilute if vinegar-based). The leaves, too, can be applied, pulped and cold, or scalded and warm. Fresh coltsfoot leaves, washed and pounded and applied as a poultice, will also bring relief. In all cases, leave on for two hours or overnight.

BULGING EYELIDS (also see Prominent Eye, p. 124)

Bulging, closed eyelids in a newborn kitten are an emergency, indicating serious infection which is likely to result in blindness. Any sign of infection in a kitten's eye must be treated immediately. Gently prise open the eyelids if they are stuck together, and bathe continually with camomile infusion (see p. 57) until the infection has cleared. It is most important to keep the eye lubricated, and to prevent closure of the eye for any length of time whilst the condition heals.

BURNS AND SCALDS

First wash the affected area well with apple cider vinegar, then ten minutes later smear a coating of honey thickly over it. Administer similar coatings until there is no more pain (long-haired breeds must have their fur clipped) then apply a light bandage over a further coating of honey to allow the wounds to heal. Skullcap, lavender, golden seal and camomile tisane should be given, four dropperfuls every hour, for the first twelve hours after the injury.

Alternatives
Raw potato pulp can be applied to burns or scalds to promote speedy relief and healing. The leaves of butterbur, applied fresh direct to the injured area, are also excellent, as is marigold ointment, St John's wort oil, and especially Swedish bitters. The drops are constantly applied to the site of the

injury so that it is kept well moistened. Give the **tisane** described above with all the alternative treatments.

Herbal Supplements
Give well-chopped **lettuce**.

CANCER

There are several herbs with which to treat cancer. They can be used generally, but they also target specific locations with great success, often bringing about a complete cure where orthodox medicine had judged the case to be hopeless.

1 ABDOMEN (including female reproductive organs): **yarrow**.
2 BLADDER (including prostate and kidney): **small-flowered willowherb**.
3 BOWEL/INTESTINES: **calamus root**.
4 BRAIN: **horsetail** and **stinging nettle**.
5 LIVER: **common club moss**.
6 LUNGS: **yarrow and calamus root**.
7 MOUTH (tongue, palate, etc.): **cleavers**; fresh **juice** and **tisane**.
8 SKIN: **cleavers**; fresh **juice** and **tisane**.
9 STOMACH: Freshly pressed **juice of wood sorrel**, 3 drops in spring water every hour.
10 THROAT (oesophagus, larynx, etc.): **mallow, cleavers**; **violet leaves** (the **tisane** is also rubbed well into the throat morning and evening).

The three great general cancer herbs are **horsetail, marigold** and **mistletoe**. The latter particularly is preventive as well as counteractive. All cancers need **horsetail poultices** to be applied directly to the affected area as well as very regular doses of the appropriate **tisane** (at least twenty dropperfuls a day—see Tumours, p. 146). Other cancer herbs (which in some cases might even work better than the exalted trio) are **red clover, rockrose, parsley** and the **leaves, tendrils** and fresh **juice** of the **grape**.

Herbal Supplements
Garlic, turnip, watercress and honey **pills** all help to eliminate cancer.

CANKER

(Adapted from advice given in *Dr Pitcairn's Complete Guide to Natural Health for Dogs and Cats*, by Richard H. Pitcairn, DVM, PhD and Susan Hubble Pitcairn: Rodale Press, USA, 1982)

If the canker is due to a simple infection, the ears should be cleaned internally with a solution consisting of half a teaspoonful of apple cider vinegar mixed into three teaspoonfuls of warm water. A cotton-wool ball should be soaked in this liquid and then applied to the inside ear. Remove as much as possible of the build-up of dark-brown matter that is a symptom of the canker, and then thoroughly wash the flesh of the interior ear with a swab of soft cotton wool moistened with the diluted vinegar, three times daily. Put ten drops of **lavender oil** into one dessertspoonful of **almond oil**, add six drops of **Swedish bitters**, warm until tepid, and administer four drops of this mixture three times daily directly into the patient's ear.

Alternatives
The ears should be washed three times daily with extract of **witch hazel**, four drops in a **tisane** of **horehound**. Cleanse with cotton-wool swabs and cotton-wool tipped ear cleaners (use these with extreme care as they can do damage). Four drops of the mixture should be put into the ear three times a day.

Tips
It is important to give the ears a good clean out every evening with **dry** cotton wool until the inside ear is as moisture-free as possible. Put a hairdryer on its lowest heat and gently waft the warm air into the patient's ear, holding the dryer at a distance of about 20cm (8in). Do this for about three minutes, and then leave the ears dry overnight until treatment is resumed in the morning.

When either the **tisane** or the **oil** is dropped into the ear, massage the ear and the area around it gently but thoroughly for a few moments afterwards.

Mite Infestation
The following lotion will bring relief:

½ fl oz (14.2 ml) almond oil
½ fl oz (14.2 ml) lavender oil
400 international units of vitamin E (from your chemist)

Mix these ingredients in a large dropper, and for a period of five days put nine drops of the mixture into the cat's ears, massaging some of the lotion thoroughly into the ear, night and morning. After each application, gently cleanse the ear with cotton wool as previously described. Dry off the ears with a hairdryer at night. If there are other areas of baldness on the head, body or limbs, these indicate further mite infestation, and should be treated with the lotion. After each application to the ears, one small drop of **eucalyptus oil** should be dropped into each ear whilst the canal is still wet and before cleaning takes place. Keep the lotion in the refrigerator, but gently warm it before treating the patient. Hot or cold drops should never be put into a cat's ear; they should be no more than pleasantly warm (test them first on your wrist to check their temperature). Wait three days, repeat the entire process, then make up this new recipe, to be administered after the second three-day interval:

Administering ear drops.

4 tsp **yellow dock root** (macerated **root**)
4 tsp **horsetail** (chopped **herb**)
1 tsp **yellow dock** (chopped **herb**)
6 tsp apple cider vinegar
20 drops **lavender oil**

Add ½ pt (150 ml) of boiling water to the **dock root** and simmer for ten minutes. Add the remaining herbs and take off the boil. Wait one minute, then strain and add the **lavender oil**. Allow to cool, and finally add the apple cider vinegar. Repeat the treatment with the new recipe as indicated above, only this time, after the initial five-day treatment period, wait two weeks before administering the final one.
Important: for both types of canker, an internal cleansing **tisane** should be taken daily. Prepare one of equal parts of **stinging nettle** and **thyme,** and give two dropperfuls three times daily until the canker has been completely banished.

Tips
If the patient's ears are very inflamed and infected, treat with a **horsetail compress** to which three drops of **lavender oil** per ear must be added. Leave the compresses on overnight. The lengthy procedure described for ridding your cat of mange mites is only necessary in its entirety if the infestation is very heavy or stubborn. Where it is slight, simplify the programme by applying the first lotion (composed of oils and vitamin E) over a single five-day period. The second half of the procedure should then be followed as instructed.

The **horsetail** and **yellow dock** solution can be used to keep mites permanently at bay. Ensure that the **infusion** is warm and rub well into the coat and ears, drying the cat with a hairdryer afterwards.

Herbal Supplements
Feed **wild garlic, watercress** and **garlic,** finely minced. Also feed honey **pills.**

CARDIAC COUGH see Heart, p. 94

CARDIOMYOPATHY see Heart, p. 94

CAT FLU (feline respiratory disease)

This is actually not influenza but a disease caused by one of two viruses, either feline viral rhinotracheitis or feline calicivirus, the first generally being the more virulent of the two. Keep the patient in a warm room, draught-free but not stuffy. Give it very warm (not hot) **marigold** and **stinging nettle tisane** with half a teaspoonful of apple cider vinegar and just the tip of a teaspoonful of honey (less than one-quarter) mixed into each dropper, four times a day, two dropperfuls each time. Gently bathe away the mucus from the eyes and nose with **camomile tisane** soaked into cotton-wool balls. Smear beneath the eyes with **marigold ointment** to prevent the mucus from the eyes sticking to the fur. It is very important to follow these nursing procedures regarding the eyes because if they are not bathed regularly with the **tisane** they may ulcerate and be permanently damaged. If ulcers appear on the tongue, give frequent mouthwashes of **cleavers**. If ulcers appear on the paws, give foot baths of **mallow** (the herb is cold-soaked overnight and warmed before use). If ulceration does occur, try the milk and **camomile** treatment detailed under Blepharospasm, p. 57. This **compress** should in any case be used on the throat overnight, and twice for a few hours during the day. A **camomile inhalation** should also be given. Pour a pint of boiling water over one heaped tablespoonful of **camomile**, suspend the cat in a cage over the steaming bowl, and throw a towel over the cage. (Do not give way to immediate protests, as the patient is often comforted after a little while by the soothing vapours. If the cat continues to be vociferous, though, it is better to forget the whole idea! Alternatively, you might be able to persuade the patient to sit on your knee with its head over the bowl and covered with a towel for a short while.) **Horsetail poultices** should be applied to the sinuses and to the chest overnight and during the day. Also administer **camomile tisane**, two dropperfuls three times a day. In the last dropperful given each time, add one drop of **Swedish bitters**.

Tips
Groom the patient and make a fuss of it. Purring helps the cat to breathe much more easily, so the longer you can keep it purring, the better. The cat should not be forced or pestered to eat. If it refuses all food, dissolve half a child's daily dose of vitamin C into one of the droppers. You can make a meat and vegetable stew with all the good healing herbs, **stinging nettle, wild garlic, garlic, watercress** and **feverfew**, included in it. The stew must be completely liquidised, as the cat's energies must all be concentrated on recovery from the disease and must not be dissipated on digestive concerns. If the cat is very feverish or debilitated, give only the herbal stew. When the worst is over, tempt the patient's appetite with small portions of its favourite treat of meat or fish.

Herbal Supplements
Feed the patient **parsley** as a tonic when it can eat normally.

CATARACT

A cloudy lens indicates a cataract (different from blue eye). If the condition is due to an existing disease (i.e. diabetes) then this must also be treated. Take a leaf of **greater celandine**, freshly washed, and rub its stem between your thumb and forefinger. The expressed juice is smeared lightly over the closed eyelid so that both corners are gently touched. This simple treatment, given daily over a number of weeks, will slowly but surely rid the eye of the cataract. Also bathe the affected eye daily with **camomile tisane. Sage tisane** must be administered, two dropperfuls three times daily.

Alternatives
A drop of **Swedish bitters** is brushed over the closed eyelid morning and evening until the condition disappears. It is better to use your washed fingertip rather than cotton wool. The **camomile** eye-bath and internal course of **sage tisane** must also be given, as detailed above.

Herbal Supplements
Feed **watercress, wild garlic, parsley,** carrots, green vegetables
and honey and **garlic pills.**

CEREBRAL OEDEMA

Chop and mince half a tablespoonful of **rest-harrow roots,**
soak them in half a pint of cold spring water, leave overnight
and strain in the morning. Warm this **tisane** until tepid, then
put in a thermos flask and administer one dropperful half an
hour before the first meal, and one dropperful half an hour
after it. Repeat in the evening. Take two flannel bags (they
can be made from hastily stitched facecloths!), put a tablespoonful of **camomile** into each one, heat in a low oven
or over a hot radiator, and when pleasantly warm apply
alternately to the patient's head, holding in place until cool,
for twenty minutes after the final dosage (morning and
evening) of **tisane** has been given. **Important:** if the oedema
has developed after heatstroke, tepid-to-cool **camomile compresses** must be substituted for the hot flannel treatment.

Alternatives
Prepare a **tisane** from the flowering stems of **lily-of-the-valley**
(the measurements in this case are half a teaspoonful of the
dried or fresh herb to half a pint of water). Give one dropperful three times daily, and make a warm **compress** of the
flowers for the cat's head (again, tepid-to-cool if the cat has
had heatstroke). Do not leave cool **compresses** on for longer
than 30 minutes. An old but effective remedy advises equal
parts of **catnip, rosemary, red sage, marjoram, wood betony**
and **pennyroyal** (one level teaspoonful each) to be added to
three pints of boiling water, simmered down to two pints,
strained, and poured boiling hot upon one ounce of **skullcap**
and a tiny pinch of **cayenne** (no more than the tip of a teaspoonful). The **infusion** is allowed to clear, and one dropperful is given every hour. Twice a day, a flannel soaked in
hot apple cider vinegar and **mustard** is applied to the soles
of the paws.

CHASTEK'S PARALYSIS see Thiamine Deficiency, p. 139

CHEMOSIS

Treat as for Blepharitis, p. 57.

COCCIDIOMYCOSIS

Treat as for Blastomycosis, p. 56.

COCCIDIOSIS

Crowded, unnatural, unhygienic conditions cause this parasitic disease. The parasites are present in the faeces. All soiled areas must be cleaned, and the cat's living quarters made healthy and hygienic. Give the patient a **calamus root tisane** (**calamus root** is left to infuse cold overnight—it must *not* be prepared with boiling water), one dropperful three times daily, and feed the **leaves** of **wild garlic**, finely minced and mixed into the daily meals and in the form of **pills**. This is an essential part of the treatment. A **speedwell tisane** should also be administered morning and evening, two dropperfuls each time.

Herbal Supplements
Garlic pills should be given regularly.

CONCUSSION

Give a **tisane** of **St John's wort, skullcap** and **white** or **wild rose**, four dropperfuls six times a day. **Swedish bitters compresses** should be applied to the back of the head (several times a day and overnight). **Golden seal** should also be given separately in a little warm milk, three dropperfuls four times a day.

Herbal Supplements
The cat should maintain a fast for 24 hours, except for honey balls given four times a day. For four days more, keep the

patient on the invalid foods described in Chapter Two. On the sixth day, the cat can begin to resume a normal diet.

CONJUNCTIVITIS

Wash the eyes regularly with **camomile tisane**. Use it also as a **compress**, morning and evening. A **speedwell, rosemary, stinging nettle** and **marigold tisane** must be given internally, two dropperfuls three times daily. A **compress** of Swedish bitters should also be applied twice a day.

Alternatives
One level tablespoonful of **cornflower** is infused in a cupful of boiling water for two minutes, and used six times as an eyewash throughout the day. A **stinging nettle, horsetail** and **thyme tisane** must also be administered, two dropperfuls four times daily. The **Swedish bitters compresses** should be applied as above.

Herbal Supplements
Give **garlic** and honey **pills, watercress** and **wild garlic**. The herbs must be finely shredded.

CONSTIPATION

A **tisane** of **wild chicory,** one dropperful in the early morning and another at noon, relieves constipation; or drop a pinch of **plaintain seeds** into a little water and give three times a day.

Alternatives
A **tisane** of **walnut leaves,** one dropperful three times daily, cures the condition, as does a **tisane** made from the **shoots** of **fennel,** one dropperful four times a day.

Herbal Supplements
The fresh **shoots** of **fennel** can be diced and fed raw to the cat. Also give **wild garlic leaves, watercress** and **feverfew.** Dried figs, combined with honey and given as **pills,** are very

effective. If the constipation is very severe or stubborn, a tiny pinch of finely ground **senna leaves** can be added to the concoction. Feed the cat the **tonic foods** listed on pp. 9–16, and ensure that the cat is given an overall healthy diet.

COUGHING

A troublesome cough can be relieved by preparing a **tisane** of **coltsfoot** with honey and a few drops of apple cider vinegar. Give this very warm, three dropperfuls every hour until symptoms ease. If the cough is bronchial, an expectorant herbal cough mixture can be made from **coltsfoot** (**leaves** and **flowers**), **rosemary**, **lungwort**, **plantain** and **horehound**. Add some lemon juice and honey, and administer in the same measure as above.

CRYPTOCOCCOSIS (fungal disease)

Treat as for blastomycosis, p. 56. In addition, alternate a **horsetail poultice** with a **marigold compress** on the sinuses, and also the abdomen if affected, for several hours a day and overnight. If the eyes are affected, a **camomile compress** must also be used.

Herbal Supplements
Watercress and **wild garlic** must be given, finely minced, in honey **pills**.

CYSTITIS

This condition is generally due to bladder stones, bladder gravel and the stagnation or concentration of urine (see cystitis under Bladder, p. 55). If you have to use dry feeds as the cat's staple diet, please also ensure that you give it supplements of grain, fruit, vegetables, herbs, honey and seaweed as detailed in **tonic foods**, pp. 9–16. In addition it is very important to administer a regular **tisane** of **small-flowered willowherb**, two dropperfuls night and morning, to cats who are taking dried feed.

I would like to offer some further recipes for the cure of cystitis, as it is such a common and unpleasant condition. Like the herbal supplements given under Blocked Bladder (p. 56), the methods below also dissolve bladder stone and gravel, cleanse the urinary tract of infection, and stop the formation of concentrated urine. (If your cat's urine is stagnant because it has to stay inside all night, or because it is reluctant to go outside in cold or wet weather, it is necessary to provide a litter tray overnight for its health and comfort.)

Barley water is an excellent remedy for cystitis. Give four dropperfuls daily, and also make up a gruel flavoured with honey for the patient's enjoyment. If the patient doesn't like the taste, you can make the gruel thin enough to feed by dropper. Give one dropperful before each meal. **Violet tisane** is a powerful dissolvent and a tonic for the bladder. Give three dropperfuls three times a day. **Cleavers** is highly efficacious in the treatment of cystitis. Give two dropperfuls four times daily. The **small-flowered willowherb** is a panacea for all bladder complaints; administer two dropperfuls night and morning. There is a potion called the '**Hippocratic kidney tonic**' which has a wonderfully cleansing and healing effect on the bladder and the urinary system. Here is the recipe:

Make a **tisane** of **violet, parsley** (or **stinging nettle**), **eyebright, cleavers, fennel, groundsel** (or meadowsweet), **small-flowered willowherb, couchgrass** (one level teaspoonful of each herb), plus two tablespoonfuls of **barley water,** in one and a half pints of water. Refrigerate, warm the **tisane** before administering to the patient, and give one dropperful four times daily. Covered and refrigerated, the medicine will last ten days, but throw away any that remains after this time.

Herbal Supplements

Watercress, cucumber, wild garlic, feverfew and **wood sorrel** are all effective remedies for cystitis. Feed the **leaves** raw, finely chopped, with honey **pills.**

CYSTS

A **horsetail poultice** is applied overnight, and **horsetail tisane** is given morning and evening, three dropperfuls each time. **Watercress** and **couchgrass** must be fed raw, finely chopped in the food and also in honey **pills** (this is an essential part of the treatment).

DEAFNESS

An old but almost magical remedy well worth a try is to moisten the acoustic duct very regularly with a cotton-wool tipped ear cleaner (take great care with this) well soaked in **Swedish bitters**. Also massage the **drops** well into the temples, around the outside ears, into the forehead, down the bridge of the nose, around the eyes (avoid contact with the eyes), and all over the back of the head. Do this six times daily. Twice a day, repeat the whole process with **lavender oil**.

DENTAL ABSCESS

Treat as for Abscess, p. 43. As dental abscesses are more difficult to treat than those elsewhere, add **thyme** and a pinch of **golden seal** to the standard **stinging nettle** and **horsetail tisane**. Another important addition to the treatment is to rub the affected tooth and gum with a few drops of **Swedish bitters** four times a day, and to give one-third of a teaspoonful internally night and morning. It is also advisable to improve the cat's general dental hygiene (see Teeth, p. 137).

DENTAL DISEASE see Teeth, p. 137

DERMATITIS see Feline Miliary Dermatitis, p. 88.

DIABETES

Diabetes Insipitus
This form of the disease occurs when the patient's kidneys are unable to condense the body's waste products into a normal quantity of urine, so the cat passes huge quantities

of weak urine. The treatment is as follows: two dropperfuls morning and evening of **stinging nettle, horsetail** and **catnip tisane**; a **compress** of **Swedish bitters** should be applied to the lungs and pancreas for the duration of an hour, once a week; an **agrimony** and **plantain tisane**, two dropperfuls mid-morning and mid-afternoon must be administered, as should a **bilberry leaf infusion**. This is prepared by boiling two tablespoonfuls of **bilberry leaves** in one pint of spring water, simmering down to half a pint, and giving the cat two warm dropperfuls three times a day. **The bilberry leaves must be picked before the berries begin to ripen,** or they will not contain the necessary myrtillin to help to cure the condition. In addition a special diet must be adhered to (see below).

Diabetes Mellitus

This is the more serious form, and is named after the sweetness of the urine, occurring because the pancreas is unable to produce sufficient insulin needed by the body cells to burn glucose, their vital energy source (insulin enables glucose to gain admission to the cell); the cells therefore signal for more glucose, so that its level rises higher and higher, eventually spilling out of the overloaded kidneys and into the urine, making it sweet. It is essential that the diet given below should be considered as a vital component of treatment.

The herbal medication is the same as for Diabetes Insipitus, except that half a dropperful of **calamus root tisane** is given six times throughout the day (two can be given an hour apart in the early morning, and four throughout the early and late evening if you are at work during the day). The **diet** consists of **celery, watercress, wild garlic, cucumber, carrot, garlic pills, onion extract pills,** the **leaves** and **shoots** of **elder,** chicory roots, salsify, asparagus, leek and especially three **stems** of **dandelion.** Whichever dietary ingredients you select from the above list, **catnip** and **dandelions** must be part of your cat's programme. Pick three full-flowering **stems** of the latter each day (the plant flowers from March to November), wash, and only then remove the **flower heads** (they keep the properties of the plant intact), chop very finely and combine with the cat's food. It is very important to ensure that the **milky** juice exuded from the **stems** is not lost. Mince all ingredients offered very finely, except for **cucumber**, which the cat will normally eat quite happily in chunks or slices. Add one or two drops of neat apple cider vinegar each day to the patient's food. You can also concoct a **diabetic tincture** which is made by crushing three large cloves of **garlic**, adding them to a pint of apple cider vinegar, and leaving the bottle to stand for a fortnight in a warm place. Mix half a small teaspoonful of the **tincture** into the food each day. Diabetes can also be caused by **shock**, so add four drops of **Dr Bach's Rescue Remedy** four times a day to the treatment given, supplanting it with the same of **Dr Bach's Rock Rose** after one week. Treatment needs to be maintained for several months.

Alternatives
Here are two old and venerated recipes for the cure of diabetes:

SWISS HERBAL INFUSION
3 tsp **Benedict's herb**
1 tsp **bilberry leaves**
1 tsp **blackberry leaves**
3 tsp **cinquefoil**
1 tsp dried **green beanpods**
1 tsp **periwinkle**

Use heaped teaspoonfuls of each herb. Dry and grind the herbs, and use one small level teaspoonful per half-cup of boiling water, infused for three minutes. Feed the entire resulting liquid by dropper throughout the day.

LINCTUS OF THE SEVEN HILLS
(a South Yorkshire wisewoman's remedy)
1 oz **prickly ash berries**
1 oz **agrimony**
1 oz **queen of the meadow (meadowsweet)**
1 oz **bistort root**
1 oz **elder shoots** and **leaves**

Bruise the **bistort**; boil in two pints of water and simmer down to one, then strain; whilst still hot, add half a small level teaspoonful of **cayenne** and one-quarter of a small teaspoonful of **olive oil**, and administer one dropperful six times daily.

DIARRHOEA

It is important to discover the cause of this condition, as it could be due to incorrect feeding, a food allergy or intestinal worms. These problems must be remedied as well as the symptoms. If the diarrhoea is due to an indefinite cause and is a chronic symptom of general debility, feed the **tonic foods** listed on pp. 9–16. Whether the cause is known or unknown, the following treatment will bring relief: take the patient off all solid food for at least 24 hours, and give regular dropperfuls of apple cider vinegar and honey (one heaped teaspoonful of each to a cup of hot spring water). Give six half-dropperfuls of **calamus root tisane** throughout the day, and two dropperfuls of **marigold tisane** night and morning. A soft linen bag (sew together two large handkerchiefs, or cut a pillowcase in two, and tack-stitch the top) filled with dried or fresh **camomile herbs** and **flowers**, warmed and bandaged on like a **poultice**, is wonderfully soothing to the patient's stomach.

Alternatives
A **sage** and **camomile tisane**, two dropperfuls four times daily, supplemented with the honey and vinegar treatment (see above) will quickly relieve diarrhoea. **Benedict's herb** is an excellent remedy for all intestinal disorders. Give two dropperfuls four times a day of the **tisane**, and half a small teaspoonful morning and evening of the **root tincture**.

Herbal Supplements
Feed **wild garlic**, **garlic pills**, and pounded **sage** in honey **pills**.

DIGESTIVE SYSTEM

One of the best herbs for the entire digestive system is **Benedict's herb**. Prepare a **tisane** and give two dropperfuls four times daily. A tonic **tincture** can also be made from the roots in the usual way. Feed one small teaspoonful in a dropper of spring water morning and evening.

DISC DISEASE

This is usually only a problem in cats after a physical trauma. If your vet is unable to treat the protrusions, it is well worth applying the following treatment.

Disc Lesions
The patient needs to be given a **horsetail bath**. Half-fill a clean bucket with fresh or dried **horsetail**, cover with cold water and leave to soak overnight. Bring to the boil the next day (the herbs and water have to be transferred gradually to a large pan, boiled, strained, and the resulting **infusion** poured directly into the cat's bath (minus the cat, of course!). Add tepid water to cool the bath to a pleasant warmth, and immerse the cat. The patient must sit (or lie if possible) so that the area of the kidneys is well-covered. The cat has to remain in the bath for at least 15 minutes, so it is a good idea to add a few drops of **lavender oil** to the bath water to promote calm and relaxation. The constant, gentle pouring of warm water over the coat whilst stroking the cat and speaking to it in a soothing tone can sometimes help. If the cat is particularly uncooperative try trickling warm water down the spine. After 15 minutes, take the patient out of the bath, wrap well in towels and, keeping it very warm, nurse for an hour, replacing the wet towels with warmed, dry ones every 15 minutes. Then dry thoroughly with a hairdryer.

Alternatives
A **poultice** of **comfrey leaves** should be applied in the morning and afternoon, and one of **comfrey roots** during the evening and overnight. A **decoction** of **peony roots** can be added to

the bath water in which the patient should be immersed as above. If this option is chosen, **peony tincture** (2 tablespoonfuls) should also be a constituent of the bath water.

Herbal Supplements
A traditional remedy is to feed crushed fresh crab in hot **sage and rosemary broth** (add the crab and simmer; take off the boil and allow to cool until warm before administering to the patient) and to apply some of the concoction to the affected parts. Slipped discs are treated as DISLOCATIONS.

Dislocations
The fresh **leaves** of **butterbur** must be applied directly to the affected area in the case of dislocation. Bandage them on as a **poultice**, changing them every few hours.

Alternatives
Comfrey leaves may be used as above, with the difference that they must be scalded before being made into a **poultice**.

Herbal Supplements
Administer as for disc diseases above.

DISTEMPER see Feline Infectious Enteritis, p. 83.

DRIBBLING

Dribbling (urinary incontinence) can be due to a number of factors. In most cases, a warm **poultice** of dried **club moss** applied to the area of the bladder overnight, and a **tisane** of **small-flowered willowherb**, two dropperfuls given morning and evening, will alleviate the problem. If it persists, rub **shepherd's purse tincture** externally into the bladder area and around the base of the spine, night and morning, halve the **small-flowered willowherb** dosage, and give four dropperfuls of **lady's mantle tisane** throughout the day. **Horsetail baths** may have to be given (see Disc Lesions, p. 77), and three dropperfuls of **horsetail tisane** four times daily. Honey in spring water should also be administered by dropper.

DRY EYE

This is a dangerous condition as it can lead to blindness, and is in any case most uncomfortable for the cat. It can be distinguished from other inflamed-eye conditions in that infected matter clings to the actual eyeball instead of accumulating in the corners of the eyes, which is where the tear-flow carries it when adequate. The eye must be bathed very regularly with **mallow tisane** and with the special eye-wash detailed on p. 57 under Blepharospasm. Mallow compresses should also be applied regularly.

EAR INFECTION

Treat as Canker, p. 63.

EAR MITES see Canker, mite infestation, p. 64.

EARS (SUNBURNED)

White or pale-coloured cats are liable to suffer from sunburned ears. It is important to rub **St John's wort oil** well into the cat's ears several times a day in hot, sunny weather (sunburn can occur even on dull days throughout the summer, so apply it whatever the weather from May onwards), paying particular attention to the tips. **Marigold ointment** should also be spread liberally on the ears when the cat comes in for the night. In both cases, the interior and exterior ear-flap should be treated. If the ears are already damaged so that flaky, scaly or scabby conditions appear on top of raised, swollen skin, moisten the areas with expressed **juice** of **greater celandine** frequently throughout the day. If these patches have become sores, bathe with warm **horsetail tisane** alternated with warmed **mallow tisane** (has to be *prepared* with cold water) and apply the **greater celandine juice** treatment as detailed above. Bruised **plantain leaves** are used as a **compress** to cover the sores. Fifteen minutes after each application of the fresh **celandine juice**, smear the ears well with **marigold ointment**. **Horsetail** and **mallow tisane** should be applied as a **compress** throughout the night. Ten dropperfuls of a **tisane** made from **marigold, horsetail, stinging nettle** and **speedwell** should be given during the day, and two of **yarrow, violets** and **golden rod** during the evening. This somewhat arduous treatment will often save the ears when squamous cell carcinoma (a form of cancer) is present.

ECLAMPSIA (milk fever)

This condition is caused in nursing queens by calcium deficiency. It can be avoided by giving the pregnant queen two dropperfuls three times daily of **stinging nettle tisane**, and by feeding her meat and vegetable stew containing boiled **stinging nettles**, as these provide an excellent source of calcium.

EMOTIONAL SHOCK

Emotional shocks and upsets are helped by a **tisane** of **golden rod,** two dropperfuls three times daily. Legend tells us that an angel of mercy brings her benison to the delicately flowered **golden rod** and so to all who partake of the herb under her divine protection. Certainly the golden-eyed Bast (ancient Egyptian goddess and protectress of cats) might be considered to be a spiritual component of this angel! All cats will benefit from **golden rod's** soothing effect in times of distress and trauma.

Herbal Supplements
Shredded **lettuce** is good for distraught cats; also give honey **pills** and cut down on the cat's protein, replacing it with vegetables and grain.

ENCEPHALITIS

Treat as for Meningitis, p. 112, with the exception that **thyme** is added to the **tisane**.

ENEMA

A gentle enema is made from an **infusion** of **stinging nettle** and **horsetail**, equal parts of each, administered tepid-to-warm. A teaspoonful of **olive oil** can be added to the mixture. One teacupful is usually all that is necessary.

Alternative
A simple method of giving an enema is to insert a peeled clove of **garlic** into the rectum at night, only care has to be taken that the first skin beneath the rind is completely intact and unbroken, otherwise the enema will be too punishing for the poor cat!

ENTERITIS

Make an infusion of the following herbs:

1 part **tormentil root**
2 parts **comfrey root**
1 part **marshmallow root**
2 parts **marigold**
1 part **goldenseal**
1 part **meadowsweet**

For measures and method see Tisanes, p. 32, and Infusions, p. 33. Give three dropperfuls three times daily. A tisane of balm must be administered half an hour before each treatment of the mixed tisane. Give four dropperfuls. It will induce vomiting; but there is no need to be alarmed, as expulsion of the morbid matter in the stomach is the only method by which to allay the symptomatic vomiting. Give the balm tisane only during the first 24 hours of the onset of symptoms.

Herbal Supplements
Put the cat on a fast for the duration of the attack (or at least throughout its height). To provide the patient with nourishment and healing whilst it is undergoing its fast, make **slippery elm** into a thick gruel and feed three small teaspoon-

fuls morning, noon and evening. Also give honey in spring water. Put one and a half level teaspoonfuls in a cup, half-fill it with warm (not hot) spring water and feed to the patient throughout the day. If there is copious vomiting, it will generally be found that one-half or one-quarter of a dropperful of the **infusion** and the honey-in-water can be ingested every fifteen minutes, and one-quarter of a teaspoonful of the gruel every half-hour. When the worst is past, replace the honey with the same measurement of apple cider vinegar and lemon juice. To ease the patient's abdominal pain, fill a linen bag with dried or fresh **camomile**, warm it, and bandage it to the cat's stomach. (Take care not to cause any pressure.)

EPILEPSY

Mistletoe is perhaps the best herb of all to counteract this condition. The **berries** are not used, only the leaves and the twigs, which are not poisonous. Prepare a standard **tisane** and give three dropperfuls three times daily. The **tincture** (bought from herbalists) should be rubbed into the heart, liver and kidney region twice a day. A **compress** of Swedish **bitters** should also be applied to the back of the head.

Alternatives
Cleavers tisane, three dropperfuls three times daily, is a herbal cure for epilepsy. The same dosage of **lady's mantle tisane** is also beneficial. An **infusion** of the **roots** of **butterbur**, two dropperfuls twice a day, will bring relief. The same dosage of **thyme tisane**, administered three weeks out of four all year round, is an excellent remedy. In all cases, the **Swedish bitters compress** treatment should be adhered to.

Tips
Although the cat may need to be comforted and made much of afterwards (some prefer to be quiet and alone for a period in a dark place) there is unfortunately nothing that can be done to alleviate the actual fit. **Lavender oil**, applied under the nose on cotton wool and rubbed into the temples afterwards, will help to ease the resultant confusion and stress. A

few drops of **Dr Bach's Rescue Remedy** will also be of great benefit. The fit will end of itself after a few moments. If the fit is prolonged, the patient must be rushed to the vet.

Herbal Supplements
Feed **garlic** and honey **pills** regularly.

FALSE PREGNANCY

A **tisane** of **feverfew**, two dropperfuls three times daily, will benefit the queen if she is pregnant, and soothe away the symptoms if she is not.

FELINE INFECTIOUS ANAEMIA

Give three dropperfuls three times daily of a **tisane** made from equal parts of **speedwell**, **agrimony** and **cleavers**. Two dropperfuls of **thyme tisane** must also be given three times a day. A **poultice** of **nasturtium** (the fresh plant) should be applied to the area of the spleen overnight. Two drops of **nasturtium tincture** should be given in a dropperful of spring water and half a small teaspoon of apple cider vinegar, night and morning.

Herbal Supplements
Boil a half-ounce of black dates with one ounce of honey. Feed the cat half a small level teaspoonful in warm water once a day. Fresh **shiitake mushrooms**, diced very finely and added to the cat's meat, are also very good. **Parsley** is a must for anaemia because of its rich iron content. **Watercress, wild garlic, garlic pills** and honey pills should also be given. Royal jelly is another remedy for anaemia. To kill the microbials that cause it, concentrate on the provision of raw **garlic**, in pill form (see above) and grated finely into the food.

FELINE INFECTIOUS ENTERITIS

This disease, more serious than ordinary enteritis but thankfully less common due to vaccination, is often referred to as feline distemper. It is a viral disease. Its treatment is the same

as that for enteritis (see p. 81), with the difference that the
tisane mixture has to be given four times throughout the day,
with the addition of a **stinging nettle tisane,** which must be
administered every two hours throughout the peak of the
illness, and every four hours thereafter. Give one and a half
dropperfuls each time. The **tisane mixture** should be made
up with two parts **meadowsweet,** and the linen bag of **camomile** must be rewarmed and (without causing any pressure)
reapplied every hour. **Nasturtium tincture** should be *very
gently* stroked into the abdomen area night and morning.
Keep the cat warm, dry, clean and comforted at all times.
Feeding the patient the recommended **slippery elm gruel** is
vitally important in the treatment of feline infectious enteritis.

Alternatives
This old remedy has been known to cure the worst and most
stubborn cases of dysentery, diarrhoea and enteritis. The
ingredients can be stored in your herbal medicine cabinet
against times of need. (It is strongly advised that for severe
cases, the following treatment should be combined with two
dropperfuls of **mistletoe tisane,** given three times daily.)

YORKSHIRE WISEWOMAN'S WORTCUNNING FOR AFFLICTED BOWELS

1 level tbsp **turkey rhubarb**
1 tsp **gum catechu** (powdered)
1 tsp **tormentil root**
1 level tbsp **barley flour**
1 tsp **gum myrrh** (powdered)
1 tsp **wild yam**
1 tsp **bayberry**
1 tsp **cinnamon**

All finely pulverised, mixed well, and passed through a fine
sieve. One-quarter of an ordinary teaspoonful is to be beaten
well with the same of the finest quality **slippery elm,** put into
a dropper filled with warm water and a drop of honey, and
fed to the ailing cat three times a day. As it begins to recover,
the whole may be made into a gruel by dispensing with the

spring water. Feed this mixture to the cat four times daily, until it is entirely well again.

FELINE INFECTIOUS PERITONITIS

The Wet Form

Where fluid accumulates in the abdomen. Give an ENEMA (see p. 81) every four hours, made up of **dandelion tisane (leaves** and **roots)** and **horsetail tisane.** A **horsetail poultice** must be applied to the entire swollen abdomen, changed every four hours, and left on overnight. Great care must be taken to ensure that the **poultice** does not cause any pressure on the abdomen. Before applying the night-time **poultice,** leave the abdomen bare for two hours, and very gently massage **nasturtium tincture** into the belly (your touch will need to be as light as thistledown to avoid giving the patient pain). Before putting on a fresh **poultice** in the morning, put one level teaspoonful of **cayenne powder** into a small bowl of very warm water (about half a pint), soak and wring out a face flannel in the **infusion,** and apply very gently all over the abdomen, soaking and wringing out again after holding the cloth in place for a moment or two. Do this for about ten minutes, and then proceed with the first **horsetail poultice** of the day. Throughout each day, the following herbal **tisane mixture** must be administered, one dropperful every hour for 12–14 hours:

   2 parts **marshmallow root**
   1 part **slippery elm**
   1 part **calamus root**
   1 part **dandelion root**
   2 parts **St John's wort**

For *'part' measures* see Tisanes, p. 32. Boil the ingredients in one pint of water and simmer down to half a pint. Take one small teaspoonful of **gum myrrh,** mix it in one table-spoonful of warm water, pour the half-pint of **tisane mixture** onto it and add one-quarter of a teaspoonful of **ginger.** When this treatment is given every hour, a **tisane** of **stinging nettle** and **horsetail**, one dropperful, must also be administered. Alternate this hourly dosage with one and half dropperfuls of **linseed tisane** (see instructions below on preparation, under The Dry Form). If there is vomiting, the two dropperfuls of **tisane** must be given in drops, one from each dropper every ten minutes. If the vomiting is severe, drops of **balm tisane** must be given until the problem is alleviated. **Horsetail** and **sage** baths are also of great benefit; but the patient *must* be kept very warm during and after the bath, and, of course, dried thoroughly, first with warmed towels, and afterwards a hairdryer.

The Dry Form
The treatment is the same as for the wet form of FIP, except that the whole area of the abdomen has to be first smeared lightly with **marigold ointment** and then covered with a large **compress** of Swedish bitters during the day. The **horsetail poultices** should be applied in the evening, changed before retiring and left on overnight. Give the **tisane mixture** exactly as prescribed above, throughout the morning and early afternoon. Then cease the treatment and give instead a **tisane** made of equal parts of **agrimony** and **cleavers tisane**, two dropperfuls every three hours until the end of the 14-hour period. During the mid-afternoon to evening period, two dropperfuls of **linseed tisane** should also be given (pour half a pint of boiling water onto one small, level teaspoonful of **linseed** and half a small, level teaspoonful of **liquorice root**, cover the vessel, keep in a warm place for four hours, then strain and refrigerate; the mixture will last for ten days in the refrigerator, but it must be warmed before it is given to the patient). Give the cat the required dosage every three hours until the 14-hour period is over.

FELINE LEUKAEMIA

Prepare a **tisane** made of equal parts of **stinging nettle, greater celandine, elder shoots, cleavers, speedwell, yarrow, marigold, blue flag, dandelion roots** and **St John's wort**. If fresh herbs can be obtained, all the better, but ensure that at least some are fresh. The **tisane** can be made up daily, or kept in the refrigerator for seven days. Always renew the **infusion** after this period of time. To make the weekly **tisane**, pour two and a half pints of spring water, just on the boil, over a teaspoonful of each of the herbs, leave to infuse for one minute, strain, put into vessels and refrigerate. The patient must be given three dropperfuls of this mixture ten times a day. **Calamus root tisane** must also be given (cold-soaked—see instructions on preparation, p. 34). Mix half a dropperful with one-quarter of a teaspoonful of **Swedish bitters** and one-quarter of a teaspoonful of honey in a little warm spring water and give six times daily, preferably half an hour before and half an hour after the patient has eaten. Put a **horsetail poultice** over the area of the liver and spleen at night, and throughout the day use **Swedish bitters** as a **compress.** If lymphosarcoma develops, fill a bottle with **marjoram** and **almond oil** and leave to steep near a heat source (or in the sun) for ten days. Then combine it with **St John's wort oil** and a few drops of **lavender oil** and rub gently into the swollen lymph nodes. (If there are swollen glands with leukaemia, this **oil** mixture will relieve them.) The fresh **leaves** of **marigold, plantain** and **butterbur** must be well washed and, whilst still wet, pounded to a pulp and applied one after the other to the swollen areas as a **poultice,** changed and alternated every two hours. Continue with the **tisane** as detailed above, and with the overnight **horsetail poultices.**

After recovery, it is a very good idea to give the patient a maintenance treatment of **stinging nettle, yarrow, marigold** and **speedwell,** three dropperfuls four times a day, as the feline leukaemia virus is extremely persistent.

Herbal Supplements
Parsley, wild garlic and **watercress** are good herbs to give in cases of leukaemia. Shred all greens very fine. Also feed honey and **garlic pills.**

FELINE MILIARY DERMATITIS

If the condition is due to flea infestation, see Fleas, p. 90. If it is due to parasitic infection, see Canker (mite infestation), p. 64. Otherwise, the patient's eczema or feline miliary dermatitis could be caused by a number of factors. First of all, check the cat's diet in case it is suffering from vitamin deficiency. Don't give it raw egg white because it contains avidin, a chemical which neutralizes biotin, an essential vitamin which the cat is consequently unable to absorb. Improve the diet (see Herbal Supplements below) and check that the dermatitis is not due to an allergic reaction. Cow's milk often causes allergy, so discontinue its provision for at least two weeks. If the eczema doesn't improve, substitute each component of the cat's diet until the source of the problem becomes apparent. If the eczema is not connected with food, check the patient's environment (even the brand of detergent used to wash the bedding, or some kinds of industrial litter, have occasionally proved to be the culprit). If the cause cannot be found, give the patient a **tisane** made of equal parts of **plantain, speedwell, stinging nettle** and **thyme**, four dropperfuls six times a day. Also give two dropperfuls of a **golden rod tisane** three times daily. A **stinging nettle** and **horsetail enema** should be given once a day until the skin has cleared. **Sage** and **horsetail baths** (given separately) are effective; also, wash the affected parts with a decoction of **speedwell**, and give half a teaspoonful of the fresh **juice** of **speedwell**, in the morning and evening. If the outbreak is very severe, **compresses** of **Swedish bitters** should be applied overnight to the stomach and kidneys.

Herbal Supplements

Feed **couchgrass, ordinary grass, catmint, valerian, watercress, parsley, wild garlic, sage, garlic** and honey **pills**. All greens have to be macerated and combined with the patient's regular food, although some cats delight in eating the chopped herbs separately. Care should be taken with **valerian**. Don't give the fresh herb, but prepare one teaspoonful of the fresh juice from the stalks and flowers instead and mix it into the patient's food. Slices of fruit, especially apple, are beneficial. Let the patient sit out in the sunshine for as long as possible.

FELINE RESPIRATORY DISEASE see Cat Flu, p. **66**

FELINE UROLITHIASIS SYNDROME see Bladder, blocked bladder, p. 56

FITS AND CONVULSIONS

If the fits are not due to epilepsy (see p. 82) they may occur because of kidney and liver disease, brain tumour, physical post-accident trauma (usually a blood clot), infections, poisons, eclampsia (milk fever) or worms. There can be a tendency to convulsion whatever the cause, however, so as well as identifying and remedying the underlying problem, the following treatment should be given: prepare a standard **tisane** of **rue** and **catnip** sweetened with honey, and administer, with or without other treatment, two dropperfuls five times daily. Also give a separate **golden rod** and **lavender tisane**, two dropperfuls three times a day, and administer **horsetail baths**. **Horsetail poultices** should also be applied to the region of the kidneys and to the back of the head (so that the base of the brain is covered) for several hours once a day, until the tendency to convulse disappears. Sadly, little can be done whilst the cat is actually in convulsion, although medical evidence seems to prove that it doesn't suffer, despite appearances to the contrary. If a cat remains in convulsion for more than a few minutes, it is in danger and must be taken to the vet immediately. **Compresses** of **rue** and **Swedish bitters**, tepid but not cold, might help if applied to the back of the head and the neck in this situation, but your overriding concern must be to place the patient in the care of your vet as soon as possible. A prolonged fit is an emergency.

FLATULENCE

An infusion of **fennel** half an hour before feeding helps this problem. Uncooked carbohydrates (peas, beans, etc.) cause flatus, as do some vegetables. Take care not to give tainted meat or fish. A cooked egg a day is good for your cat, but might be the cause of excessive flatulence. A few teaspoonfuls of yogurt in the daily diet will relieve the problem. If your cat is elderly, it may have poor muscle tone in the bowel. Follow the directions for treatment under Bowel Muscles (weak), p. 59. There could well be a chronic parasite infestation, in which case a **tisane** of equal parts of **stinging nettle**, **meadowsweet** and **thyme** would need to be administered, three dropperfuls six times daily. If there is a chronic bowel infection, give **Benedict's herb** in the same quantity. Whatever other treatment is necessary, a flatulent cat will greatly benefit from six half-dropperfuls of **calamus root** (cold-soaked overnight, then strained and warmed in the morning) given throughout the day.

Herbal Supplements
Feed three or four small meals per day, rather than two large ones, and give shredded **mint** and **lemon balm** (one small teaspoonful of each) with each meal.

FLEAS

Groom the cat daily with a fine-toothed flea comb, and wash its coat thoroughly in a bath of **thyme** and **nasturtium water**. To prepare this, put a good handful of each herb in a cloth laundry bag (available from supermarkets) and soak in a bucket half-filled with boiling water. After two minutes, strain and empty the infusion into the cat's bath; cool until comfortably warm before immersing the cat. This is a quick emergency measure; otherwise, follow procedure for standard herbal baths (p. 36). Soak the coat well (fleas can take up to four minutes to drown!) and, after repeated washings, shampoo well with a **rosemary** shampoo into which half a tablespoonful of **nasturtium tincture** has been added, together with a teaspoonful of **eucalyptus tincture**. Give the patient a really good scrub, and rinse well. If the infestation is heavy, up to three baths have to be given, following the directions above each time. Finally, dry the cat thoroughly, and give the coat a good rub with the juice of a lemon diluted in half a pint of spring water. Dry off with a hairdryer, and put a few drops of **eucalyptus tincture** into the ears, under the chin, under the tail and into the pit of each limb. Then wash the cat's bedding, its basket or bed, its litter tray, toys and food bowls in a herbal flea-repellent wash. The same procedure has to be followed for furnishings and carpets (even curtains!) in the rooms which the cat has occupied. Flea-powder the cat, its bedding, and its bed from time to time with finely ground **rosemary**, **nasturtium**, **camomile**, **eucalyptus**, **flea-bane** and **tansy**. In wet weather, a lotion prepared from **sting-ing nettle** and **nasturtium tisane** into which **lavender** and **rosemary oil** have been added (one-quarter of a teaspoonful of oil to each cup of **tisane**) will keep fleas at bay. Thorough grooming, powdering, use of the flea lotion, and frequent vacuuming of the areas in the house where the cat is allowed will control fleas, (put some of the flea powder in the vacuum bag and ensure that it is thoroughly sealed).

Herbal Supplements
Grate a small amount of **garlic** into the cat's food each day, and feed the **tonic foods** listed on pp. 9–16 to maintain its resistance.

Flea Allergy Dermatitis
Treat as above, and give a **tisane** of **thyme** and **stinging nettle**, three dropperfuls four times daily. Also give one-quarter of a teaspoonful of the fresh **juice** of **speedwell** night and morn-ing in a dropperful of spring water with one-quarter of a teaspoonful of honey and apple cider vinegar mixed into each one. Rub **nasturtium tincture** into the affected areas or, if the skin is broken, apply bruised **plantain leaves** followed by **marigold ointment**.

FORELEG PARALYSIS

Bind the leg above the paw with a **compress** of **marigold tincture** for four hours during the day, and overnight. If the patient is dragging the leg along the floor, check for sores or ulcers and apply **marigold ointment** if necessary (it has to be reapplied several times a day). If the damage to the radial nerve is very severe and will not heal, put on a **comfrey poultice** in the morning, followed by a massage with **St John's wort oil** four times during the afternoon and evening, and the application of a **compress** of **St John's wort tincture** overnight. **St John's wort tisane** must also be given, four dropperfuls three times daily. Continue the treatment until the leg is back to normal. It is far better to give this remedy a chance to heal the injured nerves than to hastily opt for an amputation.

FRACTURES

If your cat is particularly susceptible to bone fracture, and there is joint pain, stiffness and swelling, reduce its meat intake. No cat should be fed exclusively on meat, as it lacks the necessary quantities of iodine, magnesium, a number of vitamins, calcium and phosphorus. An overload of protein is also toxic. Let one-third of your cat's diet be vegetables, herbs, grains and fruit (see **tonic foods**, pp. 9–16). For the herbal treatment of fractures see the directions under Bones, p. 58.

FROSTBITE

Ear tips and tails are particularly vulnerable. Look for skin that is very pale or blue and that feels icy to the touch. Bathe the affected area with cotton-wool pads soaked in **marigold tisane** (apply warm but not hot), and smear lightly afterwards with **marigold ointment**. Also give a course of **marigold tisane** (four dropperfuls three times daily) to stimulate circulation so that the cat is not susceptible to frostbite.

GASTRITIS

Treat exactly as for diarrhoea, p. 76, only add **camomile** to the **marigold tisane**. The patient is likely to have ingested some toxic substance, so try to discover the culprit and take precautions to guard against any recurrence. If the condition does not considerably improve within 48 hours, rub **nasturtium tincture** gently into the abdomen morning and evening, and apply a **compress** of **Swedish bitters** overnight.

GLAUCOMA

Prepare a standard **tisane** of equal parts of **speedwell, stinging nettle, golden rod** and **marigold,** and give two dropperfuls three times daily. **Horsetail baths** are also necessary, as are **horsetail** and **stinging nettle enemas.** Give both twice a week with the herbal medicine until the condition clears. If it is severe, the full programme of treatment should include enemas and baths administered four times weekly. Glaucoma causes pressure on the eyeball which is very painful and disturbing for the patient. To relieve the suffering and to facilitate healing, put a few drops of **Swedish bitters** on a pad of cotton wool and secure as a **compress** over one of the eyes. Leave on for one hour, then repeat with the other eye. Do this once in the early afternoon and once in the evening. Whilst the **compress** is in place, give two dropperfuls of **horsetail tisane** (both afternoon and evening).

Herbal Supplements
Feed **couchgrass, wild garlic** and **watercress,** all chopped or shredded very fine. Also give honey **pills.**

HAEMORRHAGES see Bleeding, p. 57.

HAIRBALLS

If there is much gagging and straining, and the patient is able to eat only small amounts of food, it is probably unable to rid itself of a hairball. Prepare a **linseed tisane** by pouring half a pint of boiling water onto one small, level teaspoonful of **lin-seed** and half a teaspoonful of **liquorice root,** leave in a warm place for four hours, then strain and give three dropperfuls morning and evening until the hairball is expelled.

HEAD INJURIES

When bleeding (see p. 57) and fractures (see p. 92) have been attended to where necessary, apply **compresses** of **Swedish bitters** several times a day to the injury to prevent complications from arising. It is also a good idea to give a **tisane** of **golden rod,** three dropperfuls twice a day, to ease the patient's trauma.

Herbal Supplements

Feed the patient **cucumber** and **lettuce** (chopped fine). Also give honey **pills.**

HEART

Prepare a **tisane** of **coriander** (**leaves** or **seeds**) and **butterbur** (a **decoction** of the **roots**) and add one teaspoonful of honey and the same of apple cider vinegar per cup. Give three dropperfuls of this solution four times a day as a general tonic for the heart. Where there is congenital malformation of the heart or the great vessels or trauma to the chest, **parsley-honey wine** is very effective in bringing relief. The recipe for the wine comes from author and general practitioner Dr Hertzka (I have modified it slightly by exchanging Dr Hertzka's stipulation of wine vinegar for apple cider vinegar) and its curative virtues are highly praised by Maria Treben and others. Take ten freshly gathered **stalks** of **parsley** (with **leaves**), place them into one and three-quarter pints of organic wine (it must be organic—red or white) and add two table-spoonfuls of apple cider vinegar. Simmer gently for ten minutes on a low heat, then add ten ounces of pure honey (I would recommend a dark clover honey) and continue to simmer very gently for a further four minutes. Strain the concoction and bottle while still hot (the receptacles have to be previously rinsed with rye whisky or other strong alcohol). The bottles must be well stoppered. The sediment is beneficial and should be taken along with the wine. Give the patient two dropperfuls four times a day, or whenever breathing is difficult, rapid, or includes open-mouthed gasping. This wine will help any condition of the heart. Where the problem is a deterioration of the circulation in the actual heart muscle and other circulatory disorders, give three dropperfuls of **mistletoe tisane** three times a day. Enlargement of the heart is improved by a similar application of **agrimony tisane**. For heart failure, make a **tisane** of **corn silk, yellow deadnettle, horsetail** and **heartsease**, and give three dropperfuls four times a day. For all heart conditions, as well as administering the appropriate **tisane** and the **parsley-honey wine,** you can do nothing better for your cat than to prepare a standard **infusion** of **hawthorn** (the **leaves, flowers, twigs** and **berries** can all be used, separately or together), sweeten the **tisane** with half a tablespoonful of honey per cup, and give three dropperfuls three times a day. Of course, in cases of heart disease and failure, fluid intake must be restricted; so if you decide to put your cat on the full treatment programme outlined above (i.e. the appropriate **tisane** for the specific condition, the **parsley-honey wine** and the **hawthorn infusion**), reduce the dosage by a third in the last two instances.

Alternatives
The **leaves, flowers** and **buds** of the **wild rose** are used to make a **tisane** which fortifies and soothes the heart. Give three dropperfuls three times a day. If you cannot find **wild roses,** garden **roses** will do, especially white ones. **Cowslip tisane** is an excellent remedy for the heart. Give three dropperfuls three times a day. Also give the curative **cowslip wine,** which is made by snipping off the umbels of the flowering plant in springtime, filling a two-pint receptacle loosely with them, then pouring white wine over the flower heads until they are covered and the vessel is full. Cork the bottle and leave it near a heat source or in the sun for two weeks. Give two dropperfuls four times a day. For both the **cowslip** and

the **parsley-honey wine,** substitute apple cider vinegar if the patient also suffers from a kidney complaint, and halve the dosage if the cat reacts adversely. For the sake of the heart and the kidneys, it is a good idea to sweeten the vessel of wine with three tablespoonfuls of honey. Avicenna, a physician of the ancient East, gives this recipe to fortify and heal the heart:

AVICENNA'S TONIC

mistletoe
rue
heartsease
rosemary
catnip
pheasant's eye

Catnip is not normally prescribed for the heart, but I have included it for its relaxant and pain-relieving qualities. Make a standard **tisane** of equal parts of the six ingredients (remember that **mistletoe** needs to be cold-soaked overnight) and give four dropperfuls three times a day.

Tips
Never put a cat with an ailing heart out at night. Prevent stressful situations from arising around it, such as the teasing or boisterousness of children or other animals. Keep its environment warm, but not stuffy.

Herbal Supplements
Feed **parsley, wild garlic,** one-quarter of a crushed **kelp** tablet, **garlic** and honey **pills.** All vegetation must be shredded and chopped finely.

HEARTWORM

This condition is much harder to detect in cats than canines. It has similar symptoms to heart failure (weakness, persistent cough, gasping, staggering, reluctance to take exercise), and in fact a patient suffering from heartworm must also be treated as for anaemia and heart disease (see entries under

Anaemia, p. 50 and Heart, p. 94). To expel the worms, it is important to commence treatment in a waxing moon (i.e. between the new moon and the full moon) as the worms are active and breeding at this time (during the waning moon they become dormant and bury themselves into the host tissue, thereby making it more difficult to attack them). Begin the following treatment just after the new moon: grate a clove of garlic into a cup of skimmed milk and simmer for three minutes; give two dropperfuls three times a day of this **infusion**. Prepare a **tisane** of **thyme, stinging nettle, marigold** and **couchgrass,** three dropperfuls four times daily. The ingredients have to be fresh and two tablespoonfuls of **marigold flowers** must be used per cup of boiling water. Bathe the heart three times a day in an **infusion** of **camomile** and **wormwood,** using flannels soaked in the very warm solution and holding them to the heart for 30 seconds a time. Do this for three or four minutes, and then put on a **compress** of **Swedish bitters.** Keep it well moistened, and as well as changing the compress three times a day leave on overnight, if tolerated. Feed a few drops of **Swedish bitters** in a dropper, diluted in a solution of apple cider vinegar and spring water, and pinch of **cayenne pepper,** morning and evening. The patient must also be given **pills** of chopped **rosemary, eucalyptus leaves, cayenne** (just a pinch), **horehound** and **pumpkin seeds.** So important is the next item that I would recommend giving the **leaves** not only separately in **pill** form, but also, well minced, in the food twice daily. This important herb is **wild garlic,** which is not only an excellent remedy for all kinds of worms, but for the heart too. Don't neglect to make use of this vital ingredient in the cure of heartworm! Use fresh **wild garlic leaves,** and three of each of the **pills** per day, plus the liberal use of **wild garlic** chopped into the food, as specified.

Herbal Supplements
The heartworm is carried by mosquitoes as *microfilaria* which it injects into its victim by means of its proboscis. Therefore, it is very advisable to ensure that your cat is not tempting to the mosquito! Mosquitoes love fats, sugars, eggs, creamy milk

and cereals, so cut down on these foods during the mosquito season and give the cat pungent herbs (in **pills**, as **tisanes**, or chopped into the food) which are offensive to mosquitoes, such as **celery seed, garlic, sage, coriander, rosemary, thyme, wormwood, cayenne, onion** and **ginger**. If your cat is already suffering from heartworms, feed chopped **carrot, beetroot, horseradish, onions** and **watercress**. Also add a few drops of apple cider vinegar to its meat, and give one half of a **kelp tablet** per day.

HEATSTROKE

Remove the cat to a cool, well-ventilated place and give tepid-to-cool washes with **St John's wort tisane**, using a soft flannel. Avoid soaking the cat too much, as it must not become chilled. Also administer a **camomile** and **St John's wort tisane**, three dropperfuls four times a day for 48 hours, to help to prevent the onset of cerebral oedema (see p. 68).

Herbal Supplements
Feed **cucumber** and honey in spring water. Also give ten dropperfuls of apple cider vinegar diluted in spring water (two teaspoonfuls per cup). This can be mixed with the required honey if desired.

HERNIA (UMBILICAL)

Sometimes a queen will reject a newborn if it suffers from a pronounced umbilical hernia. This will quickly heal if washed and pounded **lady's mantle** is applied as a **compress**. The kitten will generally be able to tolerate a few drops of **lady's mantle tisane**. Use the dropper from a 10ml bottle and fill it to one-third of its length, give the **tisane** in tiny drops, and repeat every six hours until the hernia begins to reduce. It can then be left to the continually applied **poultices** to heal it completely. Don't give the **tisane** more than three times a day. If the queen continues to reject the kitten, you will have to milk about half an ounce (1ml) from her nipples every three hours to give to the kitten during its first 24 hours.

Give six feeds throughout the 24-hour period. The kitten should stay on its mother's milk for two days to absorb vital antibodies. Then you can feed a formula that your vet will provide and advise on. (Cow's milk is unsuitable for kittens.) Keep returning the kitten to the litter from time to time to see if the queen will accept it. If she persists in her rejection, don't continue to present the kitten to her, as it will become traumatised. Rear it yourself, or see if another nursing queen will accept it.

HERPES

This virus is given to kittens by a queen that is a carrier and has shed the virus particles after giving birth due to the stress involved. The kittens become infected immediately, but the antibodies in the mother's milk prevent the virus from declaring itself for a number of weeks. Treat as for Cat Flu, p. 66.

HISTOPLASMOSIS

Treat as for Blastomycosis, p. 56.

HOOKWORM

Treat as for Roundworms, p. 130.

HYPOGLYCAEMIA

Give a **stinging nettle** and **elder tisane**, four dropperfuls night and morning.

Herbal Supplements
Five fresh **dandelion stems** must be chopped finely and added to the patient's food daily. **Celery, cucumber, carrot** and **onions** keep the blood sugar level steady, as do **leek** and **asparagus.** Cut down on sugars and fats in the cat's diet, although do give a little honey in spring water. Also give apple cider vinegar diluted in spring water (two teaspoonfuls of honey, and the same of vinegar per cup of water).

ILIAC THROMBOSIS

The symptoms are dramatic and include partial or total hind leg paralysis, with the hind legs feeling very cold to the touch and the femoral pulse (under the thigh) being absent in both hind legs; shock, pain and collapse. Rush the cat to the vet immediately. Afterwards, apply a coating of **marigold ointment** to the area of the thrombosis (up the abdomen to the heart) and administer a **Swedish bitters compress**. Leave on overnight, and for four hours twice during the day. A **poultice** of **plantain leaves** should also be applied twice during the day. Give a **tisane** of **stinging nettle, marigold** and **comfrey**, four dropperfuls six times a day.

Herbal Supplements
Give those indicated under Heart, p. 94.

INCONTINENCE see Dribbling, p. 78

INFERTILITY see Abdomen, general debility, p. 42

INJURIES (General)

Apply the scalded **leaves** of **comfrey** as a **poultice** and leave on overnight. During the day, apply **comfrey tincture** as a **compress**, alternated with **poultices** made from **comfrey root**. Give a **tisane** of **golden rod, St John's wort** and **camomile**, three dropperfuls four times a day.

Alternatives
Use **compresses** of **St John's wort oil** night and day, and gently massage the area with the **oil** where appropriate (i.e. not when a massage would cause pain or when it might cause further damage to a fracture). Give the **tisane** described above.

Herbal Supplements
Feed **St John's wort,** the whole plant, chopped finely into the food.

INSECT BITES

Treat with a **poultice** of crushed **sage leaves,** and after its removal apply **St John's wort oil.** To prevent mosquito bites, rub a few drops of **lavender, rosemary,** and **eucalyptus oil** into the cat's fur during the mosquito season (no more than a few, as a strong dose would be harmful to the cat's stomach after grooming), and see **Heartworm,** p. 96 for a list of foods that render the cat internally unattractive to mosquitoes and parasites.

INTESTINES

Benedict's herb is an excellent tonic for the intestines. It will stimulate and cleanse the entire digestive tract. Give **Benedict's herb tisane** with **shepherd's purse** for intestinal bleeding. For intestinal disease, give six half-dropperfuls of **calamus root tisane** (it has to be cold-soaked overnight and given warmed the next day) separately throughout the day, and also administer a **tisane** made of equal parts of **Benedict's herb, stinging nettle, yarrow, marigold** and **speedwell.** Give four dropperfuls ten times a day. Apply **Swedish bitters** as a **compress** to the area of the abdomen. For intestinal sluggishness, give **Benedict's herb tisane** and, separately, the six half-dropperfuls of **calamus root tisane** as stipulated above. For inflammation of the intestines, the same amount of **Benedict's herb tisane** should be administered (three dropperfuls six times a day) mixed with **marigold tisane.** Apply a **horsetail poultice** overnight until the condition is healed, in addition to administering the herbal medicine.

Herbal Supplements
Feed the patient plenty of **watercress, wild garlic** and **parsley.** All herbs must be finely shredded.

JAUNDICE see Liver, hepatitis, p. 106

THE KEY-GASKELL SYNDROME

Prepare a **tisane** of **stinging nettle, yarrow, thistle, leaves** and **fruit** of the **wild** or **garden strawberry, dandelion roots** and **leaves, skullcap, St John's wort, Benedict's herb, parsley** and **horsetail,** and give six dropperfuls every two hours throughout the day. Also give six drops of **St John's wort tincture** every three hours. A separate **tisane** of **common club moss,** three dropperfuls before the first (invalid) meal of the day and three dropperfuls half an hour before a similar evening meal, must be given daily. **Compresses** of **Swedish bitters,** and **horsetail poultices** should be applied to the region of the liver and the abdomen several times throughout the day, and also overnight. Leave the **compresses** on for four hours at a time, and the **poultices** on for two. The night-time applications can stay in place for eight hours.

Herbal Supplements
The Key-Gaskell syndrome patient will suffer from constipation. To relieve this, take one pound of figs (about half a kilo), one heaped teaspoonful of very finely chopped **fennel,** the same of **couchgrass, elder** and **senna leaves,** and half a tablespoonful of **slippery elm flour.** Mince the figs thoroughly, pound the herbs and mix all together well. Form the mixture into small sausages, roll each one in the flour, and store in a ceramic container in the refrigerator. Cut off a little piece about the size of a cherry stone and feed it to the patient first thing in the morning. If the constipation remains stubborn, feed slightly more the next day; if it works too well, reduce the dosage by half. The patient should be put onto an invalid diet (a semi-fast) during the course of the disease, being fed only a selection of the special foods described in Chapter Two. Balls of honey ('honey drops') should be given regularly from the start, with a little very finely chopped or grated **garlic, watercress, parsley** and **wild garlic** folded into them. Apple cider vinegar diluted in spring

water should also be given regularly by dropper. If the patient constantly regurgitates its food and medicine, give half-dropperfuls of each every ten minutes or so. In this way, both can usually be digested. However, if vomiting is very regular, put the patient on a total fast, except for fluids (non-food fluids) and honey balls, to rest the system completely, and to allow the cat's body to mobilise its entire energy resource to fight the disease.

KIDNEYS (also see Nephritis, p. 116)

Parsley has a wonderfully cleansing and tonic effect on the entire urinary system, so wherever there is a kidney problem, offer the patient fresh, chopped **parsley** if acceptable, and if not prepare a **parsley tisane**. Supermarkets sell fresh **parsley** virtually all the year round, so never use the dried herb unless it cannot be avoided. If you grow a clump of **parsley** in a pot or in your garden, you can still use it as a **tisane** even when it is too tough and woody to shred into the food. The **parsley tisane** is so beneficial that I would recommend it as an addition to all **tisanes** prepared for the treatment of ailing kidneys. Just add it as an equal part to the recipes given below.

Where there is blood in the urine, give a **tisane** of **shepherd's purse** and **golden rod**. When there is hardening of the kidneys, make the **tisane** with **golden rod, cleaver's, yellow deadnettle** and **yarrow**. Add half a teaspoonful of **Swedish bitters** per pint of this solution. For gravel in the kidneys, treat as for cystitis, p. 71. Where there is a chronic kidney disorder, treat with a **Horsetail** and **yellow deadnettle tisane**. General sluggishness and debility due to age will be greatly helped by this **tisane**. Where there is acute kidney disease due to bacterial, viral or toxic injury, use a **horsetail, marigold, stinging nettle** and **cleavers tisane**. This recipe will also help kidney failure due to **snakebite** (see p. 133) or to serious injury or major surgery. For kidney failure due to accidents or shock (see p. 132), give **golden rod, horsetail, yellow deadnettle** and **St John's wort**. For all kidney disorders, give four dropperfuls four times daily of the appropriate **tisane. Horsetail baths** must also be given (at least two per week) and **horsetail poultices** must be applied overnight. During the day, a **compress** of **Swedish bitters** should be applied for up to six hours. The **Hippocratic kidney tonic,** under Cystitis on p. 71, is recommended.

Tips

Keep the patient free from stress (even giving unfamiliar bedding or litter, or changing the cat's environment, can contribute to stress). Give a comprehensive vitamin and mineral dietary supplement daily. Calcium, all the B vitamins, and vitamin C are particularly required. Brewer's Yeast is a good source for the B vitamins.

The patient *must* adhere to a special kidney diet. Your vet can advise on this; but the general aim will be to reduce protein, especially red meat, which contains a lot of toxins. I would advise that you cut your cat's normal protein intake by at least half, and feed a variety of herbs, fruit, grain and vegetables. The acid content of food has to be carefully monitored where there is kidney failure, but of all sugars, honey is most easily dealt with by the kidneys, and I recommend its use (although don't give more than half a small teaspoonful per day). Different acids produce different effects, however; it will generally be found very beneficial to dilute the day's ration of honey in spring water into which one-third of a teaspoonful of apple cider vinegar has been mixed. Be sure to feed small meals often, to ease the work burden of the kidneys. A small pinch of sea salt should be added to the morning meal to help to replace the salts lost due to imbalanced kidney function. When changing the patient's diet, you will need to be very patient and persistent, and to do it in tiny stages, so gradually that the cat hardly notices, although red meat should be cut out immediately.

Herbal Supplements

Feed the **tonic foods** listed on pp. 9–16, and give finely chopped **watercress, boiled stinging nettle tops, wild garlic, garlic** and honey **pills, parsley** (if the patient won't cooperate, **infuse** a small handful of **parsley** in just enough water to cover it, boil for one minute and pour the strained liquid over the food—you will, of course, include **parsley tisane** in the patient's herbal medicinal daily programme anyway). It is a good idea to do the same with a handful of **small-flowered willowherb** (mix the patient's meat, rice or other cereal with a little dry food to absorb the wetness) once daily as well. Also give plenty of **couchgrass**, and the ingredients listed under Diabetes Mellitus, p. 74.

LEUKAEMIA see Feline Leukaemia, p. 86

LICE
Treat as for fleas, p. 90. A formula of **gentian root** macerated in pure apple cider vinegar, rubbed well into the coat after thorough bathing (I recommend two baths, one given immediately after the other) is very helpful. Unlike flea infestation, which is almost unavoidable, lice infestation means that the cat is not looking after itself, and is physically and mentally depressed. The cause of this miserable listlessness must be discovered and treated. **Dr Bach's Flower Remedies** will be of particular help here.

LIGAMENTS (excessive mineralisation)

This is generally due to vitamin A poisoning. Correct the problem, put the patient on apple cider vinegar and honey diluted in spring water, use **compresses** of **Swedish bitters** and (separately) apple cider vinegar during the day and **poultices** of **comfrey roots** overnight along the spine and the back of the neck, and gently massage apple cider vinegar and **St John's wort oil** into the spine and around the back of the neck twice a day.

Herbal Supplements
Feed finely chopped **parsley** and **spinach**.

LIVER

Hepatitis (inflamed liver)
The viruses that infect the human liver cannot attack felines, nor can feline hepatitis be contracted by humans, yet the herbal treatment is similar. For chronic inflammation of the liver, give a **tisane** comprising **dandelion roots, speedwell, greater celandine, common club moss** (in this instance, only half a teaspoonful per cup of boiling water is used—measurements for the other herbs remain the same as usual), **wild chicory flowers** and **woodruff**. I consider **common club moss, dandelion** and **speedwell** to be the most important ingredients of this mixture. Give four dropperfuls six times daily.

Liver Cancer
Where growth of the connective tissue of the liver has occurred, especially if it is cancerous, give a **common club moss tisane** and apply a linen bag filled with the same herb to the area of the liver overnight. Give two dropperfuls night and morning. Use one small level teaspoonful per half-cup of boiling water. If the cancer does not go into remission, proceed with the **compresses** and **poultices** described below for cirrhosis.

Cirrhosis
The directions for treatment are the same as above, only **Swedish bitters compresses** should be applied for two or three hours during the morning and afternoon, and **horsetail poultices** during the evening and, renewed, overnight. **Agrimony, cleavers, woodruff, dandelion root** and **speedwell** combine to produce a general tonic for cirrhosis and other complaints of the liver. Give three dropperfuls six times daily. This **tisane** is particularly good for liver damage caused by toxins absorbed from the gut or other parts of the body.

Fatty Infiltration of the Liver
For this condition I would advise the **club moss tisane** in the morning (two dropperfuls) and the tonic recipe given above in the afternoon and evening, three dropperfuls four times

daily. Apply **Swedish bitters compresses** during the day and the linen bag of **common club moss** overnight (see above).

Liver Complaints Caused by Heart Disease
Give treatment as indicated under **Heart** (see p. 94) plus a **tisane** comprising **stinging nettle, yellow deadnettle** and **speedwell**. Give three dropperfuls four times a day. If fluid has to be greatly restricted, give one and a half dropperfuls of **common club moss tisane** morning and evening, abandoning all other **tisane** treatment except that for the heart disorder.

Liver Damage Caused by Poisoning
Put the patient on a fast and give a **dandelion root, speedwell, horsetail** and **stinging nettle tisane**. Give **compresses** of **Swedish bitters** over the region of the liver and **horsetail poultices** over the area of the abdomen. See poisoning, p. 122.

Failure of the Liver Caused by Bacterial or Viral Infection
Give the liver tonic **tisane** described above, and also a separate **tisane** of **stinging nettle** and **marigold**, four dropperfuls three times a day. If the condition is very stubborn, add **thyme** to the latter tisane.

Tips
The patient must be given a special liver diet—see your vet for recommendations

Herbal Supplements
It is most important to give five **flower stems** of **dandelion** each day. Cut the stems directly into the feed, making sure the milky sap is not lost. **Parsley** is also a tonic for the liver, as is **wild garlic**.

LUNGS

Bleeding in the Lungs
Give a **yarrow tisane**, three dropperfuls morning and evening.

Cancer
The treatment is the same as above, except that six half-dropperfuls of **calamus root tisane** are also given throughout the day. **Compresses** of **Swedish bitters** are applied during the day, and **horsetail poultices** overnight.

Congestion
Give a **stinging nettle** and **speedwell tisane**, four dropperfuls eight times a day, with **compresses** and **poultices** as described above. Also, make a very warm **infusion** of **ginger** and **liquorice root** into which one teaspoonful of **cayenne** is mixed, and apply it to the area of the lungs by soaking it up into flannels and placing them on the chest as hot as the patient can comfortably tolerate, holding them in position for about ten seconds, and instantly repeating the procedure. Do this for about four minutes, and then give two dropperfuls of **horsetail tisane** immediately. Repeat the treatment three times a day.

Weakened Lungs
Where the lungs have been weakened by severe infection, recovery from cancer, or are congenitally weak, give a **tisane** of **plantain** mixed with honey and apple cider vinegar (one teaspoonful of each to a cup of the **tisane**), four dropperfuls three times daily.

General Tonic for the Lungs
Equal parts of **coltsfoot, horehound, marshmallow, ground ivy, elder flowers** (or **shoots, leaves** or **twigs**), **speedwell** and **stinging nettle** are prepared as a **tisane** and given by dropper, three or four times a day. Apple cider vinegar and honey can be added, to the patient's benefit.

Herbal Supplements
Give the **tonic foods** listed on pp. 9–16, but avoid milky foods and regulate grain foods. Give plenty of fresh, green vegetables and herbs, especially **watercress, wild garlic, garlic** and honey **pills**. Pour a little apple cider vinegar, neat, over the meat and vegetable feeds, and give it diluted in spring

water by dropper (two teaspoonfuls per cup). Honey is a panacea for respiratory complaints, so give it in whatever form it is accepted. It can be diluted in spring water with the apple cider vinegar and given by dropper. **Parsley** is also an excellent tonic, so give it chopped and fresh, or poured as an infusion into the food (see directions under the Herbal Supplements recommended for Kidneys, p. 104. Cut down on the cat's protein intake. **Rose petals** also help lung complaints. Chop or cut all vegetable matter very finely.

Lung Fluke
Fast the patient for 24 hours, then give every feed with a little raw **garlic** grated into it. Also add **onion extract**. Proceed for the four-week period that the treatment is given, but be careful not to overfeed **garlic** as a large amount is an irritant to the stomach. The **tisane** must be mixed with apple cider vinegar (two teaspoonfuls per cup), and its ingredients are **stinging nettle, thyme, catnip,** and **golden seal.** Give three dropperfuls six times a day, apply **compresses** of **Swedish bitters** to the region of the lungs during the day, and a **compress** of **thyme oil** in an almond oil carrier overnight. Give the first **tisane** for ten days, and then give one comprising **yarrow, wormwood** and **horsetail** with a pinch of **cayenne** added (one good pinch per half-cup) for a further ten days. Give three dropperfuls of this **tisane** night and morning, continuing with the **compresses**, only alternating the **Swedish bitters** with a **horsetail poultice** twice during the day. Prepare a thin gruel from **slippery elm, liquorice** and **senna pods** (if they are **Alexandrian senna**, use one pod; if **Tinnevelly senna**, use two pods, which have to be soaked in a cup of warm water for six hours; remove the **pods** and add the **infusion** to the **tisane**). Administer this for four days, three dropperfuls three times a day. Finally, give a **tisane** of **couchgrass** for three days, four dropperfuls six times a day. **IMPORTANT:** if the fluke parasite infects the brain and spinal cord as well as the lungs, the relevant **compresses** and **poultices** must also be applied to the appropriate regions. Repeat the entire treatment programme if the patient is not clear of fluke eggs (your vet will test for this) after the first four-week treatment.

Tips
Unless the patient is very severely affected so that treatment
has to begin at once, start the programme on the day of the
new moon (the 24-hour fast should take place during the
preceding day). Don't feed your cat raw crab or shellfish, as
this is how infestation occurs. If the lungs are damaged or
weakened after the attack, see the advice under Weakened
Lungs and treat accordingly.

Herbal Supplements
Feed **watercress, wild garlic, couchgrass, catnip** and **parsley,**
all finely chopped, as well as raw **carrot**. Scald the carrots
briefly, as their skin may carry lung-fluke eggs. Continue with
the grated **garlic**, adding it to just one meal a day, for a few
weeks after the patient has been declared free of infestation
by your vet. Establishing this as a permanent habit will help
to keep your cat free of worms and other parasites.

Lungworm
Treat as for Roundworms, p. 130.

MALABSORPTION

This condition occurs when the small intestine is not efficient
in absorbing food, either generally or specifically. It is often
the cause of diarrhoea, of vitamin and mineral deficiency
even though the diet is adequate, of subsequent malnutrition,
anaemia, weight loss and abdominal pain. Malabsorption
often occurs because of an allergic reaction, so it is necessary
to eliminate the components of the patient's diet one by one,
for the duration of a week, to expose the allergen. To repair
the intestinal wall, and to help the small intestine to assimilate
food (whether or not its deficiency is caused by allergic reaction) give a **tisane** comprising **slippery elm, meadowsweet,
camomile** and **marigold**, three dropperfuls four times a day.
Also administer six half-dropperfuls of **calamus root tisane**
throughout the day. (The **calamus roots** have to be cold-
soaked overnight; the **tisane** is strained off and warmed
before being offered to the patient.)

Herbal Supplements
Give those listed under Diarrhoea, p. 76.

MAMMARY TUMOURS see Tumours, p. 146

MANGE

The same cleansing and disinfecting of all beds, bedding, toys, grooming equipment, carpets, floor and furniture must be carried out as for fleas (p. 90). Prepare an **infusion** of **thyme, wormwood** (in this case the whole plant is used), **violet** and **red clover**. As this is an external operation, a good handful of each herb is used. Boil the ingredients in half a pint of water for two minutes, keeping a lid on the pan while its contents simmer. Allow the solution to cool (the whole pan, well sealed, can stand in cold water to facilitate this), and apply direct to the coat, soaking hand flannels in the **infusion** and rubbing well into the skin. Treat the entire body, taking care not to miss any area, even the tail. Use the **infusion** unstrained, and repeat the treatment night and morning until the mange is entirely eliminated. I would recommend **enemas** of **quassia chips** or **stinging nettle** and **horsetail** (one a day until the condition improves) and a **tisane** of **speedwell, garlic** (one large, chopped clove per cup), **cleavers** and **elder** (**twigs, leaves, shoots, flowers,** or all four combined), to be administered in measures of three dropperfuls four times a day. If the case is severe, also rub **nasturtium tincture** well into the coat and skin twice during the day, and apply as a **compress** overnight to the affected parts. If you use a vinegar-based tincture, dilute before applying to broken skin. Just a few small drops of **Swedish bitters** can be added to the **tincture**. If the skin becomes very sore, apply **marigold ointment**; but really it is best not to use anything greasy until the mange mites have been killed, as it tends to protect them.

Herbal Supplements
Feed the **tonic foods** listed on pp. 9–16, with additional **watercress, parsley, wild garlic, garlic** and honey **pills**, diluted apple cider vinegar and neat drops of the same over the food.

MASTITIS

If a queen is refusing to feed her kittens and her mammary glands are painfully swollen and hot to the touch, she is suffering from mastitis (inflammation of the mammary glands). Steam fresh (only dried if it is impossible to obtain fresh) **shepherd's purse** (about a handful) in a sieve until it is warm and soft, place it between two thin cloths (handkerchiefs are appropriate) and either hold them against the teats or gently bandage them on. Leave for an hour, and then bathe the inflamed glands with an **infusion** of **mint** and **lettuce** (a palmful of the **leaves** of each, brewed for three minutes). Do this five or six times a day, and give a **sage tisane** into which apple cider vinegar is mixed (two small teaspoonfuls per cup), three dropperfuls four times a day.

Alternatives
The **leaves** of **dock, elder** and **camomile** (also the **flowers** of the latter, if available) can be used externally for this condition with great success. Bathe the inflamed glands at least six times a day. **St John's wort ointment** can be lightly applied last thing at night.

Herbal Supplements
Give **parsley, wild garlic, lettuce, watercress, catnip** and honey **pills**. Honey and apple cider vinegar diluted in spring water is helpful (two teaspoonfuls of honey and one teaspoonful of apple cider vinegar per cup). Chop all herbs and vegetables very finely.

MENINGITIS

Prepare a **tisane** of **stinging nettle, lavender, goldenseal, hyssop, plantain** and **marigold** and give five dropperfuls six times a day. Also make a **tisane** of **skullcap** and administer three dropperfuls every hour. Apply **Swedish bitters compresses** continually to the back of the head (leave half an hour between each **compress**, and leave each one on for two hours).

These **compresses**, together with **horsetail poultices**, can also be applied to the spine overnight.

Herbal Supplements
Fast the cat, except for the tip of a teaspoonful of finely chopped **wild garlic, garlic** and **watercress** wrapped into the middle of small honey balls, which should be rolled in **barley flour** and **slippery elm flour,** and pushed down the throat several times a day.

METRITIS

If there is inflammation of the uterus whilst the queen is nursing her kittens, her milk will contain toxins and the kittens will look and feel bloated, cry, suffer from rough coats and sore, red anuses. Until the mother has recovered, the kittens will have to be hand-reared. Give the mother a **tisane** of **horsetail, yarrow, cleavers** and **mistletoe**, four dropperfuls six times daily (the **mistletoe** has to be cold-soaked overnight—the berries are never used!) and apply **compresses** of **Swedish bitters** to the abdomen overnight.

Herbal Supplements
Treat as for Mastitis, p. 112

MIDDLE EAR

The treatment is the same as for bacterial **canker** (p. 63). Also see the treatment for deafness (p. 73) as this remedy is also effective. If the nerves of the ear are permanently damaged by infection, don't forget to try **St John's wort tisane,** four dropperfuls six times a day, and the wonderfully healing **St John's wort oil,** so good for animals, which should be put into the ears (just one or two small drops) morning and evening. This has often effected a cure.

MILIARY DERMATITIS see Feline Miliary Dermatitis, p. 88

MILK FEVER see **Eclampsia,** p. 80

MISCARRIAGE see Abdomen, general debility, p. 42

MITES see Canker, mite infestation, p. 64, and Mange, p. 111

MOTION SICKNESS

Put the patient on a fast for ten hours before undertaking a long journey, then give two dropperfuls of apple cider vinegar and honey diluted in spring water (two teaspoonfuls of honey and two of vinegar per cup). Also give large **pills** of solid honey into which a little powdered **ginger, slippery elm** and a few drops of neat apple cider vinegar have been mixed (one small, level teaspoonful of **slippery elm** and a small pinch of **ginger** per level tablespoonful of honey).

MUSCLE SPASMS

Often a symptom of shock, spinal disc disease or a reaction to surgery, painful muscle spasms which are disturbing to the patient can be relieved by a few drops of **valerian tincture** in two dropperfuls of apple cider vinegar and honey (two teaspoonfuls of honey and the same of vinegar per cup of water) administered night and morning. If there is no improvement, add a few drops of **Swedish bitters** to the diluted **valerian tincture** each time it is given.

MYELITIS AND SPINAL CORD DAMAGE

Treat as for Meningitis, p. 112, only add **thyme, comfrey** and **St John's wort** to the **tisane. Cleavers ointment** should be applied very gently to the spine three times a day, and **compresses** of **Swedish bitters** and **St John's wort tincture** should be applied separately throughout the day and night (leave one hour between each **compress** application). Very gentle massages of **yarrow** and **comfrey tincture** should be given several times a day if the condition of the spine is appropriate (they could cause more damage—ask your vet for advice). If not, apply them as separate **compresses**.

Herbal Supplements
Fast the patient, but feed balls of solid honey containing very finely chopped **yarrow**, **comfrey** and **St John's wort leaves**, the whole rolled in **barley flour** or **slippery elm flour**.

NAILS

Nail Bed Infection
Soak four tablespoons of **mallow** in a cup of cold water over-night, strain and warm (do not heat as the healing properties will be destroyed) in the morning, and, ideally, immerse the affected foot or feet in the solution for 20 minutes twice a day. If you don't have the time to spare, or if the patient will not sit patiently on your lap whilst you immerse its paw in the water (surprisingly, this is sometimes permitted!) then bandage the foot in well-soaked bandages, leaving them on for half an hour (a piece of towelling can be tied around the wet bandages to prevent the patient from wetting its environment). Do try to hold the cat's foot in the bathing **infusion** for at least a minute or two, however, as nail bed infections are difficult to cure. Afterwards, treat the infection with **marigold ointment**, and apply a **Swedish bitters compress** overnight.

Herbal Supplements
Feed the patient the **tonic foods** listed on pp. 9–16, as infections cannot take a hold unless the cat is initially slightly debilitated. Also give **watercress, couchgrass, wild garlic, parsley**, and **garlic** and honey **pills**.

Fungal Infection
Give the patient **stinging nettle tisane**, four dropperfuls six times a day, and apply **marigold ointment** and a **Swedish bitters compress** overnight.

NAVEL INFECTION

Wash the area with a few drops of apple cider vinegar diluted in spring water, dry well and apply **marigold ointment**. Repeat the treatment several times a day, and give a **thyme** and **stinging nettle tisane**, two dropperfuls three times a day. (Remember to use the very small droppers from 10ml medicine bottles when treating kittens.)

Tips
If the kitten is showing signs of distress (crying a lot), has a red, sore anus or is sluggish and cold to the touch, it may be suffering from cold stress, or the queen may be giving sour milk because she has mastitis or metritis (see p. 112 and p. 113 respectively for directions on the appropriate treatment for these conditions). If the kitten is cold, warm it by holding it in your hands for a few minutes, check that the bedding is always clean and dry, and provide artificial heat in its environment. Be careful not to heat it up rapidly, or to apply heat directly to the kitten or it will go into shock. Warmth from the hands and the breath is best, followed by the provision of a very slow increase of artificial heat some distance from the bed, in the room that the queen inhabits.

NEPHRITIS

Corn silk tisane, one dropperful every three hours until the condition improves (afterwards give one dropperful four times a day) is an excellent remedy for inflammation of the kidneys (nephritis). Also see Kidneys, p. 103, for further advice.

Alternatives
Wood sorrel tisane, four dropperfuls night and morning, will also speedily relieve the condition, but the **herb** has to be fresh.

Tips
Use the treatment outlined above in conjunction with the programme advised for general problems under Kidneys, p. 103.

Herbal Supplements
Give those advised under Kidneys, p. 103.

OBESITY

The herbs which help obesity are **stinging nettle, lady's mantle, wild chicory, asparagus** (given lightly cooked and well minced), **kale, cleavers, sage, yellow iris, redcurrant leaves** and **couchgrass**. An effective **tisane** for the condition is made from a mixture of these (you do not need to use every one listed, but be sure to include **lady's mantle, wild chicory, couchgrass,** and **stinging nettle** in your concoction). A good **tisane** to give for obesity is a combination of **dandelion** (leaves, stems, flowers), **fennel** (stems, shoots, seeds, leaves), **rosemary** (flowers, leaves, stems) and **bladderwrack** (whole plant). The dosage for all weight-reducing **tisanes** is three dropperfuls half an hour before each meal and four times throughout the day.

Tips
Do not suddenly drastically reduce your cat's rations. Cut down a little week by week so that the reduction is hardly noticed. If you have been accustomed to feeding a lot of junk food or fattening treats, gradually replace these with titbits such as boiled fish and poultry, a little **catnip**, and pieces of wholemeal toast spread with solid honey. Bones, too, can be given, as they are lasting and promote the production of digestive enzymes and the metabolic rate; but they *must* be given raw, as bones become brittle and splinter easily if they are cooked, and are therefore dangerous to the cat. Pieces of melon and **cucumber** are usually enjoyed, as well as slices of apple and a range of berries. These can be fed in yogurt, which will aid the digestive process and so work against obesity.

Herbal Supplements
Feed **parsley, feverfew, watercress, fennel** and green vegetables (especially **asparagus**), all chopped, shredded or minced finely.

OBSTRUCTED BOWEL see Bowel Muscles (weak), p. 59

OSTEOSARCOMA see Tumours, p. 146; Bones, bone diseases, p. 59

PAIN

For a cat's pain, apply **horsetail poultices** to the affected area(s) alternated with **compresses** of **Swedish bitters**. Give a **tisane** of **camomile** and **catnip**, four dropperfuls six times a day, or as required.

PANCREAS

See the herbs listed under Diabetes (p. 73) for the ingredients of a **tisane** which will act as a tonic to the pancreas. Use it to help with digestive problems and to ward off diabetes and pancreatitis.

Pancreatitis
Apply **horsetail poultices** and **Swedish bitters compresses** alternately throughout the night and day. Pancreatitis is a very serious, agonising condition, so you will need to be meticulous and devoted in your nursing if the patient is to recover. However, the **poultice** or **compress** need only be changed once during the night. Prepare a **tisane** of **calamus roots** (they have to be cold-soaked overnight) and give six half-dropperfuls a day. Three times a day, make up a thin gruel of honey, **slippery elm** and half a teaspoonful of **Swedish bitters,** and give three dropperfuls morning, noon and evening. (You can prepare one-quarter of a cupful to provide the whole daily dosage, and add to it three teaspoonfuls of **Swedish bitters.**) A **tisane** of **stinging nettle, marigold, yarrow, catnip, elder, mint** (three parts) and **mistletoe** (for measures, see Tisanes, p. 32) must be administered ten times a day. Ideally, three dropperfuls of the **tisane** should be given each time, but if the patient regurgitates it, give a few drops every ten to fifteen minutes. Once or twice a day, bathe the general region of the pancreas with very warm **St John's wort tisane**

into which a few drops of **St John's wort oil** have been mixed, and administer a few drops of the **tisane** (*without* the oil) at the same time. This is such a horrible and dangerous condition that I would advocate the use of spoken charms while the medication is administered to alleviate it, even if you would normally feel disinclined to resort to such methods (see Chapter Ten).

PANLEUKOPAENIA see Feline Infectious Enteritis, p. 83

PARALYSIS

This condition can be caused by parasites, especially ticks (see p. 141). Check for internal and external intruders and treat as appropriate (see Canker, Mite Infestation, p. 64, and Mange, p. 111, for advice on the treatment for mites). Radial nerve paralysis is another common cause. For advice on how to treat it see Foreleg Paralysis, p. 92.

Give a **tisane** of **sage**, **thyme**, **comfrey** and **St John's wort**, six dropperfuls four times a day. Also apply **compresses** of **Swedish bitters**, **yarrow**, **St John's wort** and **comfrey tincture** to the affected parts. Don't forget that these **compresses** must be kept warm. Each of the above **tinctures** should be applied separately. Also soak a flannel in a hot **infusion** of **cayenne**, **lavender**, **marjoram** and **thyme** and apply, comfortably warm, to the back of the head, the spine and the paralysed limb. **Compresses** of **Swedish bitters** should also be applied to the back of the head and the spine. Twice a day, give the paralysed regions a rub with an **infusion** of **mustard seed** (let it brew for five minutes before using). If the seed is difficult to obtain, use **mustard powder**.

Herbal Supplements

Fast the cat for three days, except for balls of honey containing finely grated **garlic**, **yarrow**, **St John's wort**, **comfrey** and a pinch of **cayenne** (one added ingredient per ball of honey). These little balls have to be pushed down the throat. Give two or three (keep them very small), morning, noon and evening. Apple cider vinegar diluted in spring water is also helpful. **Cayenne** stimulates the blood, and three small pinches a day, inside honey balls, should be given. Wash them down with the herbal medicine or diluted apple cider vinegar. After the third fasting day, begin to feed the invalid foods listed in Chapter Two. After two days, a normal diet can be resumed.

PERICARDIUM

Problems occur when bacterial or viral infection attacks the heart's muscular walls. This surrounding sac is called the pericardium. Apply **horsetail poultices** and **Swedish bitters compresses** over the region of the heart, and prepare a **tisane** of **horsetail** (2 parts), **marigold** (4 parts), **hartstongue** , **tansy, vervain, valerian root** and **parsley** (for measures, see Tisanes, p. 32). Simmer for one minute, then pour the **tisane** over half a tablespoonful of **American valerian.** Wait for five minutes, then strain and give four dropperfuls every two hours. Apply flannels soaked in a very warm **decoction** of **camomile** and **wormwood** for ten minutes each time the medication is given, resoaking and replacing every two minutes (the solution has to be kept very warm).

There is a marvellous anti-spasmodic tincture concocted by Dr William Fox, the nineteenth-century botanical physician of Sheffield. It is an excellent remedy for the pain and anxiety occasioned by inflammation of the pericardium, and is well worth taking the trouble to prepare.

DR FOX'S TINCTURE
4 parts **black cohosh (snakeroot)**
1 part **gum myrrh**
½ part **lobelia seeds**
1 part **skullcap**
1 part **skunk cabbage**
½ part **cayenne powder**

For measures and method see Tinctures, p. 34. These ingredients must be infused for two weeks in a pint of apple cider vinegar. Use a closely stoppered or sealed vessel, and give it a good shake once a day. It should be kept warm, near a radiator or in the sun, while the herbs infuse. Strain through a fine sieve. The sediment must not be used. Four drops of this **tincture,** in honey and spring water (two teaspoonfuls of honey per cup) are to be given by dropper four times a day.

Herbal Supplements
See those given under Heart, p. 94.

PLAQUE see Teeth, p. 137

PLEURISY

Give a **tisane** prepared from **coltsfoot** and **horsetail** sweetened with honey (two teaspoonfuls per cup), three dropperfuls five times a day, throughout the day. Twice in the morning and twice in the evening, give a **comfrey root tisane** into which a few drops of **Swedish bitters** have been mixed, two dropperfuls only. The fresh **leaves** of **coltsfoot** should be washed, crushed, and the pulp applied warm to the chest as a **poultice.** Give four of these throughout the day, and at night apply a **horsetail poultice.** These are for the cat's chest, but at the corresponding point on its back apply a **Swedish bitters compress.** Do this twice during the day. Three times a day, give the hot flannel treatment with **camomile** and **wormwood** described under Pericardium, p. 120.

Herbal Supplements
Give those listed under Lungs, congestion, p. 108.

PNEUMONIA

The treatment is the same as for pleurisy (see above), the only difference being that a **thyme** and **plantain tisane,** plus the **Swedish bitters,** is given instead of the **comfrey root tisane.** Additionally, dropperfuls of lemon juice and apple cider vinegar, a few drops in each dropper diluted with honey and spring water (two teaspoonfuls of honey per cup) are given regularly throughout the day, one every two hours.

POISONING

Immediate action is essential. Contact your vet without delay to find the antidote, and meanwhile prepare an emetic to induce vomiting. Mix one level tablespoonful of **mustard powder** with warm spring water, just enough to make it liquid, and give it all by dropper. One large heaped teaspoonful of table salt or sea salt in half a small cup of warm water, administered by teaspoon or dropper, is another method. Herbal emetics include **balm, ipecacuanha, lobelia, radish** and **senega**. A strong **infusion** must be made in each case, although as the **mustard powder** or salt methods are so quick and easy you may prefer to utilise one of them. Keep the patient warm and clean whilst vomiting occurs, and afterwards give an aperient (laxative and evacuant) to cleanse the bowels. It needs to be powerful, so use a **tisane** of **aloe, buckthorn, cascara sagrada, rhubarb root** or **senna. Senna pods** are easy to keep on hand and are therefore a good choice, only there will be no time to cold-soak them as usual. Instead, pour boiling water over five pods, let them infuse for five minutes, crush them well under water, strain, cool the cup containing the **pods** and the **infusion** by standing it in cold water (don't let it overturn) and administer as soon as the solution has reached a comfortable temperature (give very warm, but not hot). Give half the cupful at first, then the second half six hours later. After this, repeat the dosage night and morning for the first three days. During this time, the patient must be put on a fast, except for tepid spring water, honey, **tisanes** and the laxative water. Give balls of solid honey about the size of a fingernail to which a very few drops of apple cider vinegar have been added, rolled in a minute amount of **slippery elm** flour, immediately after poisoning has taken place (two or three an hour, pushed gently down the throat). After the first four hours, reduce the number to one per hour, and then to one every three hours after a further six-hour period. Also give three dropperfuls of **stinging nettle** and **horsetail tisane** in the morning and evening and three dropperfuls of **dandelion root tisane** three times a day. Twenty dropperfuls of spring water must also be given throughout the day for the first three days. After this time, discontinue the **stinging nettle** and **horsetail tisane** (continue with the **dandelion root tisane**) and give a **tisane** of **rue** and **hyssop**, half a small level teaspoonful only of **rue** per cup. Give four dropperfuls six times daily.

A highly effective aperient water to give to a poisoned animal, more effective even than **senna water**, is produced from an old Russian recipe:

RUSSIAN APERIENT WATER

1½ tbsp **senna leaves**
1 tbsp **sassafras bark**
½ tsp Spanish juice or **liquorice**
½ tsp **cloves**
2 tbsp honey
½ tsp **ginger** (bruised)
½ tsp **cayenne**

Boil these ingredients in three pints of water for half an hour. When cold, strain, and add one pound of Epsom salts and two ounces of apple cider vinegar. Stopper well, and lay the bottles on their sides during storage. This will keep the water good for six months or more. Give the patient three dropperfuls three times a day during times of difficulty or emergency.

Herbal Supplements

After the initial three-day fast, feed the patient **watercress**, **parsley**, **wild garlic** and **dandelion stems** and **leaves**. Mince all green matter very fine.

POLYPS

Give a **horsetail tisane**, four dropperfuls six times a day, apply **horsetail poultices** to the abdomen or the anal area, especially overnight (don't cover the anal passage!) and give **horsetail baths** twice a week.

Herbal Supplements
Give **watercress, parsley** and **wild garlic**, all finely chopped.

PROMINENT EYE

A bulging eye may be caused by a number of factors. The eye may be injured or infected, or an infection may have spread outwards from the sinuses to cause the condition. Glaucoma may be present, or, more seriously, cancer, either of the eye itself, or growing behind it. Consult your vet immediately to discover the cause of the symptom. If the eye is infected, treat as for blue eye, p. 58. If the eye is injured, proceed as directed under Blepharospasm, p. 57. However, if the injury is very serious, **St John's wort tisane, oil** and **tincture** should be used as a regularly applied **compress** during the day, and a poultice of **comfrey roots** overnight. The scalded **leaves** of **comfrey** also make an excellent **poultice**, as does **comfrey tincture**. These **poultices** can also be used as an extra aid if the eye infection (see above) is very severe. For both injuries and infections, a **stinging nettle** and a **St John's wort tisane** should be given, four dropperfuls four times a day. If the problem is cancer, a **marigold tisane** should be given, five dropperfuls ten times a day, and a separate **violet tisane**, three dropperfuls six times a day. **Marigold ointment**, fresh **juice** and **tincture** should all be used as very regularly applied **compresses** (allow an hour between each application), and, in between these, washings of a mixture of **horsetail** and **marigold tisane** should be given. Bathe the affected eye continuously for about ten minutes. **Horsetail** and **Swedish bitters compresses** should be applied overnight. If the problem is glaucoma, see p. 93 for advice.

PYLORIC SPHINCTER

Problems occur, especially in kittens, when the muscle that seals the stomach and permits the passage of food to the small intestine suffers from a 'stricture' or blockage. This causes projectile vomiting, particularly in kittens when they are given their first solid foods and the pyloric sphincter can only open sufficiently to allow liquids through, but not solids. Treat as indicated under Bowel Muscles (weak), p. 59.

Your vet must always diagnose the cause of projectile vomiting (rush the patient to the surgery), as if there is a total bowel obstruction the cat will be in great danger and distress. If the problem is due to the pyloric sphincter, commence the treatment outlined above, with an additional **tisane** of **liquorice** and **dandelion roots** if the patient is an adult cat. The dosage is three dropperfuls four times daily. If the patient is a kitten, don't give the aforementioned aperient **tisane**, and be sure to administer the one required (**lady's mantle** and **shepherd's purse**) in the appropriate measure for kittens.

PYOMETRA

Treat as for metritis, p. 113, only add two parts **lady's mantle** to the **tisane**, and increase the measure of **cleavers** to two parts. Also add one-third of a teaspoonful of **Swedish bitters** to the first and last dose of the **tisane** as it is administered each day. **Yarrow baths** are recommended. Please note that a vet must be consulted at the outset, and if the queen's condition is advanced, she will need to have a hysterectomy. The disease is caused by the development of small cysts after the thickening of the uterine wall (usually due to the presence of initial ovarian cysts). These lead to inflammation, and the uterus fills with pus. Signs are: a swollen abdomen; an offensive vulval discharge (unless the cervix remains closed, in which case there will be no discharge, but an increased swelling of the abdomen); dullness; thirst; loss of appetite; lethargy; poor physical condition.

RABIES

In the UK, it is illegal to treat an animal suffering from the rabies virus, as by law it must be destroyed, although there is evidence to suggest that rabies is responsive to treatment. It may just be possible to treat a cat before the 'madness' starts, and so save it from this fate. In fact the madness is only a symptom, like coughing or sneezing in colds and flu, of the virus ensuring that it perpetuates itself by causing the irritation which produces the required behaviour. If a cure can be found, even after madness has commenced, the cat will make a full recovery both mentally and physically. A Native American remedy is to take the bark from the root of the common **ash tree**, two level tablespoonfuls per cup of spring water, boil gently for ten minutes, immerse the animal in the **decoction** and also administer freely by mouth (about ten dropperfuls per hour, or more if possible). Dr Fox, the Sheffield botanical physician, received a letter from a Mr Hubbard of Illinois, reporting that he and his brother were bitten by a mad dog when they were boys, together with a sheep from a flock nearby, and that while his father was preparing the remedy, the sheep began to exhibit signs of hydrophobia, becoming frenzied and eventually collapsing. As in his father's experience the remedy was untried, he poured a good pint or so over the prostrate sheep, hoping to ascertain whether he could depend upon it as a cure for his sons. He continued:

> Four hours after the drenching had been given, to the astonishment of all, the animal got up and went quietly with the flock to graze. My brother and myself continued to take the medicine for eight or ten days, one gill three times a day [a gill is half a cupful or a quarter of a pint—in some districts it denoted half a pint]. No effects of the dread poison were ever discovered on either of us.

An old English remedy is to use the seeds and the keys (the seed cases) of the **ash** in the same way, but in this case the Native American method of using the **bark** from the **roots** is much more effective. Another method described by a Saxon forester who was reluctant to take his secret to the grave with him is to wash the wound well immediately with warm water and vinegar (apple cider vinegar is best), rub dry, and then apply a few drops of hydrochloric acid to neutralise and destroy the poison in the infected saliva. This, at least, is not so ruthless a remedy as that used by Emily Brontë when she was bitten by a mad dog whilst offering it a drink of water outside Haworth Parsonage, who applied a red-hot domestic iron to the affected part!

If you suspect your cat has been bitten by a rabid animal, put the methods above into practice at once, fast the patient and, night and morning, give an enema of **lobelia, cayenne, rhubarb** and **tincture** of **gum myrrh**, just two drops of this, and one-quarter of a teaspoonful of the other herbs in a small cupful of boiling water which must be allowed to cool to blood heat before being administered as an enema. After its initial wash with neat apple cider vinegar, keep the wound wet with **gum myrrh tincture**, washing it frequently. At night, apply a **poultice** of **bloodroot, horsetail** and **lobelia**, fresh if possible. Put a small teaspoonful of **Dr Fox's tincture** into a teaspoonful of spring water (see Pericardium, p. 120) and give every hour by dropper with the **ash root bark tisane**, which should also be given every hour, six dropperfuls a time. Feed nothing but the honey balls described under poisoning, p. 122, and keep the patient very warm. This programme of treatment should continue for three days, after which small amounts of food can be offered. Continue treatment for ten days after the cat has ended its fast. If no symptoms are presented, the patient is clear. **Important: protect yourself from being bitten or scratched at all times** (the virus lives in the saliva, but if the cat licks its paw, its claws may infect you).

Tips
Because the herbal medication is needed so urgently after infection by rabies, it is a good idea to make up the necessary **tinctures,** and to keep the requisite **herbs** in **powder** form (especially the **ash root bark**) in your herbal medicine cabinet. Don't keep any herbal medicine for more than twelve months, however, as after the duration of a year its healing virtues begin to fade away).

Herbal Supplements
Give those listed under Poisoning, p. 122.

RHEUMATISM

So many herbs are helpful for this condition that it may be apposite here to raise the question of astrology. Many authorities think that astrology will become a precise and exalted science in the future, a spiritually exalted science which will combine with herbalism to bring perfect health to the occupants of the earth. Dr Bach, the inspired doctor who formulated the world-famous *Flower Remedies*, tells of his far memories of the miraculous bird and animal doctors in ancient India, whose skill and knowledge were almost superhuman. The rags and tatters of such sublime arts that remain today simply bid the herb-healer to group herbs for cats under those ruled by the sun and the moon, for throughout history, cats have been deeply associated with both, with day and night, male and female and cosmic balance. It would be too complex to enter here into a discussion of individual astrological correspondences, but you may find it interesting to decide whether your cat is a moon cat or a sun cat (see below), and to treat the patient with the appropriate herbs. Give moon herbs for moon cats and sun herbs for sun cats. If the results are unsatisfactory, the cat may need to cross over to a herb mixture corresponding to its opposite nature to restore interior balance. Moon cats are mysterious, secretive, aloof, magnetic, dainty, fastidious, bossy, coolly arrogant, dignified, regal and love the night. Sun cats are extrovert, amiable, love open spaces (they will sprawl out in the middle of the room rather than hide or find an unobtrusive corner to curl up in), show off, possess charisma and are majestic and condescending in their bearing. They are easily offended, love the sun and the daylight hours, and require a lot of sympathy and fuss if they are unwell. Of course these definitions are generalisations, but I hope they will help you to intuit the polarity of your cat's nature. Give one of the following **tisanes**:

- **Herbal Potion for Sun Cats: camomile, St John's wort** and **mistletoe** (the last to be cold-soaked). Give three dropperfuls four times a day, and rub the affected joints with **rosemary** and **camomile oil.**

- **Herbal Potion for Moon Cats:**   willow, watercress and cleavers. The dosage is the same as above. Rub the affected joints with **agrimony ointment**.

Other excellent herbs for rheumatism are **parsley, comfrey, thyme, stinging nettle, horsetail, dandelion roots** and **parsley**. I would recommend the addition of **parsley** and **stinging nettle** to any **tisane** prepared to counteract rheumatism.

Herbal Supplements
Feed fresh **watercress, parsley, wild garlic, garlic** and plenty of honey **pills** with a few drops of neat apple cider vinegar added. Also give fresh **chickweed** and one-quarter of a **kelp tablet** daily. Pour apple cider vinegar over the food and give diluted in spring water. Do not give more than half a table-spoonful of apple cider vinegar per day.

RICKETS

Prepare a **tisane** of **yarrow** and **stinging nettle**, and give four dropperfuls four times a day. Also give the patient regular baths containing a strong **decoction** of walnut leaves (four good handfuls, steeped overnight in a bucket of cold water and heated until very warm, strained and added to the bath, which should be taken first thing in the morning and last thing at night). If the case is severe, give an additional **tisane** of **marigold** and a few drops of **Swedish bitters**, three dropperfuls night and morning.

Herbal Supplements
Give **parsley** and **stinging nettle tops** boiled in a little milk, also plenty of honey **pills** and as many as the patient will accept of the **tonic foods** listed on pp. 9–16.

RINGWORM

Crush the **leaves** and **stems** of **borage**, and apply the expressed juice directly onto the seat of infection. Give a **marigold tisane**, three dropperfuls four times a day, especially half an hour before and half an hour after each meal.

Alternatives
Follow the same procedure as above, substituting the fresh
juice of houseleek, and administer the same **tisane**.

Herbal Supplements
Ringworm is a fungal disease which healthy, resistant tissue
fends off. Feed a selection of the **tonic foods** listed on pp. 9–
16, and especially feed **garlic, watercress, celery** and **wild
garlic**. Make sure that all of these are finely grated or
shredded.

RODENT ULCERS see Ulcers, rodent, p. 149.

ROUNDWORMS

Commence the treatment during the waxing of the moon (see
'Heartworm', p. 96), putting the cat on a fast for two days
(one day only if the patient is a kitten), giving only two
dropperfuls every two hours containing a few drops of apple
cider vinegar in spring water. On the night before the end of
the fast, give one tablespoon of **castor oil** (one teaspoon for
a kitten). The next morning, give no more than four **garlic
pills** with **wild garlic leaves** and **pumpkin seeds** chopped finely
and mixed into them. Half an hour afterwards, give another
tablespoonful (or teaspoonful) of the **castor oil**. Thirty
minutes later, give a warm, very runny feed of milk, **slippery
elm, flaked oats** and honey (about one-quarter of a cupful).
Give three of these meals a day for three days, continuing
with the herbal **pills** but giving only two of them on the
second and third morning. Throughout these three days give
a **tisane** of **marigold** (in this case, two level tablespoonfuls of
the fresh or dried flowers have to be used per cup of boiling
water—infuse for only one minute and reduce to the normal
dosage after 48 hours), three dropperfuls four times a day.
Continue the **tisane** treatment for two weeks, likewise the
two morning herbal **pills**, although the **pumpkin seeds** can
be discontinued after the first three days. Before retiring at
night, give the patient six dropperfuls of a honey, **feverfew**

and **couchgrass tisane**. This should be continued for a week. After the three days on the semi-liquid diet described above, the patient can return to its normal food, but for a period of two months after the commencement of treatment, include a small teaspoonful of grated **carrot** and **garlic** in the diet. During the three-day treatment period, **enemas** of **marigold** and **wormwood** should be given, slightly less than one-quarter of a pint, morning and evening.

Herbal Supplements
Feed **parsley, wild garlic** and **watercress**, all finely minced. Also give the **tonic foods** listed on pp. 9–16, to ensure that the system is strong and healthy and able to resist infestation by worms.

RUNNY EYE

Give **yarrow tisane**, four dropperfuls three times a day. Mix together **eyebright** (1 part), **Benedict's herb** (1 part), **speedwell** (1 part), **comfrey** (2 parts), **valerian** (2 parts), **camomile** (2 parts), **lady's mantle** (2 parts) and **rue** (1 part). (For measures and methods, see Tisanes, p. 32). Take half a tablespoonful of this mixture, soak it in a pint of cold spring water overnight, bring to the boil the following day, simmer for one minute, add a pinch of sea salt, stir well and leave to infuse for three minutes. When the solution is comfortably warm, soak a piece of cloth in it and hold against the runny eye for half a minute. Continue to bathe the eye for half an hour. Repeat each day until all symptoms have disappeared.

Herbal Supplements
Give **watercress, wild garlic, parsley** and **fennel**, all finely chopped.

SALMONELLA

Treat as for Poisoning (see p. 122), but increase the dosage of diluted apple cider vinegar.

SHOCK

Shock is a serious condition and can quickly lead to death if its effects (which cause physiological changes) are not dealt with immediately. A cat in shock will exhibit certain symptoms such as panting, cold paws and ears, a weak, racing heart, inability to stand with floppy limbs and a glazed, distant expression with the pupils dilated, cold, pale or faintly blue gums, and no proper response when it is called, petted or nursed.

Treatment must begin without delay. Take the patient to a warm, safe, quiet environment, wrap it loosely in a blanket, putting into its folds a comfortably warm (*not* hot) rubber water bottle. It is most important to ensure that you do not make the cat hot, as this increases stress. Let it be very comfortably warm, free from draughts, yet well ventilated and at ease. Talk to it softly and soothingly, making sure that you do not convey your own anxiety. Calling its name soothingly but firmly at frequent intervals is helpful. Stroke the patient very gently and rhythmically along the spine. Every half-hour, give a few drops of **Dr Bach's Rescue Remedy** in a dropperful of honey, spring water and apple cider vinegar (four good teaspoonfuls of honey and the same of apple cider vinegar to a cup of spring water). Put some drops of **lavender oil** on a cloth and hold it just below the cat's nose for about 30 seconds every five minutes. After an hour, do the same with **rosemary oil**. Later, when the cat is feeling better, it can be given a **tisane** of **golden rod** and **camomile**, four dropperfuls every three hours. If any limbs are paralysed due to injury, add **St John's wort** to the **tisane** and apply the scalded, crushed **leaves** of **comfrey** to the region as an overnight **poultice**.

SIGHT

To improve defective vision, give a **tisane** of **eyebright, speedwell** and **horsetail**, three dropperfuls four times a day, and bathe the eyes night and morning in a solution of **eyebright, fennel, speedwell** and **loosestrife**. (**Note:** One level tablespoonful of **loosestrife** is to be used per half-pint of boiling water. Add one-quarter of a small level teaspoonful of sea salt to this solution, and leave to infuse for half an hour before straining and using.) Once in the morning and evening, give three dropperfuls of **lady's mantle tisane**, and after bathing, dry the eyes well. Take a fresh **leaf** of **greater celandine**, wash and bruise the stem between your thumb and forefinger, the expressed juice is then smeared gently over the closed eyes and into the corners. **Shepherd's purse tincture** in a weak saline solution should also be applied three times a day.

Herbal Supplements
Give **fennel, watercress, wild garlic, parsley, carrot** and honey **pills.**

Small Eye
The treatment is the same as is outlined under Sight.

Sunken Eye
Treat as directed under Sight, except that an additional **St John's wort tisane** must be given, three dropperfuls four times a day, and alternate **compresses** of **shepherd's purse tincture** and **St John's wort oil** should be applied to the afflicted eye. Dilute the tincture if it is vinegar-based.

SLIPPING KNEECAP

Apply **comfrey leaves** as a **poultice** overnight, and rub **shepherd's purse tincture** into the affected part six times daily. Internally, give **lady's mantle tisane**, three dropperfuls four times a day.

SNAKEBITE

Treat the same as for rabies, p. 125 (the **ash roots bark** remedy) and **poisoning**, p. 122. In addition, treat the wound with fresh **plantain juice** (expressed from the leaves and dabbed around the edge of the punctures), and afterwards apply a **horsetail poultice**, night and morning, for no longer than two hours.

SPRAINS see Bones, p. 58.

STEATITIS (pansteatitis, yellow fat disease)

This occurs when the cat consumes food containing too many unsaturated fatty acids such as those of fish oil. Lumps appear under the skin which cause distress and sensitivity, the cat runs a fever, loses interest in food and cannot bear to be handled. Give the patient strong supplements of vitamin E (available from your vet or pet shops) and give a **stinging nettle** and **dandelion root tisane**, four dropperfuls six times a day.

STINGS

Apply the fresh, crushed leaves of **plantain** to all insect stings, snakebites or dog bites. Hold them in place, then attach them as a **poultice**.

Alternatives
Apply **gentian leaves** or the **leaves** of **lady's mantle**, fresh, bruised and applied direct. A **Swedish bitters compress**, left on overnight, will heal painful and poisonous swellings caused by insect stings.

Herbal Supplements
Feed **parsley, mint, catnip, wild garlic** and **watercress**, chopped finely.

STROKE

Threatening
Give a **mistletoe tisane** (cold-soaked overnight and then warmed a little in the morning before administering), three dropperfuls night and morning, and four dropperfuls of **sage tisane** twice throughout the day. Apply a **compress of Swedish bitters** to the area of the heart overnight, and twice during the day bathe the brain and heart region in a tepid-to-cool **decoction** of **camomile** and **wormwood**. This treatment will

reduce the severity of a stroke if the signs appear (loss of consciousness; loss of function down one side of the body, either the face alone or the face and limbs being affected; a stupefied, mentally depressed state with dilated pupils; staggering, pacing and circling consistently to the right or left; abnormal responses), but it has to be given immediately, so administer the **sage tisane** at once and put the **mistletoe** to soak cold for four hours before use (more can then be cold-soaked properly overnight to use in the morning). The **bathing** and **compress** should also be given without delay. Continue treatment for a week.

Aftercare
Give the **mistletoe tisane** as described above for six weeks, then gradually reduce it so that two dropperfuls are given each time for a further three weeks, and then for the next three weeks only two dropperfuls of the **tisane** are to be given in the morning. In addition, from the beginning four dropperfuls of a **tisane** comprising **cornflower, fennel, St John's wort, lily of the valley, speedwell, lavender, balm, rosemary** and **sage** should be given three times a day. Apply **Swedish bitters compresses** to the head for an hour each day, and if the eyes or limbs remain affected, massage gently with **St John's wort** and **shepherd's purse tincture** twice during the day, and last thing at night give a similar massage with **St John's wort** and **thyme oil. Comfrey leaf poultices** can be applied very warm to the paralysed areas, and left on overnight. Such dedicated nursing will be rewarded with a noticeable improvement, often a complete recovery.

STYES

Treat as for conjunctivitis, p. 70.

TAILS (broken)

Treat as for broken **bones** (see p. 58), but also give **St John's wort tisane**, three dropperfuls four times a day, and after the break has healed, massage gently with **St John's wort oil** night and morning. Feed plenty of honey **pills** mixed with a few drops of apple cider vinegar while the tail is healing, for some weeks afterwards. This will help the severed nerves to recover.

TAPEWORM

Begin the treatment three days before the full moon. It is important to remember that this worm, the great monster of the parasitic worms, propagates itself by breaking off segments of its body, which then grow into new worms. Therefore there are always several growths of the worm in the intestines existing simultaneously, making it necessary to follow through with the programme of medication every other moon three or four times, to be entirely certain of destroying them. **IMPORTANT**: the herb I recommend, which is **oil of male fern**, is toxic if taken in any quantity. The dose is half a small teaspoonful, or seven drops, twice a day. If this is ineffective, it may be increased to one teaspoonful or 15 drops; but wait a week before recommencing treatment. Put the patient on a semi-fast; the last meal of the day should be given at least two hours before administering the second dose of medicine. Mix seven drops, or half a small teaspoonful, of **male fern oil** (this is not easy to purchase nowadays, so you may have to buy a **male fern*** in a pot from a garden centre) into a little spring water with apple cider vinegar and honey, and give once in the morning, and the same dose once in the evening. Soak two **senna pods** overnight, add a pinch of **ginger** to the **infusion,** and give by dropper the first and third morning of the treatment, two hours after administering the **male fern oil**. On the third day, mix together a teaspoonful of pure lemon juice, a teaspoonful of honey, a tablespoonful of hot spring water, and add the **male fern oil** to this solution. Administer by dropper, night and morning. On the morning of the fourth day, give a **tisane** of **camomile** and **slippery elm,** three dropperfuls, and again four times throughout the day. Repeat this treatment in eight weeks' time, and again eight

---

* See directions for preparation of OILS, p. 31.

weeks later. Keep the cat on the **tisane** of **camomile** and **slippery elm**, two dropperfuls night and morning, for two weeks after the cessation of treatment at the end of the fourth day, to soothe and heal any ulceration of the intestines that the tapeworm might have caused. This programme of treatment should thoroughly cleanse the patient, not only of the worm itself but also of the unhealthy matter in the intestine which allows worms to establish themselves in spite of the natural defences of the body against such infestation.

Note: if the case is very stubborn and the treatment outlined above does not entirely destroy the tapeworms, follow the treatment for roundworms at the commencement of the next new moon for ten days, and then proceed with the tapeworm treatment as directed.

Herbal Supplements
Feed the **tonic foods** listed on pp. 9–16, and the herbs and vegetables listed under Roundworms, p. 130.

TEETH

Teeth can be cleaned using **flowering lavender, sage leaves,** or a piece of fresh lemon. Wear gloves to protect from involuntary biting! Where caries is present (tooth decay), give regular washings of the whole mouth with **horsetail tisane,** and bathe the gums night and morning with a strong **decoction** of **sage** and **rosemary leaves.** A little **clove oil** dropped into cavities will relieve pain — repeat every few hours. Where there is bad breath (halitosis is a symptom of caries) give washings of **lavender** and **wormwood,** also gently scrub the gums, tongue and the whole oral cavity with the **tisane** and give it internally, four dropperfuls three times a day. Washings given with a **decoction** of **walnut leaves** are also good. A strong **infusion** of **lavender, water dock** and **sanicle** will clear gum disease, strengthen the gums and tighten loose teeth. A soft toothbrush can be used, dipped frequently in the **tisane** or **decoction,** to massage and scrub the teeth and gums.

Herbal Supplements

Give **watercress, parsley, feverfew, wild garlic, mint, couch-grass, catnip** and **comfrey**, also figs, raisins, dates, dried apricots, cucumber, corn, oats, half a **kelp tablet** a day, and also raw bones. All except the cucumber must be finely chopped.

TETANUS

Fortunately very rare in cats, when this killer disease strikes, we turn once again to the healing 'golden angel' behind the benign virtues of **golden rod**. First wash the **leaves, stems** and **flowers** (or just the **leaves**, if nothing else is available) very briefly in cold water, pulp, and apply direct to the wound as a **poultice**. Leave this on for three hours, and then apply a bread **poultice**. Leave on for two hours, remove, let the air get to the wound for half an hour, and then apply another **golden rod poultice**. This should be left on for four hours, then removed, and another applied after 30 minutes. Do this until bedtime, and then for the overnight **poultice** add a few drops of **Swedish bitters** to the **golden rod pulp**, and apply very warm. Give a **golden rod, stinging nettle** and **skullcap** tisane with a few drops of **Swedish bitters** added to the third dropper, six dropperfuls every three hours. Fast the patient, except for balls of solid honey mixed with neat drops of apple cider vinegar, which should be pushed down the throat, one every hour, for ten hours during the day. Give an **enema of horsetail, meadowsweet, dock** and **golden rod**, one small cupful night and morning. On the second day, the honey balls can be reduced to one every two hours. Continue the treatment until all symptoms disappear, and then continue only with the overnight **poultice**, the **tisane** and the honey treatment (one ball every four hours) for one month. When, within the month, the wound has healed completely, it will no longer be necessary to apply the night-time **poultice**, but do continue the **tisane** and honey treatment for the full month, as specified. When muscle stiffening and cramping occur, a **poultice** of **Swedish bitters** and **acid tincture of lobelia** (use a good few drops of the latter until the bandage is well moistened) applied warm, will bring speedy relief.

Alternatives

Apply alternate **golden rod** and bread **poultices** to the wound, changing every two hours, and leaving 30 minutes before each reapplication. Administer one-quarter of a small teaspoonful of **acid tincture of lobelia** and the same of **Dr Fox's tincture** (see under Pericardium, p. 120) three times a day. Also give the honey treatment as described above.

A second alternative is to give, twice a day, an **enema** of one-quarter of a teaspoonful each of **lobelia, gum myrrh, rhubarb** and **valerian,** and a good pinch of **cayenne** in one-quarter of a pint of **raspberry leaf tisane.** Also give **cayenne** and **lobelia tisane,** three dropperfuls every hour until the muscles relax. Apply very warm bags of **camomile** (thin linen bags can be speedily made by sewing together two handkerchiefs) to the stiffened muscles, and particularly to the abdomen. Reapply as soon as their warmth begins to fade. They can be quickly and easily heated by placing them between hot water bottles. Do this until the cramps subside. After the first day, discontinue the first tisane, and give a **tisane** of **camomile, skullcap** and **stinging nettle,** three dropperfuls four times a day, for a period of two weeks. Keep the patient warm and well-rested throughout this time, and give plenty of honey balls each day (at least four).

Tips

If the patient's jaw is locked, curl back the lip, find a gap at the side of the mouth, and empty the dropper into it, tilting the cat's head back so that it has to swallow. Feed the **tisanes** this way, also the required honey, which can be put into spring water. Add a few drops of **Dr Bach's Rescue Remedy** to the honey every hour.

THIAMINE DEFICIENCY

This condition is usually caused by feeding the cat too much raw fish, which contains thiaminase, a destroyer of thiamine. Herbs, vegetables and grain contain plenty of thiamine, so give these with any commercial feed to ensure that your cat receives its daily requirement. Sometimes physical or

emotional stress brings about the condition. Take the cat to
the vet for an injection of thiamine, correct its diet by giving
the foods listed above, avoid overcooking any meals you
might prepare for your cat, and give a **tisane** of **dandelion**
(**roots** and **leaves**), **parsley**, **skullcap** and **stinging nettle**, three
dropperfuls six times a day. If nervous signs such as loss of
balance, walking with the head down and claws extended,
have begun, add **camomile** and **St John's wort** to the **tisane**
mixture. If vomiting is a problem (although **camomile** and
skullcap will greatly alleviate the condition, two components
of the advised **tisane** described above), give four dropperfuls
of **Iceland moss tisane** (it has to be boiled for two minutes
and then left to stand for ten) in the morning and evening.

Herbal Supplements
Give the **tonic foods** listed on pp. 9–16.

THREADWORMS

Treat as for roundworms, p. 130, but also give an **enema**
night and morning of a strong **decoction** of **cotton lavender**
(almost certainly available from your nearest garden centre).

THYROID

Make a **tisane** of **cleavers** and **mallow**, which has to be given
three times a day in 'sips' or half-dropperfuls, eight at a time.
Don't be tempted to cut corners and administer in whole
dropperfuls, because this would not have the internal washing
effect on the throat that is so much needed where there are
thyroid problems. When you have made the daily requirement of the **tisane**, don't throw away the used herbs; make
them into a **poultice** by draining them off (don't wring or
squeeze them), mixing them with **barley flour** and applying
very warm as a **poultice** around the throat. Do this in the
evening and leave on overnight. During the day, apply two
horsetail poultices, two hours apart, for two hours' duration
each, and, two hours later, a **compress** of **Swedish bitters**, to
be left on for four hours. One-third of a pint or 180ml per

day must be taken of a **tisane** comprising **marigold, stinging nettle** and **yarrow**. Give by dropper every two hours. Four times a day, two drops only of **Swedish bitters** are given, in half a dropperful of spring water, half an hour before and half an hour after the morning and evening meal. Half a teaspoonful of the white pith inside the stem of the **common reed** is mixed with one teaspoonful of grated **garlic**; half added to the morning meal, half to the evening meal. One fresh yolk of a medium-size hen's egg (free range, please) is given as a supplement each day as well, although be careful not to give any of the raw white of the egg, as this is harmful for cats.

Herbal Supplements
Give **parsley, wild garlic, garlic**, honey, apple cider vinegar and half a **kelp tablet** daily.

TICKS

There are ticks which secrete a nerve toxin in their salivary glands. These are dangerous and while some cats develop a resistance to them, others are affected and, once signs of poisoning have started, will die within 24 hours or less (depending on how many ticks they are carrying). The signs are coughing, gasping, retching, strange calls, and then shortly afterwards the cat begins to collapse, paralysis sets in from the tail and hindquarters towards the head, until eventually the breathing becomes laboured and the animal expires from respiratory failure. Long before this distressing outcome is allowed to develop, of course, action can be taken to save the cat. First, search the patient to find the culprit (look carefully, there may be more than one) and remove it by placing an inverted bottle of strong alcohol, apple cider vinegar or methylated spirits over the parasite, which will quickly open its jaws and drop off. Don't touch the tick or put pressure on it in any way, as you will squeeze out more poison from its salivary glands into the cat's system. If there is no other way, burning it with a match or lighter will get rid of it, but obviously there is a danger of hurting the cat, and perhaps we should not be unnecessarily cruel even to ticks! Painting the tick with nail varnish is another way of persuading it to drop off. Then rush the cat to the vet for an injection of anti-tick serum. If for some reason you are unable to get to the vet, give the cat **garlic** and honey **pills** every half hour, or make an **infusion** of **garlic** in spring water, add honey (two good teaspoonfuls per cup of water) and feed it by dropper, six every half hour. Give also a **tisane** of **eucalyptus, golden rod, thyme, horseradish root, marigold, nasturtium** and **watercress** (two or three of these will do if you cannot obtain them all in the limited amount of time you will have to effect a recovery), four dropperfuls every half-hour. Put bread **poultices** over the areas where the ticks were attached, changing them every two hours, and apply a **Swedish bitters compress** overnight. Fast the patient, and continue the treatment for 72 hours, reducing the dosage to one dropperful of the **garlic** and honey **tisane** (or one **garlic** and honey **pill**) and one dropperful of the other **tisane** every hour after the first six hours, and then the same every three hours after the initial 24. After the first day, only the overnight **Swedish bitters compress** need be applied, and the patient can gradually return to normal feeding.

Tips
The highly poisonous ticks generally only occur in Australia and some southern states of the USA. If symptoms persist after the three-day treatment, add two parts of **St John's wort** to the **tisane** recipe given above, and administer four dropperfuls every two hours until the symptoms disappear. If you find poisonous ticks on your cat and you need time, perhaps a few hours, to assemble the herbal remedies, look for some **common** or **ribwort plantain**, take some of the **leaves**, bruise them, and hold them in place directly over the areas to which the ticks had attached themselves (obviously you will have disposed of them first). Make your cat unattractive to ticks by giving it a daily rub with **rosemary, lavender** or **lemon oil** in the summer and early autumn (don't overdo it, or the cat will have an upset stomach after cleaning itself) and feeding it **kelp** (one-quarter of a **tablet** per day), **pills** of

rue, and drops of **Swedish bitters** diluted in spring water and apple cider vinegar from May to the end of October. Drops of **rosemary** and **lemon oil** have to be applied in a carrier of **almond oil**.

TONSILLITIS

Agrimony and **mallow tisane** is a soothing remedy for tonsillitis, whether the condition is a symptom of cat flu or whether it exists independently. The **mallow** has to be cold-soaked overnight, strained, and the **infusion** added to the **agrimony tisane**, which should be allowed to cool to blood-heat beforehand. Give five dropperfuls four times a day. It is helpful to administer it in half-dropperfuls so that it can more thoroughly wash the throat. If a lot of pus forms around the tonsils, the patient will be in considerable pain. The prescribed **tisane**, together with **poultices** made from the **mallow** residue mixed with **barley flour** and applied to the throat for two hours, bring real relief. **Horsetail poultices** and compresses of **Swedish bitters** can also be applied to ease the pain and inflammation. Small honey balls, mixed with a few drops of neat apple cider vinegar, pushed gently down the throat, one every hour until symptoms ease, are also very effective pain-relievers. A stew of fresh **stinging nettle tops, cayenne** and **ginger** (just a pinch of the latter two ingredients) is soothing and nutritious for the tonsillitis patient.

TOXOPLASMOSIS

Where there is acute generalised infection, give a **tisane** of **gum myrrh, nasturtium, wormwood, thyme, stinging nettle, cleavers** and **plantain**, four dropperfuls every hour for 14 hours of the day, each day for two weeks. If the patient does not respond satisfactorily, give more (don't exceed seven dropperfuls per hour). A good pinch of **cayenne** in the **tea mixture** is helpful, as is a daily **horsetail steam bath**. Pour boiling water into a basin containing two good double handfuls of **horsetail**, and suspend the patient a little way above it in a carrying cage with a large towel thrown over the cage. **Poultices** of **horsetail** should be applied overnight to the spleen, and **compresses** of **Swedish bitters** to the same region during the day. Give one **enema** a day of **stinging nettle** and **horsetail**. Raw shredded **garlic**, the shredded **leaves** of **rue** and **wild garlic**, shredded **parsley** and **watercress**, with a few drops of neat apple cider vinegar, should be mixed into honey balls, one type of herb per ball, and pushed down the throat, one every hour for eight hours a day. This is a very important part of the treatment, especially the provision of raw **garlic**, which will greatly assist in eliminating the disease.

Tips
In the acute form, the toxoplasmosis outbreak will only last for about two weeks, but for its duration, you need to dedicate yourself to saving your cat's life by carefully following the treatment procedure outlined above, or the cat may not survive. If one of the vital organs is attacked, you will need to give some of the following as a separate **tisane**, four dropperfuls six times a day:

- brain: **St John's wort**
- kidneys: **golden rod**
- liver: **dandelion roots** and **leaves** with **stems**
- heart: **parsley-honey wine** (see Heart, p. 94) and **hawthorn**
- eyes: **loosestrife**, **speedwell** and **eyebright**; given internally and as an eyewash
- pregnant queens: **yarrow** and **lady's mantle**

Where there is chronic generalised infection, the treatment is the same as above, only the **tisane** should be administered in dosages of four dropperfuls six times a day, and one **compress** once a day, with the **horsetail poultice** applied overnight two or three times a week. Treatment usually has to be given for several weeks. **Enemas** and **steam baths** are optional, but feed the herb and honey balls several times a day. One or more of the cat's organs will be affected, so look at the list above to determine which additional **tisane** should be administered to the patient. After the cat has recovered, it is a good idea to put the patient on a short course of **skullcap** and **gentian**

tisane, about three dropperfuls four times a day for two or three weeks.

IMPORTANT: toxoplasmosis is easily transferred to humans! Don't handle raw or undercooked meat with bare hands; don't allow your hands to come in contact with the soil if the cat uses the garden as a toilet (*toxoplasma gondii* exist in the soil anyway, so it is as well to be careful to wear gloves when gardening if there is any broken skin on the hands); empty litter trays every day, wearing disposable gloves, and afterwards disinfect them.

TUBERCULOSIS

The **leaves** and **flowers** of **coltsfoot** are used to make a **tisane** with honey and apple cider vinegar, which is administered very warm, six dropperfuls six times a day. **Compresses** of **Swedish bitters** and **poultices** of **horsetail** are applied during the day and overnight to the region of the lungs, back and front. The chest area must be bathed with very warm flannels soaked in hot apple cider vinegar. The patient must be rubbed down twice a day with an **infusion** of **cayenne**, salt and apple cider vinegar (two good teaspoonfuls of each boiled in a cup of the vinegar) and then dried vigorously (but not roughly) with a coarse towel. Keep the patient quiet and well-rested. Give an **enema** of **stinging nettle** and **horsetail** twice a week. After the first five days, reduce the **coltsfoot tisane** with honey and apple cider vinegar to three dropperfuls every three hours, and prepare the following medicine:

4 parts **liquorice root**
1 part **wild cherry bark**
1 part **horehound**
1 part **vervain**
2 parts **centaury**
1 part **boneset**
(For measures see TISANES, p. 32)

Add two and a half pints of water and boil down to two pints. Strain, add half a teaspoonful of **cayenne** (a small, level teaspoonful) and one tablespoonful of **raspberry tincture of lobelia,** and administer six dropperfuls four times a day. (Keep the medicine in the refrigerator, but warm well before administering.) **Slippery elm** with honey must also be given, three dropperfuls four times a day.

Continue with this treatment for two weeks, then change to the following:

4 parts **wild cherry bark**
1 part **comfrey root**
1 part **mouse-ear**
2 parts **columba**
2 parts **ground ivy**
1 part **Peruvian bark**

Prepare the medicine exactly as described above, making the same additions, and continue with the **coltsfoot tisane** (the reduced dose) as before. Also continue with the **enemas, poultices, compresses** and the hot flannel treatment until the patient has recovered.

Herbal Supplements
Give balls of solid honey encasing grated **garlic, wild garlic, watercress, chickweed** and **parsley,** all finely chopped.

TUMOURS

For all types of tumour in every location, **horsetail** is utilised as a **poultice.** These should be applied in the morning and afternoon for two or three hours, and then again overnight. Between times during the day a **compress** of **Swedish bitters** is applied, and left on for three to four hours. For external growths and tumours the fresh, pulped **leaves** of **violet** together with the fresh **leaves** of **hogweed** and **plantain** are also applied together as a **poultice** continually throughout the day and overnight. Leave 20 minutes between each application, and rub the growth gently with fresh **speedwell** and **wood sorrel juice** three or four times before administering the next **poultice.** These **poultices** should remain on for about two hours. The treatment is intensive, but it usually only needs to be continued for two weeks, after which period the **poultices** can be restricted to morning and evening applications for a further two weeks, and then discontinued altogether if the patient is clear. Give the following **tisanes** for all tumours, but it is important to look under Cancer (p. 62) to find the specific herb for the particular location of the cat's tumour. This herb should be added to the mixed **tisane** given below, *and* administered as a separate **tisane**, four dropperfuls six times a day. Moreover, the herbal residue from the specific cancer herb **tisane** should be mixed with **barley flour** and put on as a **poultice** first thing in the morning, before the first **violet, hogweed** and **plantain poultice** of the day is applied, and last thing in the evening before the **horsetail poultice** is secured for the night. The **tisanes** are: four dropperfuls of **horsetail tisane**, given half an hour before the morning meal and evening meals; four dropperfuls eight times a day of a **tisane** prepared from **marigold, yarrow, stinging nettle, mallow** (cold-soaked overnight and added to the warm mixed **tisane** in the morning), **violet, parsley, couchgrass,** and two drops of **wood sorrel juice** per prepared half-cup of the **tisane**, plus the addition of the specific for your cat's tumour (don't forget to *also* give the latter as a separate **tisane**, four dropperfuls six times a day).

Alternatives
Prepare a **tisane** using equal parts of this old remedy:

DR FOX'S CURE FOR CANCER
quassia chips
yellow dock root
bittersweet (American)
cinquefoil
agrimony

Add two pints of water and boil down to one pint. Add half a small level teaspoonful of **cayenne,** and, when cold, half a tablespoonful of **decoction** of **red Jamaica sarsparilla.** Give six dropperfuls four times a day.

When the cancer is foetid and emits an offensive smell, a charcoal **poultice** can be applied with great advantage. Simmer half a pint of yeast in the oven, and while it remains hot mix the charcoal with the yeast until it is of a proper consistency for the **poultice** (i.e. a paste). **Poultice** the cancer as often as required; place a thin gauze or muslin upon the cancer before applying the **poultice**. This process will stimulate the absorbents to take up the foreign deposit; if a bleeding cancer, liberally use powdered **Peruvian bark** and **gum myrrh** before applying the **poultice**. **Poultice** the cancer as often as possible. If the tumour is well advanced, **poultice** it with **slippery elm, lobelia** and **blood root** in equal parts, at the same time washing the surrounding area several times with **Peruvian bark tisane**. If this treatment is persevered with, it will seldom fail to cure.

The following is a very good cancer liniment of great power:

2 tbsp **tincture** of **blue iris**
1 tbsp **tincture** of **blood root**
½ tbsp **tincture** of **red clover**

Mix them all together, then saturate a cloth in the solution and apply it two or three times a day. Cancers in the early stages have been cured by simply washing the ulcer with a strong **decoction** of the **root** of the **yellow dock,** applied as warm as the patient could bear it. Wash and scrape the roots of fresh **docks** fine, to lay on the cancer as a **poultice**; keep them moist and change them three times a day.

IMPORTANT: the first alternative mentioned above (Dr Fox's cure for cancer) can be used to cure benign tumours as well as malignant growths; use only half the stated amount of **tisanes**.

ULCERS

Mouth

These continuous sores can prevent the cat from feeding, and are painful and disturbing to the patient, causing it to paw at the mouth and salivate. Give washings of **cleavers tisane** by administering six half-dropperfuls four times a day. Also give a **lady's mantle** and **mallow** (cold-soaked overnight and added to the warm **lady's mantle** in the morning) **tisane**, three dropperfuls four times a day. Some **catnip** can be added to help relieve the pain and calm the patient. Space out the applications so that the cat has the benefit of treatment about every two hours.

Tips
Ulcers are a common feature of cat flu. If they also appear on the paws, treat with **marigold ointment** and **mallow** footbaths. Should they fail to respond, apply a warm **comfrey root poultice**.

Rodent
These very painful ulcers are not contracted from rats or mice as originally believed, although their cause is still uncertain. It seems they might arise from general debility of, or allergic reactions which affect, the stomach and liver. The treatment outlined above is usually quickly effective, but there are some very stubborn cases which fail to respond to regular treatment, either herbal or veterinary. If your cat is among the unfortunate, the following herbal programme will almost certainly effect a cure, or at least improve the situation and relieve the patient. Take these ingredients:

1 tsp **rue**
½ tbsp **American bittersweet**
1 tsp **ground ivy**
1 tsp **wood sanicle**
1 tsp **agrimony**
1 tsp **bogbean**
1 tsp **raspberry leaves**
1 tsp **parsley**
2 tbsp **honey**
4 tbsp **apple cider vinegar**

Put in one and a half pints of water, boil down to a pint, add a pinch of **ginger** and a pinch of **cayenne** and give six

dropperfuls four times a day. In addition, give three dropperfuls four times a day of **couchgrass, elder, wormwood**
and **wild chicory** to keep the bowels open. **Poultice** external
ulcers with **slippery elm, lobelia** and **blood root** mixed with
a strong **decoction** of **oak bark**, three times a day. If the
ulcer is in or on the mouth, wash repeatedly with **cleavers**
or **mallow tisane** (it doesn't matter if the cat swallows a lot—
both **tisanes** are beneficial). A little of the **decoction** smeared
on the wound, together with **marigold ointment**, brings relief.
A double **infusion** of **balm** (i.e. two rounded teaspoonfuls to
a cup of boiling water) twice a week, to rid the system of
impurities, is very helpful. Give six dropperfuls half an hour
before feeding in the morning, and six dropperfuls half an
hour before lunch on the two cleansing days. The same
number of **horsetail steam baths**, given for the same reason,
will also greatly benefit the patient.

Tips
These painful and persistent 'rodent' ulcers will also respond
to the treatments for Cancer (see pp. 62 and 146), especially
the cancer **liniments** and **poultices**. The treatment does not
have to be so drastic and urgent, of course. Cut down on the
amount of **tisanes** and **poultices** by about half.

Herbal Supplements
Feed **watercress, wild garlic, garlic** (only a moderate amount
as it can irritate the stomach), **feverfew, parsley, mint, couchgrass, catmint,** and plenty of honey **pills** mixed with a few
drops of neat apple cider vinegar. Also give the **tonic foods**
listed on pp. 9–16.

UPPER RESPIRATORY TRACT INFECTION (urti)

Treat as for **cat flu** (actually feline respiratory disease), p. 66,
with the exception that as well as **camomile** eye-washes, a
decoction of **stinging nettle, thyme, marigold** and **nasturtium**
should be applied continually to the eyes, and should be given
morning and evening as a **tisane**, with a few drops of **tincture**
of **gum myrrh** added, four dropperfuls each time.

VIRAL INFECTIONS

The **tisane mixture** given above (for urti) is very good for all viral and infectious diseases generally. **Horsetail** and **Swedish bitters poultices**, or **poultices** of **blood root, lobelia** and **slippery elm** mixed with a strong **decoction** of **oak bark** applied to the infected part, or to the region of the affected organs, are highly beneficial.

VITAMIN A POISONING

Too much of this essential vitamin can be absorbed by cats who are fed an excess of liver, or are given overdoses of cod liver oil or vitamin and mineral supplements. The signs are a stiff neck, pain, foreleg lameness, abnormalities in gait and posture, and an inability to attend to proper grooming. This is because the imbalance of vitamin A has caused minerals to be deposited in the ligaments of the backbone. Normally flexible and elastic, they then become hard and rigid. Abnormal bone formation also occurs in the neck and back vertebrae, causing the cat pain and difficulty of movement. Correct the diet immediately on diagnosis. Give massages with **myrrh, clove** and **lavender oil** (the first two need to be diluted in an almond carrier oil) to counteract the patient's limitation of movement, and encourage constant, but very gentle, exercise. Give plenty of solid honey balls mixed with neat apple cider vinegar, and dropperfuls of apple cider vinegar diluted in spring water, because both these substances carry off unwanted calcium deposits in the body (the dosage is strong—about six tablespoonfuls of apple cider vinegar to a cup of spring water). The herbal treatment is as follows: four dropperfuls of **horsetail tisane** half an hour before the morning meal, and the same half an hour before the evening meal; four dropperfuls of **stinging nettle tisane** six times throughout the day, accompanied by two drops of **Swedish bitters** every other time the dose is administered (i.e. three times a day). **Compresses of Swedish bitters** are applied for four hours a day along the spine and the back of the neck. Do this in the morning, and in the afternoon apply **compresses of**

cabbage leaves. Heat them with an iron and apply comfortably hot directly onto the skin of the neck and backbone,
holding them in place with a cloth until they cool, and then
reapplying. Do this for 20 minutes. At night, apply a **compress** of **hogweed**. Wash and pulp the **leaves**, apply them
directly to the skin and bandage them on, to remain secured
overnight. Alternate with **comfrey root poultices** to be left
on overnight in the same way, also apply **compresses** of the
scalded **leaves of comfrey**, and give a thorough rub with
comfrey tincture, two or three times a day. Once or twice a
week, **horsetail baths**, to which a handful of fresh **comfrey
leaves** has been added, should be given. In this way, even
advanced cases of vitamin A poisoning can be restored to
normality.

VOMITING

Cats often induce vomiting, especially through eating **couchgrass** and other herbs. They are simply following a natural
method of internal cleansing. Of course, there are circumstances where continual vomiting is dangerous and distressing
for the cat, in cases of debilitating illness, for instance, or
when it is in SHOCK. In these cases, a soothing **tisane** of
gentian and **sage**, with **skullcap** added if the cat is nervous
or agitated, will usually calm the vomiting very quickly. If
the condition is very severe, take a handful of **spearmint** (or
ordinary **mint**), a teaspoonful each of **cloves**, **cinnamon** and
rhubarb, and pour over these one pint of boiling water.
Sweeten with one good tablespoonful of honey when it has
cooled down to blood heat, and administer six dropperfuls
every 20 minutes. If the vomiting is due to food poisoning,
give half-dropperfuls of apple cider vinegar diluted in spring
water, one every few minutes until symptoms abate.

VULVAL DISCHARGE

If a queen's vulval discharge is abnormal and evil-smelling,
it indicates a uterine infection. It is essential to take her to
the vet in case she has retained a dead kitten or placenta. A

tisane of **marigold, nasturtium, yarrow** and **lady's mantle,** six dropperfuls every half-hour, will help. **Swedish bitters compresses** and **horsetail poultices** should be continuously applied to the abdomen. If she develops a putrid fever, give two small teaspoonfuls of fresh yeast in water every three hours.

WOUNDS

Wash the wound in saline solution and clip away any matted fur. Cover the wound with clean, fresh green leaves, secured by a bandage moistened with cold water. Change daily, and ensure that the bandage is clean before replacing it. **Plantain leaves** are best, followed by **comfrey, geranium, Benedict's herb, nasturtium, butterbur, mallow, sorrel, yellow dock, castor oil, cabbage, lettuce** or **hops.**

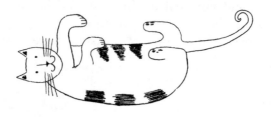

Chapter Five

Guide to Common Herbs

This chapter describes 29 common herbs that can be found in the garden, along waysides, in woods or wasteground. Also described is Swedish bitters (see Useful Addresses for a mail order supplier). Other herbs mentioned in this book may be found in the appendix, accompanied by their Latin classifications. **Please note:** the herbs lobelia and blood root are poisonous if more than the stated dose is given. These herbs should not be administered to kittens or young cats. If you have a small cat, halve the dose. They are American herbs, and can only be bought in Britain from herbalist suppliers (the lobelia cited is the Indian tobacco plant, not the trailing lobelia available from garden centres). Care with wormwood and rue is also advisable. These can only be given to kittens in the specific doses stated (see Chapter Three); no more than one-quarter of the standard preparation dose should be given.

Remember that many herbs are becoming scarce in the wild due to the destruction of their natural habitats. It is always better if you can to grow your own plants from seed purchased from a supplier.

AGRIMONY (*Agrimonia eupatoria*)

This tall, upright plant, which flowers from June to September, grows on banks, by waysides, in woodland clearings, field sides, along country paths and on wasteland. The stiff spike bears a multitude of small, yellow flowers shaped like the wild rose. The toothed, pinnate leaves are divided into many leaflets, giving them a fern-like appearance.

Agrimony is a potent healer for **sore throats, tonsillitis, infections of the mouth** and general mouth and throat discomfort caused by **feline respiratory disease.** It is of great benefit for **ailments of the lungs, stomach, liver, kidney and bladder,** particularly **cirrhosis of the liver.** It helps **rheumatism, poor digestion** and **back pain,** and is excellent for

enlargement of the heart and disorders of the spleen. It is also a good wound herb, and is very successful in the treatment of anaemia. The tisane is used for all the above disorders, but agrimony baths will also greatly assist recovery. Agrimony ointment is very helpful for sores, especially those that develop when there is foreleg paralysis. It is also good for diseases of the eye. Agrimony can be used to prepare tisanes, infusions, decoctions, baths and ointment.

The ancient Egyptians thought highly of this plant, and made frequent use of it to heal themselves and their animals. It is associated with clear soul vision and purity of perception of the spiritual worlds.

BENEDICT'S HERB, HERB BENNET, AVENS, WOOD AVENS (*Geum urbanum*)

Benedict's herb is a perennial plant, common in woods, hedges and waysides, growing from a fragrant rhizome which bears abundantly branched, downy stems up to one foot

(30cm) in height. The leaves are large and three-lobed, and their edges are toothed. The five yellow petals of the flowers stand well apart, and the green sepals show between them. These glowing, pale yellow flowers have earned it the somewhat flamboyant and gaudy country name of 'goldy star of the earth'. It is a wonderful cure-all for **disorders of the digestive system**, and will regulate **diarrhoea** and **constipation**, however stubborn the condition. It will halt **dysentery, cleanse the intestines of mucus deposits**, and **allay vomiting**. Regular washings of the mouth and the throat with the tisane clear **gingivitis** and other **gum disorders**, and will relieve **sore throats**. Taken as a decoction in the spring (use roots), Benedict's herb **purifies the system** and will remove **obstructions of the liver**. It cures **halitosis**, and **stimulates a poor appetite**. As a **poultice** applied to **wounds**, it will quickly **reduce inflammation**. Taken as a tonic over time, it reduces **weakness** and **debility**. Benedict's herb is used for tisanes, infusions, decoctions (of roots), poultices, compresses and tincture.

In folklore, it was called 'the Blessed herb', and was designated St Benedict's herb because it was considered a general antidote to poisoning. It is said that a monk presented St Benedict with a goblet of secretly poisoned wine, but when the saint pronounced a blessing over it as a matter of course, the poison, being a sort of devil, flew out of it with such force that the vessel was shivered to smithereens, the crime of the would-be poisoner being thus exposed. The herb is associated with the soul quality of invincibility, and with the mystery of the resurrection.

BUTTERBUR, BOG RHUBARB (*Petasites hybridus*)

This plant, more striking for its oddity than its beauty, grows along the margins of rivers, near ponds and lakes, in ditches and marshes and damp meadows. It will also choose a wood, field or roadside where the water-level tends to be high. The leaves can grow to an enormous size, and in fact the Greek name for the herb signifies an umbrella or a head covering. They are vaguely heart-shaped and form points like teeth around the edges, are downy underneath, have a thick, strong

stem, and grow to a height of three feet (90cm). The plump, white flower-stalk, however, usually only attains a height of six to twelve inches (15–30cm) and produces a spike of flowers varying from off-white to pink. These are surrounded by circular green bracts, which soon turn into black burrs which are ferocious cleavers if they manage to attach themselves to clothes or hair. The roots are used to cure **fevers**, and should be gathered before the plant has flowered. Butterbur tisane is also good for **fevers, shortness of breath** and **epilepsy**. The leaves are applied as fresh ointment for **sprains, back problems, dislocations** and for all **burns, scalds, cancerous ulcers** and **wounds**. It is a tonic for the **heart, kidneys** and **bladder**, dispels **asthma**, and drives away **colds**. It revives **depressed spirits, eliminates worms,** and the powdered root banishes **feline acne** and **feline miliary dermatitis**.

Make a decoction from the roots, or grind them and stir half a small level teaspoonful into warm honey and apple cider vinegar diluted in spring water (about half a cupful). Give this amount by dropper twice throughout the day.

Tisanes can be prepared from butterbur, also tinctures (for back pain) and fresh ointment.

The flowers of butterbur are particularly rich in nectar, so much so that Swedish bee-keepers plant the herb beside their hives so that the bees can gather it to make honey. Throughout history, it has saved many from death by plague. It was used in love-divinations, and was said to cause visions of a future spouse to arise. The plant is associated with shelter and protection, both physical, psychic and spiritual.

CALAMUS, SWEET FLAG, SWEET SEDGE (*Acorus calamus*)

Calamus is an aquatic plant, quite reed-like in appearance and similar to the yellow iris. It is found in ditches, by lakes and streams, in marshy meadows and nodding along the brink of small rivers. It can be distinguished from the iris by the well-defined, crimped edges of its leaves, and by their sweet fragrance when chafed. The flower spike bears dense clusters of yellow flowers tinged with green. The erect, sword-shaped leaves are yellowish-green, tapering to pink at their base. Its roots, flowers and leaves are all delightfully aromatic. The plant does not flower unless it is standing in water. Its healing is in its roots, and they are, with Benedict's herb, perhaps the best tonic for the **digestive system** in existence. The entire digestive tract is strengthened, **flatulence** and the **digestive weakness** that causes it are banished, the **stomach** and **intestines** are cleansed of **excess mucus**, and the **appetite** is improved, when you give your cat six half-dropperfuls per day of a cold infusion of calamus root (warmed before being administered!) for a period of time. The infusion also helps **glandular disorders**, **anaemia** and **dropsy**. **Kidney ailments** and **food allergies** are also alleviated and healed, **weak, watering eyes** are restored to normal, and the **entire system purified** by these powerful healing drops. Ear tips or other extremities that have been damaged by **frostbite** respond well if they are bathed continually in a solution of calamus that has been cold-infused as usual overnight, the whole boiled for one minute in the morning, and then left to steep for five minutes.

This decoction has to be applied to the damaged regions at a temperature only slightly warmer than tepid. The regular cold-infusion also helps to banish **fevers** and **ulcers**. For any disease of the **stomach** and the **digestive system,** be it of the **liver, gall bladder, spleen** or **pancreas,** the calamus root infusion is invaluable. Use with other specific herbs for the condition (see Chapter Four), especially Benedict's herb, if the patient does not respond. Calamus is also excellent for all **nervous disorders,** and the **infirmities** and **palsy** of **old age.**

Calamus can be used to make decoctions, baths, infusions, washes, juice (wash the fresh roots thoroughly and put them in the juice extractor), oil (good for inhalations and aroma-therapy) and tincture (obtained by macerating the finely-chopped rhizome in apple cider vinegar for fourteen days). Infusions are always cold-soaked.

Calamus was used to strew churches (one of the claims of extravagance brought against poor Cardinal Wolsey at his trial was that he loved to strew his floors with this herb, expensive because it had to be imported from Norfolk!) and is linked with incense and ritual—a mysterious property of the plant is that it gives off so much heat within the spathe at the time of flowering that the temperature rises significantly within and above the plant. It is associated with worship, adoration and a spiritual state of grace.

CAMOMILE (*Matricaria chamomilla*)

Blooming from May to August in cornfields and along country waysides, meadows and grassland, camomile has curly, lacy leaves and separate white, daisy-like flowerheads with mossy yellow centres borne on a long stalk. The white petals commonly droop downwards around the yellow disc florets, like a white fringe around a yellow cushion. The herb has a spicy scent rather like the aroma of fresh apples (its name means 'ground-apple'). This herbal panacea is excellent for **kittens;** administer in all cases of **stomach pain, upsets, wind, gastritis, internal inflammation** because the queen is suffering from **metritis** (see Chapter Four), **restlessness** and

fever. It will also benefit adult cats similarly, and can be given for all **abdominal** and **uterine disorders, inflammation of the testicles, wounds, toothache, eruptions,** and as a steam bath for **colds** and **feline respiratory disease.** It is of particular benefit for **inflamed eyes** and **conjunctivitis,** and in fact all **eye problems** will benefit from camomile compresses and washes. A pillow filled with warmed camomile and applied to **areas of inflammation** and **pain** gives wonderful relief. Camomile baths, or a strong decoction rubbed regularly into the fur (dry off afterwards with a hairdryer) will improve the **coat** and give it an attractive gloss. **Fevers, back** and **rheumatic pains** are eased by internal applications of the tisane and regular massages with camomile oil. **Cystitis** and other **bladder problems** are helped by compresses of an infusion of camomile flowers applied to the site of the bladder, or by poultices of fresh ointment similarly applied. They have to be put on warm, and kept warm. **Nervous disorders** are soothed by the tisane, and the oil, given as a massage to **paralysed limbs,** brings back life and movement. The infusion is a tonic for **kidney** and **urinary tract problems,** and camomile boiled in milk (honey can be added) and applied as a compress is helpful in cases of **blepharospasm, protrusion of the eyeball (prominent eye)** and **blue eye**. These compresses applied overnight, and continual washings with the infusion during the day, are good for **dry eye**. Maria Treben tells of an old recipe for **deafness** used by the 'camomile witch', that entailed frying green field onion (*Ornithogalum caudatum*) in camomile oil and dropping it, comfortably warm, regularly into the ear-canal. Camomile flowers can be used as a poultice to significantly **reduce the swelling caused by abscesses**. Bags may also be loosely stuffed with the flowers and steeped for a minute in boiling water, before being allowed to cool to a comfortable heat and applied as a fomentation for **abscesses**, or a decoction of camomile flowers and crushed poppy-heads can be used as a very warm fomentation (use face flannels) for the relief and healing of **dental** and **general abscesses**. Camomile can be used to make infusions, tisanes, decoctions, fresh and standard ointment, washings and baths, tincture, oil, fresh juice and fomentations.

The secret of its medicinal powers lies mainly in its yellow stamens, and, appropriately enough, the ancient Egyptians dedicated this plant to their sun gods, Osiris and Ra. In folklore, camomile was considered to be the only sure protection against nightmares, and the evil spirits who inflicted them. It is therefore linked with psychic protection and the holy marriage of the sun and the moon (the spirit and the psyche) symbolised by its white petals surrounding the golden disc floret, yet folding back vertically to acknowledge the ascendancy of the spirit (the white moon psyche, or mind, bowing as handmaiden to the ineffable fire of the spiritual sun). The spiritual potency of camomile is the divine peace created by the spiritual principle of balance.

CATNIP, CATMINT (*Nepeta cataria*)

A common sight amongst hedgerows, on grassy wastelands and in fields, meadows and ditch banks, catnip has a tall, downy stem which during midsummer bears a spike of white or lavender-hued flowers. Cats and other creatures eat the plant, and give themselves a massage in it, in order to benefit from its medicinal value. It will sometimes cause cats to grow pensive and dreamy. Catnip is a **digestive** plant, and will heal **colic, flatulence** and **internal inflammation**. It halts **coughs**, and is a gentle, safe and efficient **painkiller**. Catnip is used for tisanes, infusions and tincture. It can also be given to cats, in very small doses, as salad greens (no more than half a teaspoonful daily).

It is advisable not to let cats chew the roots of this plant (they are invested with a similar fragrance to the leaves) as it could over-excite them. It is only the roots that have the sinister effect that people fear so much nowadays as far as their cats are concerned. The rest of the plant is harmless if taken in small doses. The root is said to be inhabited by a Viking-like spirit of valour and combat, and to make those who partake of it very fierce and quarrelsome (the Vikings revered these qualities, and were delighted if their children expressed them). There is a folk legend concerning a certain hangman, who was unable to countenance doing what a hangman has to do until he had chewed a piece of the root! The herb is associated with the goddess Chaos, and with her unruly but highly creative energies.

CLEAVERS, GOOSEGRASS, STICKY WILLIE (*Galium aparine*)

There are three varieties of bedstraw, *Galium aparine, Galium verum* and *Galium mollugo*. *Galium aparine* has hooked hairs which make it very sticky to the touch. Its flexible, trailing stems cling to other plants, and it can grow to the top of the tallest hedge or post. The circlets of leaves grow round the square stems like many-rayed stars. The four-petalled flowers grow in little white clusters. *Galium verum* (Lady's bedstraw) has very thin stems and eight thread-like leaves arranged in circles. There are masses of tiny yellow flowers branching from the axils of the leaves. It grows chiefly on dry banks in coastal areas. *Galium mollugo* (hedge bedstraw) is similar, although its leaves are a little larger, and it has white flowers. They all flower from June to August, but

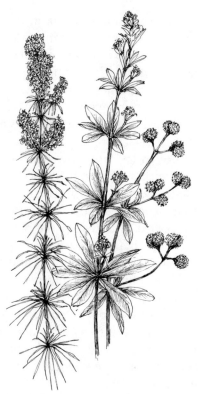

Left: lady's *bedstraw* (Galium Verum); right: Cleavers *(Galicum aparine).*

Galium aparine is the only climber. I always use this variety, simply because it is by far the most common.

Cleavers is a great purifier, and will flush the toxins from the **liver, kidneys, pancreas** and **spleen. Disorders of the uterus,** the **lymphatic** system and the **skin** are helped by this herb. The fresh juice, applied to cases of **feline acne** and **eczema,** quickly alleviates the problem, as do regular washings of the infected areas with cleavers tisane. These washes should also be given to promote the healing of **wounds** and **abscesses.** Further internal uses of the tisane include the treatment of **epilepsy, anaemia, dropsy, nervous complaints** and **constriction of the vocal cord.** Toms suffering from **blocked bladder** will be greatly helped by regular doses of cleavers tisane (partial blockages only—complete blockages require the immediate attention of the vet) as the tea dissolves gravelly deposits in the bladder. **Cancer of the tongue** and **mouth** is greatly helped by cleavers tisane, as are other **cancerous growths**. The fresh juice, ointment, and application of the tisane both internally and externally are all used together to combat cancerous conditions. Cleavers is used to make tisanes, infusions, decoctions, fresh juice and ointment.

Lady's bedstraw (*Galium verum*) is so called because it was supposedly used to create a bed for Mary to give birth in Bethlehem. It gives off a sweet scent of honey when crushed, and was said to bring ease to Mary's pains. It is associated with the soul quality of charity, and with the spiritual principle of eternal replenishment, or self-giving.

COLTSFOOT (*Tussilago farfara*)

The bright yellow flowers of coltsfoot are among the first to appear in springtime. They appear in February, opening before the plant has developed any leaves. Small, hairy, leafy bracts grow up the sturdy stem, and the flower bud is enclosed by a ring of green bracts. The flower head, like a big golden daisy, consists of an outer ring of ray florets and an inner 'button' of tube-like disc florets. Later in the year the large, coarse leaves appear, shaped somewhat like a shield with five points and slightly toothed edges. Marshy grounds, wasteland, the banks of dykes, rivers and railway embankments are carpeted with these early flowers. It is most particularly a chest herb, with powerful **expectorant** and **anti-inflammatory** properties. It is excellent for cases of **bronchitis, bronchial asthma, pleurisy, feline respiratory disease,** the **chest problems** that accompany a range of feline **fungal diseases,** and can be administered with confidence in the early stages of **tuberculosis of the lungs**. It can be given with honey and lemon when **coughing** is a **persistent problem**. Coltsfoot leaves, which appear in late May, are richer in medicinal virtues than the flowers. A poultice of fresh ointment made from them is very beneficial for the chest in cases of **pneumonia** and **swellings** due to **bruising**. Make a compress from a long-brewed decoction of the leaves for **wounds** that will not heal, and the **sores** and **ulcers** caused by **foreleg paralysis**.

Steam baths should be prepared from the leaves and flowers of coltsfoot to help **chronic bronchitis** and **shortness of breath**. Also apply a compress to the chest made from a strong infusion, and give plenty of the tisane, for this condition. Half a small teaspoonful of the expressed juice, taken in warm spring water mixed with honey, twice daily, is also most effective, and will benefit cats suffering from **asthma**. **Ear infections** are helped by the fresh juice, too. Warm the juice and drop frequently into the ear, regularly but sparingly. **Insect bites** can also be treated with coltsfoot juice. Coltsfoot can be used to make tisanes, infusions, decoctions, compresses, poultices, steam baths, tincture and fresh juice.

In folklore, it was called 'the son before the father' because of the appearance of the flowers before the leaves. It was chosen as a signature for apothecaries, its flowers being painted as a sign on the doorposts of their shops. It has to do with the soul quality of 'taking the first breath' and with the spiritual quality of initiation. Strangely enough, it is one of the great therapeutic smoking herbs (taken to relieve any condition that obstructs the breath) and formed the predominant basis of the Herbal Tobacco, so popular in Britain until World War II.

COMFREY, KNITBONE (*Symphytum officinale*)

This vigorous, stately plant grows in marshy fields and ditches, in the vicinity of streams and gravel pits, on wasteland and rubbish dumps, and on low-lying roadsides. The funnel-shaped flowers, which are out through May and June, droop prettily in little bouquets. They are often deep red, but vary from creamy yellow to blue or purple. The large, stalked, lance-shaped leaves are coarse; the stem is covered with stiff hairs that are prickly to the touch. Comfrey is esteemed as a truly remarkable **wound** and **bone-setting** herb. The tincture is particularly effective in curing **rheumatism** and **swollen joints**, even where arthritis has caused extensive damage. For **paralysis**, this tincture can be astonishing in its effects. Massage well into the joints and muscles of the affected parts several times a day. Where the **paralysis** is due to **strain**,

shock, **dislocation** or **sprain,** apply the scalded leaves of comfrey as a poultice. A second poultice, made from the roots
(well ground), stirred into a little hot water and one-quarter
of a teaspoonful of corn oil, spread on a piece of cloth,
applied appropriately and then bound lightly as usual, is used
for **bony protrusions, infected** and **fractured bone, ulcers,**
neck and **back pain,** and **general stiffness of the joints.** A
cold-infused tisane, prepared overnight from the roots, is
good for **digestive ailments, bronchitis, internal bleeding in
the stomach, lungs** or **bowels, pleurisy** and **internal ulcers.**
The scalded comfrey leaf poultice is of much value in the
relief and healing of **abscesses,** and has been known to halt
gangrene. The tincture is also an excellent compress for
wounds, injuries and **bone fractures.** The fresh leaves of comfrey, added to a bath, also help **bone fractures, pain in the
bones, rheumatism, slipped discs** and **poor circulation.**

Comfrey can be used to prepare a cold-infused tisane from
the roots (see above), decoctions, tincture, fresh and standard
ointment, an ordinary tisane prepared from a rounded tea-

spoonful of the minced roots which is infused for three minutes, root poultices, scalded leaf poultices, compresses (use the tincture) and baths. The standard tisane is very good for **internal haemorrhage** and **stomach, liver** and **lung ulcers.**

Monks grew comfrey in their physic gardens, and it gradually became a favourite plant of cottagers. It is rich in mucilage and gum, and 'has the property as no other herb of knitting and binding together that which has become severed'. It is linked with the soul qualities of comfort and healing compassion, and is associated with the spiritual principles of integration, wholeness and renewal.

COMMON CLUB MOSS, STAG'S HORN CLUB MOSS, GROUND PINE (*Lycopodium clavatum*)

The evergreen common club moss, although to be found all over the world, occurs throughout Britain mainly on the moors of the northern counties. It is a rambler with long trailers which sprout small, soft, forked branches as they creep along the forest floor. After some years, the plant

develops a yellow-green flower spike which contains the medicinal spores used by herbalists as a dusting powder for skin conditions. However, the whole plant can be used with great success for a number of ailments. A poultice, and one or two baths using common club moss, will bring relief and healing to toms suffering from **cystitis, gravel in the bladder** and **blocked bladder**. A small linen bag filled with the moss should be applied by bandage wherever there are **muscle cramps** due to **viral disease, shock** or **injury**. Both **cirrhosis** and **cancer of the liver** are greatly helped by this radium-rich plant. Apply the herb-bag and give four dropperfuls of the standard tisane night and morning. It also gives excellent results in cases of **rheumatism, chronic constipation, gravel in the kidneys, renal colic** and **hepatitis**. If your cat suffers from diarrhoea or a weak digestive system, give only half the stated dose and combine with six half-dropperfuls of calamus root tisane daily. The tisane gives impressive results when used to combat **disorders of the urinary tract** and the **reproductive organs**, and will bring relief in cases of **inflammation and hardening of the testes**. Common club moss can be used to prepare tisanes, poultices, herb-bags, tincture and baths.

Mosses are considered to be the first group of plants to colonise the earth, and their spores are everywhere in the air about us (which is why watery or damp places green over quickly). They are linked with the soul quality of pioneership, and symbolise ancient wisdom and the spiritual principle of abundance.

COWSLIP, PAIGLE (*Primula veris*)

The pretty cowslip comes into bloom throughout April and May, inhabiting damp meadows, ditch banks, slopes and pastures. The leaves are pale green and crinkled, and form a rosette close to the ground, from which the flower stalks arise, daintily hung with drooping umbels of sunlight-yellow flowers. They can be readily bought nowadays from garden centres and flower markets. Cowslip tisane helps with all **nervous disorders** and **antisocial behaviour**, especially when combined with lavender and St John's wort. It is a tonic for

the **heart** and the **blood**, and **purifies the system**, making it
an excellent remedy for **rheumatic complaints**. It is also of
great value in treating **inflammation of the heart muscle,
all heart disorders, dropsy** and **tendency to stroke**. Make a
decoction of cowslip root mixed with a teaspoonful of honey
and apple cider vinegar to **cleanse and stimulate the kidneys**
and to **rid the bladder of gravel and stones**. Use the decoction
mixed with the tisane as a healing tonic for the **brain,** and
for **paralytic disorders**. Cowslip is suitable for the making of
tisanes, decoctions, oil and tincture.

Stories in folklore abound concerning this lovely flower.
One of my favourites is that of a young girl who was near
death, and fading fast. She longed to enjoy one last spring,
and as she was virtually taking her last breath, she pointed
to the open cottage door where some cowslips grew, and said
to her mother 'I only wish that I could live as long as those
cowslips.' From that moment on, she grew stronger, until the
next day she was in radiant health and the cowslips had
bloomed. As the flowers burgeoned, she became more and
more beautiful, until people were almost afraid of her loveli-
ness, it was so strange and unearthly. One day a young farmer
stopped by, and was so entranced by her beauty that he
impulsively gathered the cowslips growing by the door, to
offer them to her as a bouquet. The girl gave a cry and at
once fell into a coma, her hand clasping the cowslips. In the
morning she was dead, with the flowers withered against her
breast. Sensitives perceive a strong angelic and fairy presence
behind the cowslip. It is associated with the goddess, or the
Divine Woman offering the keys to heaven. It teaches us that
it is the soul, the unworldly inner self, which holds the keys
to the spiritual worlds, available to us here and now whilst
still on earth. The cowslip is commonly called 'keys of heaven'
by country-dwellers.

DANDELION (*Taraxacum officinale*)

This bright, golden-flowered plant flowers throughout the
early spring and summer. The rich green leaves have edges
like jagged teeth, and there is one soft, furry, flower head to

each upright stalk. They look like small marigolds, and in fact an alternative country name for the dandelion is the field marigold. They grow everywhere, and carpet waste places with their radiant, cheerful blooms. The dandelion is a supreme **liver** herb, and it also gives excellent results in the treatment of **gall bladder complaints**. It can be used for **eczema** and **feline miliary dermatitis**, and is a healing tonic for the **spleen**. Serve a finely-chopped teaspoonful of dandelion leaves and stems (the leaves are best gathered before, and the stems during, the time of flowering, but both are valuable at all times) to your cat each day, either mixed with the meat or cereal feed (potatoes, corn and rice mix particularly well) or tucked into herbal pills. This dietary supplement will increase the flow of gastric juices and cleanse the patient's stomach of all morbid, unhealthy deposits which are fed upon by internal parasites, and are the reason why some cats make such good hosts for these unwelcome colonists, whilst some are able to readily repel their attacks. **Metabolic disturbances** will also be helped by the tisane and the fresh greens, as will other **digestive disorders, glandular swellings, ailments of the spleen,** and all **rheumatic problems**. For **hepatitis** and **every liver complaint,** not only should the tisane and the greens be taken daily, but two of the stems should be pounded on a ceramic surface, and then the whole (stems and the expressed milky sap) taken up with slippery elm flour, rolled into balls and given as pills. The same treatment is necessary for **diabetic cats.**

Dandelion tisane is made from the roots, which are cold-soaked overnight, brought just to the boil in the morning, strained, allowed to cool to blood heat, and administered. It is best taken half an hour before and after food. The plant can also be used to make tincture, and to supply greens and herbal pills, as described.

The name of the dandelion is a corruption of the French *dent de lion*, meaning lion's tooth. The ancient Greeks also linked this plant with the lion. It is interesting to note that it has associations with the Egyptian sphinx, the lion with the human head. Esoterically, this is a symbol of the spirit contained in matter, and in fact, according to arcane lore, the dandelion's role is to succour the binding of body and soul together, so that the spirit may function on planet earth. This is done on a subtle plane under the administration of the great Earth Mother, who creates bodies for all her children to inhabit. Her sacred signature is said to be the white, milk-like sap of the plant.

GOLDEN ROD (*Solidago virgaurea*)

This elegant plant, with its upright stems, leaves of clear green and masses of golden star-like flowers, grows on banks and hillsides, in woods and copses, in clearings, on damp ground and on ditch sides. It flowers from the end of June to October. The blossoms are gathered to treat **intestinal ulceration** and **bleeding of the intestines,** as well as **dysentery, vomiting** and **flatulence.** Used together, the flowers and leaves yield a tisane which is a first-rate medicine for **kidney ailments.** It is also excellent for treatment of the **urinary tract** and for all **bladder complaints.** In combination with cleavers and yellow or white deadnettle, it assists greatly where there is **renal failure** or **hardening of the kidneys.** It brings swift relief to cats suffering from **blocked bladder** or **cystitis.** It is recorded that in 1788 a young boy whose bladder had virtually petrified, was healed completely after taking golden rod tea for some time. He passed fifteen large stones as big as pebbles, fifty over the size of a pea, and a large quantity of gravel! It is also a **wound herb.** Make a poultice from the leaves and blossoms, or a compress from a tisane made of the same, and give the tisane internally. For cats suffering from **nervous stress** or **extreme emotional shock,** the tisane is a blessing, as it brings comfort and restores well-being. Golden rod can be used to make tisanes, poultices, compresses and tincture.

The Latin name is rooted in *solidare,* for the plant is known as a vulnerary, or one that 'makes whole', and was considered a panacea for all ills. Some people say that there is an angel of mercy behind the vibration of this plant. It is associated with the spiritual qualities of mercy and consolation.

GREATER CELANDINE, SWALLOW WORT, TETTERWORT (*Chelidonium majus*)

The stem of this perennial plant (not related to the lesser celandine except by the colour of its flowers) is slender, round and slightly hairy; it grows from 1½–3 feet high (45–90cm) and forms many branches; the points where the branches join the stem are swollen and jointed, and break very easily. When this happens, the plant emits a bright orange-coloured juice, which is strongly and unpleasantly rank. The yellowish-green leaves, almost grey underneath, are very thin, and resemble oak leaves. The flowers are arranged at the ends of the stems in loose umbels and are a pretty sunrise yellow, blooming

from May until late autumn. It is found by old walls, on waste ground and in hedges, almost always nearby human dwellings. It **cleanses the blood** and **stimulates the circulation**, and, taken in quantity, especially with stinging nettle and elder shoots, helps in cases of **leukaemia**. The greater celandine is another powerful **liver herb**, also benefiting the **metabolism, the kidneys** and **the gall bladder**. The juice is extracted, and half a cupful of this is mixed with one cupful of spring water into which two tablespoonfuls of apple cider vinegar have been added; this is given in warmed dropperfuls several times throughout the day. The juice, used externally, is successful in the treatment of **ringworm, malignant skin diseases, cataract, spots on the cornea, defective vision,** and a **bleeding or detached retina.** A homoeopathic tincture of greater celandine is available from chemists and herbalists for these disorders, but for **cataract** and **impaired vision,** the fresh juice is best. It is obtained by bruising a washed, wet leaf-stem of greater celandine between the forefinger and thumb, and then smearing it over the closed eyelid and into the corners. It is not actually rubbed into the eye. Take care when treating your cat in this way, as your skin should not absorb any quantity of the juice (it is an irritant in large doses). An infusion of the herb, with two tablespoonfuls of apple cider vinegar added per cup, and the addition of a few aniseeds, is helpful in removing obstructions of the liver and gall bladder. Greater celandine can be used to make the infusion described above, also standard tisanes, juice and the homoeopathic tincture referred to (it is better to buy this than to attempt to prepare it yourself).

In folklore, the greater celandine (the true celandine) has always been associated with swallows, because it comes into flower when these harbingers of summer arrive, and fades at their departure. It is still sometimes called swallow wort in country districts. It was believed that the parent birds used it to bestow supernaturally clear sight on their young. It is linked with the soul quality of reawakening and with the spiritual principle of resurgence.

HORSETAIL, BOTTLEBRUSH, SHAVE GRASS, MARE'S TAIL (*Equisetum arvense*)

This is a common plant, often found in damp soil, but also growing along waysides, in fields, hedgerows and on railway embankments. It has a lime-green stalk, ringed at intervals with whorls of small green branches. When the plants are fully grown, they look like miniature pine trees. It grows from early spring until the autumn. It has wonderful **blood-staunching powers**, and the tisane, taken internally, will halt **haemorrhages** and **vomiting of blood**. Standard poultices are applied to **infected wounds**, **cancerous growths** and **ulcers**, and the tisane is given regularly by mouth. For **kidney** and **bladder problems**, **gravel** and **stones**, the same treatment is applied. Give horsetail tisane on a daily basis to old cats, to guard against **rheumatic problems** and **nervous disorders**, also **sluggishness of the digestive system** and **kidneys** which is so often a problem in old age. Horsetail is primarily a **kidney herb,** and to treat complaints of this organ, the tisane

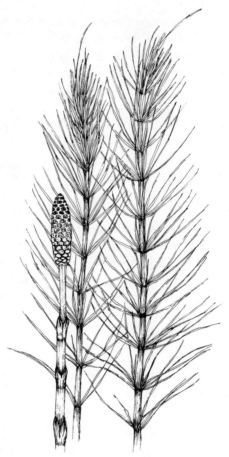

is given regularly, poultices are applied, and horsetail baths
are also used to complete the therapy. For **bladder mucus**
and **bladder cramps**, employ a horsetail steam bath as well
as the poultices and tisane. The herb is an impressive **diuretic**,
and will relieve **water retention** in the **pericardium, pleura,**
and that which is caused by **under-functioning of the kidneys.**
In any illness, if **water retention** occurs whilst administering
herbal medicine, discontinue it for a few days, and give the
patient only horsetail tisane. The accumulation of fluid will
soon disperse. **Visual impairment** is often rectified by this
herb, due to its **cleansing and stimulation of the kidneys.** For
allergic skin conditions, and **feline miliary dermatitis,** the
tisane, plus continual washings and compresses of a strong

decoction of horsetail, are most beneficial. These are also useful for **infections of the nail bed, caries, bony projections, diarrhoea** and **herpes.** Where **bleeding of the lungs, intestines** or **uterus** occurs, or any severe **haemorrhaging** from an injury, etc., the dosage of the herb has to be doubled or trebled to be certain of halting it. Normal strength tisanes can be used for **hardening of the arteries, tonsillitis, inflammation of the mouth, inflammation and bleeding of the gums, chronic bronchitis** and **tuberculosis.** This simple tisane even **counteracts** and **destroys tumours,** if it is administered with diligent regularity for a protracted period. It dissolves **polyps,** soothes **stomach gripes,** combats **liver and gall bladder attacks,** and relieves **congestions** which **cause pressure on the heart. Disc lesions** are caused to disappear through the therapeutic virtues of horsetail baths, accompanied by the application of the tisane. Horsetail is suitable for tisanes, strong infusions, poultices, baths, fresh ointment, compresses and tincture.

It is interesting that horsetail is associated by appearance with the pine tree, and by name with the horse, because the pine is the tree of the sun, and the horse is a creature of the sun. Horsetail is a herb of the sun, and is linked with the soul quality of nobility, and with the symbol of spiritual intelligence.

INDIAN CORN, ORNAMENTAL MAIZE, SWEET CORN (*Zea mays*)

This is the fruit of the sweet corn crop. The ears are hung with fine, webby material called 'corn silk'. It has medicinal virtues, and can be bought from herbalists. The tisane is an excellent treatment for **obesity,** and as it is a **powerful diuretic** it can be used for **all complaints of the bladder** and **kidneys,** especially **stones, oedema, fluid in the heart, nephritis, cystitis, renal colic** and **rheumatism.** Put one teaspoonful only into a little water and apple cider vinegar (one teaspoonful of apple cider vinegar per tablespoonful of water), take up by dropper, and administer every three hours. Corn silk can be used as a tisane, infusion and tincture.

It is sacred to the goddess Ceres, ancient presiding deity over cereals. It is associated with the soul quality of giving, and is a symbol of the spiritual principle of abundance. Corn silk filaments are said to represent the mystical veil of Ceres.

LADY'S MANTLE, LION'S FOOT (*Alchemilla vulgaris*)

Considered a magical herb by the ancients, this is an unusual plant which has an air of protectiveness. The leaf, shaped like a mantle or a shoulder-wrap with seven points, bears a dewdrop at its centre early in the morning, because it spreads itself out like a receiving hand. This precious dew (the distilled essence of mother earth) was collected on glass plates by alchemists to be used in their alchemical processes. Wherever the stem branches, one of these 'receiving hands' carefully encircles the branching point while the stem of the leaf itself again encircles the stalk with a sheath. The plant suggests that which is embracing, cherishing, protecting. The flowers are golden-green, and blossom in the time of the cuckoo, from April until the end of June. It is interesting that this

yellow-green is the colour of the zodiacal Cancer, the sign of the moon, of women and the goddess (the cuckoo is also a symbol of the goddess). Lady's mantle is indeed a herb for feminine disorders, and should be given as a tisane for all abdominal ailments, **injuries after delivery, debility of the abdomen during and after birth, inclination to miscarry,** to **strengthen the developing foetuses and the womb,** for **inflammation of the abdomen** and **prolapse of the uterus.** Also use fresh ointment poultices and lady's mantle baths. The poultices and tisanes will bring rapid healing to **wounds, infected** and **neglected sores,** and to **bleeding jaws after the removal of teeth.** It is good for **wound fever,** brings back strength to **weakened muscles and limbs,** is a tonic for **anaemia,** and is helpful in cases of **epilepsy.** It brings healing, too, to **ulcers, stings** and **cuts,** and will aid **obesity,** especially in queens. **Diabetic cats** should be treated with the tea regularly and frequently, and given occasional lady's mantle baths. Application of the tisane, together with repeated washings around the area of the heart with a strong infusion of the herb, will bring great relief to **disorders of the heart muscle.** In particular, lady's mantle is used, in conjunction with shepherd's purse, for **paralysis,** especially **foreleg paralysis,** and for **all incurable disorders of the muscles.** Use lady's mantle for tisanes, infusions, poultices, compresses, fresh ointment, tincture, washings and baths.

In folklore lady's mantle was associated with the Virgin Mary, and is linked with the soul quality of maternal nurturing. It is associated with the mystical golden egg, the precious cosmic egg in which each individual spirit is contained, so that no matter what the horrific disturbances and onslaughts at the earthly level, the vital essence of a person or creature cannot be destroyed or harmed, and remains eternally intact.

MALLOW, COMMON MALLOW, BLUE MALLOW, HIGH MALLOW (*Malva sylvestris*)

The large-leafed variety of this herb (*Lavatera arborea*) is a majestic plant, although it tends to creep if not well-staked. It has large, dancing flowers of mauve, lilac-pink or white

with a blush of red, and can be obtained from garden centres and flower markets. The wild, small-leafed mallow creates a pretty mound of foliage and flowers with a purple, deep- to pale-pink hue. From this mound, creeping stems emerge, eventually forming a larger cushion of foliage. The leaves are club-shaped, on dainty stems, and it flowers from June to September. Mallow grows by walls, along paths and way-sides, and on any grassy ground near human dwellings. The cold-infused tea is particularly helpful for **inflammations of the mucous membranes of the body,** so it is useful for infec-tions throughout the **bladder, mouth** and **gastrointestinal tract,** for **gastritis,** and **ulceration of the stomach and intes-tines.** Stir slippery elm flour into a mallow leaf decoction to help internal ulcers. It is very good for **asthma, bronchitis, coughs, tonsillitis, dry mouth** and **feline respiratory disease.** It is also effective for **emphysema,** especially when the warmed dregs of the tisane are used to make a poultice for the chest. If kept very warm, it can be left on overnight. It is an excellent remedy for **dry eye.** Wash the eyes very fre-quently with the warm tisane, and make eye compresses to leave on overnight. Washings of the tisane are good for **aller-gic cats**. Bathe the affected places regularly, even if only around the mouth and nose. **Wounds, swellings, ulcers** and **fractures** are helped by these washings. For **inflammation of the throat** and even **throat cancer**, mallow tisane is used to wash the throat every hour each day until symptoms cease, and overnight a poultice, made from the tisane residue mixed with barley flour, is applied to the throat and kept very warm. Use mallow to make tisanes, infusions, decoctions, tincture, poult-ices, compresses, washings and baths. Mallow is always cold-soaked overnight.

Pythagoras tells us that mallow was the first messenger sent by the gods to earth to indicate to humankind that the gods sympathised with our sorrows and sufferings, and took pity on our woes. It was a revered plant for this reason, and is associated with the soul quality of compassion, and with the spiritual dynamics earthing the divine healing essence.

MARIGOLD, POT MARIGOLD (*Calendula officinalis*)

Orange, golden or a burnished variation of these shades, all marigolds have the same healing properties. It is above all else a **cancer** herb, but it also brings great relief in cases of **inflammation of the liver**. It **purifies the blood,** so **stimulating the circulation** and bringing swift healing to **wounds**. Where they will not heal, or where the cat is clearly **in pain** whilst they are doing so, marigold ointment, either the salve or the fresh ointment applied as a poultice, will soothe away the distress in a short time. The ointment is also of use for **frost-bite, burns, scalds** and **skin conditions**. Baths or washings of the tisane help quickly where there is **fungal infection of the genitals** and in **anal irritation**. The tincture is excellent for **sores, ulcers, swellings, wounds, bruises and sprains, feline acne** and **eczema, feline miliary dermatitis** and **glossitis** (swell-ing and ulceration of the tongue in felines); dilute it and apply it as a compress. The diluted tincture (one part water, one part tincture) is very good when combined with St John's wort oil for **haws** (protrusion of the third eyelid). All **eye problems** are helped by marigold tincture and washings of the tisane and infusion. The ointment can also be applied to the eyelids to heal **blepharitis**. The tisane helps **ailments of the gastrointestinal tract, internal ulcers and blood or bacteria in the urine**. **Fevers, dropsy** and **viral infections**, especially **herpes**, are also firmly counteracted by this tea. The ointment and the tisane are used in all cases of **fungal disease** (actinomycosis, blastomycosis, coccidiomycosis, cryptococcosis, histoplasmosis, ringworm, etc.), and the tisane is used in conjunction with calamus roots and Benedict's herb for chronic or severe **diarrhoea**. For a **pining, grief-stricken, shocked** or **depressed cat**, make a standard tisane from the blossoms, and administer in the usual way. Rub the bruised flower head on a **wasp** or **bee sting**, or any **sting** or **bite** from a **poisonous insect**, to immediately **relieve the pain** and **disinfect the site of the wound**.

Marigold is a well-known garden flower, and can easily be obtained from any garden centre. It can be used to make tisanes, infusions, fresh and standard ointments, compresses, poultices, juice, tincture, oil, baths and washings.

An old country name for the marigold is summer's bride, because it faithfully follows the sun, unfolding its petals in the sun's light and closing them again as soon as it fades. It symbolised constancy and endurance in love, and was often used in wedding garlands and love charms. It protected against evil witchcraft, and its appearance in a dream was a sign of coming riches. It is linked with Mary bringing forth Christ, the light of the world, signified by the golden sun (mari-gold), and is esoterically associated with the gifts of the soul (divine woman or goddess) and the eternal riches of the spirit, which cannot be exhausted or 'spent'.

MISTLETOE (*Viscum album*)

This evergreen plant attaches itself to pines and deciduous trees, especially oaks and apple trees. It forms a round bush, bears white, sticky, moon-like berries which are poisonous, and has golden-green leaves which swoop out from the tops of their branching stalks like little pairs of wings. Only the leaves and twigs are suitable for use. They should be gathered from early October to mid-December, and from the beginning of March to the end of April. The plant is only of medicinal use at this time. The cold-soaked tisane is given in cases of **chronic cramps, frostbite, hardening of the arteries, stroke, bleeding of the lungs** and **intestines, disorders of the uterus,** especially **haemorrhaging,** and as a general **blood-stauncher,** good for **nosebleeds** and **wounds.** Mistletoe also heals **poor circulation, lack of energy** and **unwillingness to take normal exercise, heart disorders,** and **visual defects.** Maria Treben cites it as the best herb for **all heart and circulatory complaints.** It also benefits the entire **glandular system,** aiding the **metabolism** and stimulating the **pancreas,** so healing **diabetes.** It is very good for cases of **hormonal imbalance.** It also **fights and prevents cancer,** and **counteracts epilepsy.** Mistletoe is prepared as a cold infusion. The leaves and twigs can also be used to make tincture and juice.

Mistletoe is the 'Golden Bough' of classical legend, and was considered a sacred, wonder-working plant by the Druids and the Vikings. The Druids cut it ceremonially with a golden sickle during their holy solstice festivals, and the Norsemen feared and revered it, attributing to it terrible and supernatural powers, although in ancient Scandinavia it was the plant of peace, hung up outside the home to denote the certainty of a safe welcome within. In Britain, it was a protective plant, and was called All Heal, because it cured a multitude of diseases and conditions, settled quarrels (hence kissing under the mistletoe) and was an antidote to poisons. Mistletoe is 'in between the worlds' because it is neither of the earth or the air. It has been discovered recently that it grows only on cancerous parts of tree-boughs, which it heals, so it cannot really be called a parasite. Only birds (which have a strong esoteric connection with angels) can propagate it, carrying the sticky seeds on their beaks, or depositing them undigested in droppings. Seeds put into water or soil do not germinate. Whilst some plants help to bind the body to the soul, mistletoe binds the soul to the body—but not quite, retaining the freedom of the heavenly worlds for the spiritual beings of earth, symbolised by its ambivalent stature. It is the mediator between heaven and earth, but it can never be claimed by the earth. Its mission is to lift what is earthly into the spiritual spheres. It is an angel bound by a single fingertip, pointing the way upwards to freedom. Only birds can give it birth, and only the wise trees can sustain it.

PLANTAIN, RIBWORT, SNAKE PLANTAIN, JACK STRAW (*Plantago lanceolata*)

This esteemed plant grows by waysides, on grassy banks, in ditches, meadows, and along the edges of woods. It rises on its long, thin stalk from a rosette of often rather crumpled looking ribbed leaves with slightly toothed edges, the shape of tongues of flame. The flower spikes on top of the leggy stems are black, and look like little cones. The broad-leafed plantain (common plantain, *Plantago major*) is similar, although, as its name implies, it has broader leaves and

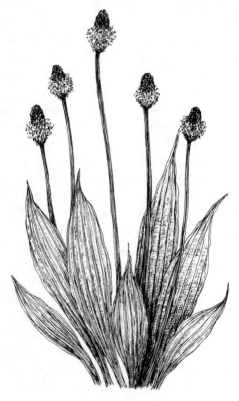

the flower spike is longer, with purple anthers rather than the blackish anthers of the ribbed plantain. Both types have the same healing properties. Plantain is used for the entire range of **diseases of the respiratory organs**, particularly **congested lungs, bronchial asthma**, and **tuberculosis of the lungs**. The whole plant is utilised for these conditions. It **purifies the blood, the lungs** and **the stomach**, and is good for **bad blood, kidney disorders, eczema, herpes** and **coughs**. It helps **convalescents**, especially when they need to **gain weight**. It also helps with **liver** and **bladder diseases**, especially when used with an equal measure of thyme. Plantain is an impressive **wound herb**, and when washed, bruised and placed on the open wound, the leaves bring rapid healing. They are also good for **cuts, scratches, dog bites, snake bites** and **stings and bites from poisonous insects**. The fresh, bruised leaves have been used to treat **cancerous** and other **aberrant growths**, and for **malignant glandular disorders**. Marjoram oil is dabbed well onto the appropriate parts, and bruised plantain leaves are laid over the oil and held in place by a bandage. For cats suffering from **iliac thrombosis**, the fresh leaves, crushed and applied at the site of the thrombosis along the aorta (up the abdomen to the heart), should be regularly administered after the patient has been treated by the vet (also see directions for further treatment given under Iliac Thrombosis, p. 100). Plantain can be used to make tisanes, infusions, fresh ointment, poultices and dressings from the fresh leaves.

In folklore, plantain is known as the herb which springs up wherever the British settled or colonised (as mentioned in 'Hiawatha' by Longfellow) and is still called 'Slan-lus', or plant of healing, in parts of the Scottish Highlands. It does seem to have an affinity with Britain, and was revered by the Anglo-Saxons. It appears in the old 'Lacnunga', the most ancient source of Anglo-Saxon medicine, as 'Waybroed' (now 'waybread', another country name for the herb), one of nine sacred herbs. It is associated with the soul-quality of valour, and is linked with the spiritual ritual of 'slaying the dragon'. It is a panacea for all venom, whether from insects, snakes, hydrophobic animals, or that released by plague and thought-energy.

SHEPHERD'S PURSE, WITCHES' POUCHES,
PICK-POCKET (*Capsella bursa-pastoris*)

Shepherd's purse grows by waysides, on grass verges and
grassy wasteland, in ditches and in gardens. The dainty white
flowers, not a vivid white and of which only a few are ever
open together, form an almost flat head. Below these flowers
the fruit stalks continue growing, like little pairs of delicate
outstretched arms growing in a row up the main stalk, their
'hands' being the tiny heart-shaped-pouches or purses that
give the plant its name. The leaves grow close to the ground
in rosettes. They are irregular-toothed and somewhat untidy-
looking. Poultices of shepherd's purse are very beneficial for
nursing queens showing signs of **eclampsia**. Apply them to

the swollen, inflamed teats to bring speedy relief. For all **internal** and **external bleeding**, shepherd's purse tisane should be given, because it is a **wound** and **haemorrhage herb**. Its other great virtue is that the tincture is uniquely helpful in cases of **muscular complaints**. In all instances of **limb and muscular atrophy**, massage the appropriate area well six times a day with the tincture, and give two to four dropperfuls of lady's mantle tisane four to six times a day, depending on the severity of the condition. Baths are also very helpful. Shepherd's purse can be used to make tisanes, baths, infusions, decoctions, poultices and tincture.

In folklore, shepherd's purse and its little pouches were reputed to be beloved of fairies and witches, who kept treasure in them. Shepherds, because of their pastoral careers, were considered to be allies of the good fairies. The plant is linked with the soul quality of the penetration of illusion, in that precious things are often hidden in mundane and unlovely caskets or exteriors, and the spiritual mystery of hidden treasure.

SMALL-FLOWERED WILLOWHERB (*Epilobium parviflorum*)

When gathering this plant it is important not to mistake it for its cousin, the stately rosebay willowherb, as its properties worsen the conditions which the smaller, more delicate small-flowered variety so successfully alleviate. It grows to about two feet in height (60cm). The leaves are darkish-green, stems thin and upright, though waving and flexible, and it bears flowers from deep to the palest pink. The small, fragile blooms stand on top of long willowy pods, like eyes on the end of stalks. When the flowers stop blooming, these pods open to reveal the downy seeds, protected by long, soft, grey-white hairs. It grows by walls, in gardens, along waysides, favouring semi-shade. It is a potent healer for all **bladder** and **kidney disorders**, and is of help in cases of **blocked bladder, cystitis, scanty** or **stagnant urine** and **suppression of urine**. It can even be used to treat **bladder** or **kidney cancer**. The

small-flowered willowherb is used for infusions and tisanes only.

The willowherb tends to grow where ancient buildings have been cleared, or where fire has ravaged the ground, even though it usually prefers a site near rivers and waterways. It is this connection with moving bodies of water, with the urinary system, with what we might perceive as flushing out and clearing away, showing its affinity with sites where this has taken place in nature and in human civilisation, that links the willowherbs with the unfettering of blocked energies and the spiritual principle of creative destruction. It is an 'out with the old, in with the new' herb, one of which feng shui experts would no doubt approve!

Important: take care not to gather the great hairy willow-herb, which has fleshy stems, grows much taller and has flowers considerably larger than the small-flowered variety, as this is a poisonous plant.

SPEEDWELL, HEATH SPEEDWELL, FLUELLEN
(*Veronica officinalis*)

The speedwell or veronica forms large, dense, low-growing clumps, from which long trailers extend, bearing tiny blue flowers with a dash of violet. The leaves are pleasantly rounded, and it is these round, splayed leaves that distinguish it from chickweed. It is an inhabitant of clearings, fields, hedgerows, grassy wastes and particularly lawns. It has a strong purifying action, and will clear **bronchitis, digestive disorders** and **asthma**. It is also effective in the treatment of **sores, eczema,** and **ulcers,** especially where these are of the moist, weeping kind. It rids the **intestines** of **mucus** and **unhealthy deposits.** It is also used for **liver** and **spleen disorders** in company with other herbs (especially stinging nettle and dandelion; eyebright and vervain are also beneficial).

It relieves **rheumatism** and prevents **furring of the arteries**. Speedwell has a reputation for **improving the vision**, and an **eye-wash** made from a decoction of the plant will soothe away **conjunctivitis** and many other **eye disorders**. Speedwell may be used for infusions, tisanes, compresses, decoctions (good for washing wounds before applying compresses), fresh juice, fresh ointment, poultices, eye-washes and tincture.

'Fluellen' is an old, evocative name for speedwell, deriving from the old Welsh for 'the herb of St Llywelyn'. The Welsh considered speedwell to be a mystical herb, endowed with supernatural healing virtues. It is associated with the saintly qualities of the ancient Celtic holy man, and is an emblem of miracles.

STINGING NETTLE (*Urtica dioica*)

One of nature's most potent herbs, and certainly one of my personal favourites, the stinging nettle is a tall, handsome plant. It turns from an emerald, almost luminous green in the spring, to a darker, ranker green in the summer. It grows everywhere, in cities and countryside, near human dwellings, on wasteland, pastures, waysides and grass verges, under hedges and in gardens. It has broad, heart-shaped leaves tapering to a fine point, and bears a multitude of small, green flowers in long, branched clusters springing from the axils of the leaves, which scatter pollen copiously. The whole plant has a downy appearance, and also sports many, more spear-like, stinging hairs. Their attacks may be alleviated by bruising dock leaves and rubbing the afflicted parts. (Dock is almost always growing nearby to provide salve for nettle-rash.) It is used to treat **rheumatism**, **arthritis** and **defective circulation**, but it also **relieves depression, eliminates bronchitis** and **reduces the risk of haemorrhage**. It is perhaps the best **blood herb**, which it **purifies** and **renews**. It **cleanses the stomach** and the **circulatory system**, ridding the body of **eczema** and other **chronic skin disorders** in the process. It rids the whole body of toxins, is a **tonic for the pancreas**, lowering the blood sugar and protecting from **diabetes**. It sweeps away **disorders, discomfort** and **infections of the uri-**

nary tract, releases **suppressed urine** and defeats **constipation**. It will benefit **weak** and **sickly** cats. It is an excellent herb with which to treat **allergies** and **viral infections**, and it will also counteract **cancer**, especially of the **stomach**. **Leukaemia** may be treated with the stinging nettle in company with other herbs (particularly yarrow, marigold and speedwell), and it is also successful in cases of **anaemia**. It has an impressive record, too, in the treatment of **liver**, **gall bladder**, **spleen**, **stomach** and **lung disorders**, also **ulcers** and **vascular constriction**. A decoction prepared from the roots is a first-rate remedy for **dissolving renal stones** and other **internal obstructions**. The fresh ointment is used to bring wonderfully swift and cooling relief to any area of the body that is painfully **swollen** and **infected**. Use the stinging nettle to make tisanes, infusions, decoctions, compresses, poultices, fresh ointment, baths and tincture.

The stinging nettle is reputed to have been brought to earth by an angel, to heal humankind. It was spread to ease the bitterness and gall of the earthly experience (symbolised by its sting). It is associated with the spiritual dynamics of revelation.

ST JOHN'S WORT (*Hypericum perforatum*)

This mystical herb of the wayside has an abundance of yellow flowers which bloom from late June onwards, their five petals spreading outwards like the rays of a medieval sun. The leaves grow in pairs; they are small, narrow and stalkless. Pairs of slender, flowering branches grow numerously from the axils of the leaves on the erect main stem. The upper branches are the first to flower. It grows along roadsides, in meadows, hedgerows, woodland, and in wild, remote places. It is an excellent **wound herb,** and is beneficial for all **nerve injuries.**

Highly-strung, hysterical cats, or those who have suffered **emotional** or **physical trauma**, should be given St John's wort tisane, baths and regular rubs with the oil. This oil is also used for all **wounds** and **swellings**, especially **glandular swellings**; massages with the herb benefit **rheumatism, arthritis** and **back pain**. It is also soothing for **sunburn, scalds, grazes** and **burns**. St John's wort is suitable for the preparation of tisanes, infusions, fresh ointment, compresses, juice, poultices, oil, tincture and baths.

Folklore connects the free-flowing red sap of this plant with the wounds and the blood of Christ. There is an old tradition that the plant moves about secretly at night, to avoid being gathered before St John's eve, when its healing properties come into full sway. It is associated with the soul quality of sacrifice, and the spiritual principles of redemption and mercy.

SWEDISH BITTERS

The recipe for Swedish bitters is to be found in Maria Treben's wonderful herbal *Health Through God's Pharmacy*. It has 11 ingredients which are the components of a recipe found amongst the papers of a famous Swedish physician, Dr Samst, after his death in a riding accident aged 104. The medicine is taken in drops, used as a lotion or to make a compress. It is a panacea, and has effected many miraculous cures. It can be bought as a preparation made with alcohol, or as a do-it-yourself pack, which can be prepared with apple cider vinegar instead of alcohol. This is my preference, as I dislike giving alcohol to animals, and the apple cider vinegar does not dry out the skin when Swedish bitters is applied as a compress. Maria Treben assures readers that according to stringent laboratory tests, the herbs drown the alcohol and the whole is considered as medicine, so if you prefer to buy the ready-made compound, don't be afraid to give it to your cat, even where under normal circumstances, alcohol would be prohibited (for heart and liver complaints, for example). However, as apple cider vinegar is such a great healer in itself, it makes sense to add its properties to the already considerable virtues of the bitters. They can be given for any complaint, either as a compress, to be left on for four hours or overnight, or as oral drops, half a teaspoonful in a dropperful of spring water morning and evening. Often they give results when all else has failed. See Useful Addresses for availability.

WILD GARLIC, RAMSONS (*Allium ursinum*)

This woodland plant has a very acrid taste and smell. The broad, glossy leaves, quite similar in appearance to those of lily of the valley, spread over the ground like a carpet beneath the trees, appearing at the end of March. The flowers bloom in May, blossoming at the top of the long, thin, pale-green leafless flower stalk as an umbel of white, star-like flowers. The leaves die back in late summer, and the bulbs lie dormant

beneath the soil until the following spring. It particularly favours ash and beech woodland. Wild garlic cannot be used to make tisanes, because the healing virtues in its leaves are destroyed by heat. It has to be given, finely snipped or chopped, as a green salad. Most cats will accept it in their meat or mixed with potatoes or rice. If not, put it into honey pills. It **cleanses the blood** and the **entire system,** and is excellent for **feline miliary dermatitis** and other **skin conditions.** It is a **tonic for the brain, stomach** and **intestines,** and will calm **diarrhoea,** even when severe or persistent. It cures **worms,** even the worst cases, and **stimulates intestinal activity,** so helping **constipation** and **flatulence.** It is also very effective in the treatment of **heart disorders, hardening and furring of the arteries, bronchitis, shortness of breath, colic, herpes, rheumatism, dropsy** and **tuberculosis. Wounds** are helped to **heal quickly** when the fresh juice, expressed from the leaves, is applied as a compress or, if the wound needs air, applied simply as a lotion. Wild garlic can be used as fresh greens (offer the fresh leaves from March until the end of May, thereafter mince the bulbs and leaves into a pulp, add warm milk and give one teaspoonful per day), fresh juice and tincture.

All the garlics have vigorous purifying and protective powers, and long before Bram Stoker wrote his famous *Dracula*, it was used extensively throughout Romania and Hungary to ward off evil spirits and vampires. Theophrastus relates that the ancient Greeks placed cloves of garlic on the piles of stones at crossroads as a supper for Hecate, queen of dark witchcraft, and Pliny records that garlic and onion were invoked as deities by the ancient Egyptians on the swearing of oaths. European folklore claimed that if a morsel of the bulb was chewed by anyone running a race, his competitors would be prevented from outstripping him. Garlic is linked with the soul quality of wise restraint, and with the spiritual principle of the absorption of darkness into light.

YARROW, MILFOIL, SOLDIER'S WOUNDWORT
(*Achillea millefolium*)

The flowers grow in large umbels, rather like cow parsley, only the plant is smaller and the flowers more closely clustered. They are like little daisies, pink, pale lilac or white in colour. The plants grow to a height of about one or two feet (30–60cm). The leaves are very feathery in appearance. It grows everywhere, amongst the grass, in meadows, pastures and by the roadside.

Yarrow has been called the herb of mercy, because it is excellent for **feminine complaints**. All **abdominal disorders**, even **cancer**, are greatly helped by this herb. When a queen suffers

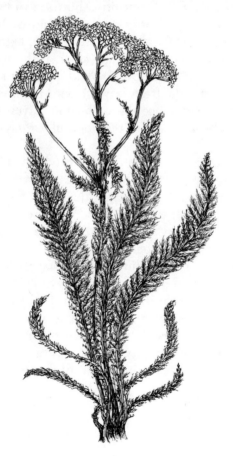

from **inflammation of the ovaries** or **prolapse of the uterus,** give her yarrow tisane and yarrow baths as regularly as possible. For **feline respiratory disease,** use yarrow tisane, very warm, to relieve **congestion** and the discomfort of **running eyes.** Give the eyes a wash with the tea as well as administering it internally. **Blepharospasm** and **blepharitis** are also helped by the regular internal and external application of yarrow tisane. It has a powerful healing effect on the **bone marrow,** renewing and cleansing the blood. It should therefore be used in all diseases of the **bone** and **bone marrow.** It halts bleeding in the **lungs** and the **stomach,** and is good for **flatulence, indigestion** and **abdominal cramps.** It soothes and heals the **gastrointestinal tract,** calms **diarrhoea,** relieves **constipation,** and stimulates a **poor appetite.** It acts as a boost to the **kidneys,** relieves **rheumatic** and **back pain,** and is good for the **circulation** and therefore the **heart.** The tea also dispels **sadness** and **moroseness,** and the fresh pulped leaves, put onto a **decaying tooth,** will take the pain away, and help to halt the **putrefaction** and **decay.** Washing the coat with a **decoction** of yarrow is very helpful for **feline alopecia** (hair loss) and for **feline miliary dermatitis.** It is an excellent cure for all **fevers,** and will quickly staunch the **bleeding** of **wounds** and **nosebleeds.**

Yarrow can be used to make tisanes, infusions, decoctions, tinctures, ointment, poultices, compresses, oil and baths. When making the ointment, use plenty of flowers, if available, and add a measure of raspberry leaves for every measure of yarrow. This ointment is particularly good for **anal irritation** and the **healing of wounds.**

Yarrow is a herb of protection and fidelity in folklore, and is linked medicinally and supernaturally with mothers and babies, which associates it with the Virgin and the Christ-child or the Goddess and her children (all the creatures of the earth), and esoterically with the wisdom of the heart.

YELLOW DEADNETTLE (*Lamium galeobdolon*)

This appealing plant is usually to be found near areas colonised by the stinging nettle, and looks similar, except that its foliage is generally a lighter green, and the upper pairs of leaves support circles of golden-yellow flowers, clustering together like long, shapely hoods back to back in a ring. It grows in woodland, damp hedgerows, meadows and waste-land. With its companion plant, the white deadnettle, which is similar except that it bears more rounded, bell-like flowers (poetic country names for the two are the yellow and white archangel) and is much more common, the yellow deadnettle is of use to the queen because it is a panacea for all **feminine disorders** and **complaints of the abdomen,** and to the tom because it brings healing in cases of **scanty urine, painful urination, cystitis** and **blocked bladder. Kidney disease** and **fluid retention in the heart** are helped by these herbs, as are **digestive disorders, feline miliary dermatitis** and **ulcers. Bladder malfunction, chill in the bladder with accompanying mucus,** and **nephritis,** respond to the medicinal properties of both plants. Baths with a strong decoction of white or yellow deadnettle added, boost their healing virtues. Yellow dead-nettle, golden rod and cleavers make up an excellent tisane for the treatment of **hardening of the kidneys.** The yellow and white deadnettle can be used for tisanes, infusions, decoc-tions, compresses, poultices, fresh ointment, tincture and baths.

In folklore, there is a story that the virtues of these flowers were revealed by angels to a monk—perhaps they were Michael and Gabriel, angels of the sun and the moon. The white archangel represents the soul quality of pure devotion, whilst the yellow archangel is a symbol of secret spiritual joy.

Chapter Six

The Bach Flower Remedies

Dr Edward Bach was born in 1886 in England, of Welsh extraction (his name is pronounced 'Batch'). He studied orthodox medicine at University College Hospital, London, and although he qualified as a surgeon and later as a bacteriologist, and established a highly successful practice near Harley Street, he became dissatisfied with the conventional philosophy of isolating disease and attacking it with allopathic medicines and surgery. He felt that this military approach to illness was often unsatisfactory, because the bombarded and suppressed disease, although seeming to disappear, often returned shortly afterwards in a much more aggressive form which could not be counteracted. He wished to develop a method of healing with the principles of purity, simplicity and wholeness as its underlying philosophy. He believed that medicine should treat the person, not the disease. In removing the disease from centre-stage, one no longer entered into combat with it. In fact, it was ignored, and the focus was firmly placed on the disharmony within the patient, their extremes (likes and dislikes), their fears and anxieties, their needs and vulnerabilities.

Whilst attending a dinner party in 1928, he underwent a

revelation. Observing the many different guests, he suddenly realised that their various characteristics actually represented several clearly-defined types of person and that these types would react in a certain way to illness and affliction. Using his intuition and his deep knowledge of nature and herbs, he visited Wales (intimations of Nelferch, the Welsh herb-healing fairy woman of the enchanted mountain lake are, for me, delightfully indicated here!) and collected two plants, *mimulus* and *impatiens*. He prepared these in the same way as he made his oral vaccines (the Seven Bach Nosodes, which were renowned for their efficacy, and which he had developed some years previously, combining the principles of homoeo-pathy and his extensive knowledge of orthodox medicine) and prescribed them according to the personality of his patients, with outstandingly successful results.

A year later, he closed down his laboratory and his busy practice, and journeyed to Wales to seek further natural reme-dies. Wandering in a dewy meadow one morning at sunrise, it occurred to him that each dewdrop, warmed by the sun, would become the distilled essence of the plant it bejewelled; and he refined a method of preparing his remedies from pure water. He went on to develop 38 in all, suffering the symp-toms of each condition until he discovered the flower or tree which healed them.

Dr Bach's belief was that when harmony was restored to the soul through the healing properties of the remedies, the natural life-force, released from the cramping and blockages which manifest as disease, would course freely through the whole being of the patient, and restore lost health, simply throwing off the invading condition. Plants and plant souls inhabited the earth before humankind, and plant wisdom and power understands how the life-energy is channelled through all the levels of a conscious being, so sustaining a perfect balance between body, mind, soul and spirit. Therefore the plant essence, which is spiritual in kind, can work on our subtle bodies and their emanations, bringing these into attunement so that we are at one, or in harmony, with the wholeness of creation both within and without. This is not quite the same as herbalism, which does treat the disease or condition directly; but I believe that the cosmic and soul qualities of plants *do* play upon the subtle bodies of the patient receiving herbal treatment in much the same way, and that this is how they are so often able to effect such a powerful and complete cure. Nevertheless, the soul types of earthly beings, being so finely attuned to Dr Bach's 38 plants, are wonderfully assisted by them in recovering lost harmony; and so the application of the remedies is a boost to herbalism, and will even effect a cure entirely on their own.

The Bach Flower Remedies are very effective when used to treat animals, because they do not offer intellectual resistance as we do, and so do not encumber and delay the healing process. Everyone who has a cat companion is aware of its distinct personality, and it is this personality which should be treated by the appropriate remedy, or remedies. They can be found on sale in herbalists, and even in the larger Boots chemists nowadays, where they are accompanied by leaflets explaining their origins and how to administer them (which is simple, just a few drops are put in the drinking water or milk, or straight onto the tongue, four or more times a day).

I highly recommend the use of these remedies as companions to the herbal healing recipes and directions given in this book, as they heighten and speed the healing process. Your cat cannot be harmed or overdosed by them, and they can be freely given even when the patient is taking veterinary-prescribed medication.

As descriptions of the remedies are geared towards human personalities rather than animal, I will try to give a feline interpretation below:

AGRIMONY: try to pretend that nothing is wrong with them, even when they are very ill.
ASPEN: the paranoid cat, full of fears of unknown origin.
BEECH: arrogant cats who do not suffer fools gladly.
CENTAURY: cats whose will can be overridden by dominant companion animals and who will surrender food to them, even though they have not taken their fill.
CERATO: follow the lead of other companion animals; are often led into 'scrapes'.

CHERRY PLUM: distraught after trauma; for those who have been badly treated, and who display loss of control, vicious rages, and antisocial behaviour.

CHESTNUT BUD: cannot learn by experience and continually repeat the same mistakes; poor at understanding their human companion's wishes and rules.

CHICORY: very possessive of either their own space, or a human or animal companion's affection; demand attention, express selfishness and make a terrible fuss if they are neglected in any way (according to their standards!).

CLEMATIS: indifference, inattentiveness, dreaminess and mental absence.

CRAB APPLE: over-fastidious, even for felines; tend to be disgusted by physical human contact, and cleanse themselves over-exaggeratedly after being touched (this behaviour is normal to a certain degree—look for obsessive all-over disinfecting and obvious disgust).

ELM: sudden loss of confidence and ability in a normally self-assured, independent cat.

GENTIAN: easily becomes despondent, easily discouraged and dejected.

GORSE: suffering from extreme depression, seeming weary of life.

HEATHER: very needy cats who demand a lot of fuss and are very vocal and complaining, always sympathy-seeking if something is wrong, however trivial.

HOLLY: jealous, envious, resentful, revengeful and suspicious, express hatred towards other animals or humans.

HONEYSUCKLE: pining, for a lost environment or for an absent human or animal friend.

HORNBEAM: suffering from mental or physical exhaustion after illness or trauma; convalescents, or for those who need to develop 'backbone', as they are suffering uncertainty from their unaccustomed lack of strength and well-being.

IMPATIENS: irritable, impatient and short-tempered.

LARCH: hesitancy due to lack of self-confidence; seem to have an inferiority complex, anticipate failure, have to be coaxed to make a necessary leap from a tree or a wall, dither and lack conviction in deciding what they wish to do (to come in or stay out, to be nursed or left alone, etc.).

MIMULUS: nervousness; apprehension; fear of known things; shyness; timidity.

MUSTARD: melancholy, saturnine, moody.

OAK: for valiant cats, who struggle on in illness or injury, and have to be persuaded to keep still; who will not give in, or who are inclined to nervous illness.

OLIVE: completely exhausted, drained cats who have come to the end of their strength and spirits.

PINE: sensitive conscience, readily feeling very guilty for any wrongdoing, or for what it is afraid may be interpreted as wrongdoing (something falls off the shelf in its vicinity, for instance, and it behaves guiltily, although not at fault).

RED CHESTNUT: excessive fear and anxiety, running after human or animal friends to see where they are if they leave the room, etc.; seems to know when others are in distress or ill and is full of sympathy, which it demonstrates.

ROCKROSE: terror, extreme fear or panic.

ROCK WATER: egocentric, rigid, inflexible personality, expressing nobility of character but whose dignity is of paramount importance to its well-being; if ever lost, such cats are deeply humiliated, offended and resentful; they will not forgive you if you witness their fall from grace.

SCLERANTHUS: becomes travel-sick, is uncertain and indecisive in its behaviour, has mood swings and frequent digestive upsets.

STAR OF BETHLEHEM: all the effects of shock following a bad fright or an injury.

SWEET CHESTNUT: very serious cases of depression, nervous illness and trauma, when the cat has reached the outer limits of its endurance.

VERVAIN: very highly-strung, stressed, tense cats, who seem almost liable to nervous breakdown when under strain, and who easily become over-excited.

VINE: dominant, inflexible, proud of their achievements (hunting, fighting, producing litters, etc.), autocratic, arrogant and proud.

WALNUT: a remedy that is protective against powerful influences (uncharacteristic bad behaviour due to psychic atmosphere, stress factors outside your control, bad habits caught from association with a dominant animal friend outside the home) and which assists adjustment to any major transition or change (moving house, neutering, parting with kittens, changing owners, etc.).

WATER VIOLET: proud, superior, aloof, reserved and like to isolate themselves.

WHITE CHESTNUT: suffer from nervous habits, lack of concentration, obsessive behaviour (those who are likely to give themselves lick-sores, for instance), who cannot let go of destructive behaviour-patterns.

WILD OAT: restless cats who exhibit signs of dissatisfaction, resentment, despondency, uncertainty, and unpredictability.

WILD ROSE: apathetic, resigned, lethargic and uninterested. They are bored with life and unhappy, but prefer a sleepy moroseness to an assertive reaction against the circumstances which disagree with them.

WILLOW: for the resentful, repressed cat who takes bitter offence and often clearly feels badly done-to, and who enjoys threatening or attacking other cats or companion animals.

RESCUE REMEDY: a composite of CHERRY PLUM, CLEMATIS, IMPATIENS, ROCKROSE and STAR OF BETHLEHEM, to be given in times of accident, emergency, great emotional or nervous suffering, after serious operations, traumatic births, after fights with other cats or attacks by other animals, terror or severe mental trauma (a house-move, for instance).

One of the many advantages of this pure and simple system of healing is that the little bottles can be carried around in a pocket or handbag without any inconvenience, so that if travelling with your cat you can have Rescue Remedy on hand in case of emergency, and administer treatment from other bottles as regularly as necessary if the cat is on a course of therapy.

Chapter Seven

Crystal Healing for Cats

Although a wide range of crystals can be used to treat cats, there are six powerful healers that I have found particularly helpful for animals. For each stone, use one to put in a pouch at the bottom of the cat's bed, and another to put into the drinking water for three hours before it is given to the cat. This can be done with milk, too. Simply pour into a basin, put in the prepared stone (see below), cover, and leave for three hours in a cool place before offering to the cat. The crystal must be removed from all liquids before they are given to the cat.

BOTSWANA AGATE   This is a dark crystal with a clearly defined white 'eye' (the more obvious the eye, the better the crystal seems to work). It is a good healer, slow and steady, with stabilising, fortifying energies.
BLOODSTONE   This stone is said to have formed when drops of Christ's blood fell to earth at the crucifixion and instantly crystallised. It improves the circulation and is a healer for all blood-related ailments. In former times it was used to staunch haemorrhages. It is also a tonic for the brain and the circulatory system. It detoxifies the body,

helping rheumatism and affected hips and joints. It is good for the queen at the time of birthing, bringing ease and protection.

CARNELIAN A general healer, particularly good for the abdomen and the entire digestive tract. It is beneficial for the kidneys, for difficult emotions, and for the allergic cat. It is very protective, and heals jealousy and envy. It inspires self-confidence and courage and a sunny nature. It is helpful for the blood, for infections and for balancing the thyroid.

GREEN AVENTURINE This stone will reconnect the patient to the natural world, severance from which is so problematic and disharmonious for cats. It is excellent for strengthening and healing the heart, and calms nervousness. It helps skin conditions, asthma and allergies. Also use as described in Triangulation (p. 208).

RUTILE QUARTZ This is a potent healer which clears blockages and is good for bronchitis and congestion of the lungs. It energises the system, anchors and integrates the life-force into the body (helpful after accidents, injury or surgery) and helps to restructure body cells.

RED AND YELLOW JASPER Jasper is a good, gradual, reliable healer, and is excellent for disorders of the pancreas, gall bladder, spleen, stomach, bowels, liver and kidneys. It deals efficiently with gross, heavy, malignant energies. It removes blocks in the liver and the bile ducts, and cleanses the adrenal glands. It also counteracts and prevents cancer. Use yellow jasper for liver complaints and an ailing stomach, and red for the bowels, also generally for the organs and muscles of elimination, including the bladder. Both stones are used in the treatment of cancer.

PREPARING THE CRYSTALS

First and foremost, wash your crystals under the stream of water from the cold tap. Then, place them in a bowl of spring water, and add two tablespoonfuls of apple cider vinegar. Cover the bowl and leave to soak for a few hours. Remove them, hold each one in the palm of your left hand, imagine your heart as a golden glowing star, and say, 'I bless this crystal in the name of the Divine Spirit, and dedicate it to the highest good. I ask the angels of the Divine Spirit to cleanse it of all consciousness which is not its own or is not that with which I programme it.' Let the light from the star in your heart shine out over the crystal, and in an act of imagination, place the crystal in the golden glow of your heart, where there is a cave for safekeeping. Your crystal is now blessed, dedicated and cleansed, and is ready to be programmed. Do this by simply cupping it in your left palm, holding it to your heart and intoning your cat's name slowly three times. Speak to the crystal (it is a centre of conscious-ness) and make a clearly worded request that it should bring healing to your cat (always refer to your cat by its name). Ask for specific healing ('may the healing power go to the liver, the heart, the stomach, to help with . . . . . .'s nervous problem, or aggressive or disobedience problem', etc.). Then, again from your own heart, put into the crystal the quality in which you wish your cat to be bathed (life-energy, love, healing from the angels, peace and calm, consolation, etc.). Do this not so much mentally, but in an act of imagination centred in the heart, so that you really feel the quality with which you are imbuing the crystal. Then apply as directed.

MAINTAINING CARE

If your cat takes a long time to recover, you will need to repeat the cleansing and dedication ceremonies occasionally. What is most important, however, is to wash the crystals every day. You only need to hold them under the stream from the cold tap for a second. If this is not done, the crystal power becomes clogged and unclean.

TRIANGULATION

While the cat is asleep or resting in its bed, bless, cleanse and dedicate three green aventurines, and place them to form the points of a triangle so that the cat is in the centre of the imaginarily-described triangle. Leave in place for as long as the cat will cooperate!

TIPS

If the cat keeps throwing the pouch out of bed, place the rededicated, blessed and cleansed crystal on a photograph of the patient. On the other hand, your cat might be very cooperative and actually help you to choose an appropriate crystal. Put a handful of the required crystals (one sort at a time) on the floor in front of it, and see if the cat starts to examine, or indicate in any other way, one particular crystal from the homogenous selection.

It may be helpful to note that the Botswana agate and the green aventurine are endowed with particular healing virtues in tune with the animal kingdom.

Chapter Eight

Spiritual Healing

Spiritual healing is a very simple and natural form of the art, and it is very effective for animals, as they do not erect mental barriers or consciously resist the inflow of subtle energy in the way that humans sometimes do.

Sit comfortably either with the cat beside you or on your lap. It is through the mystery of the breath that the spiritual worlds are drawn upon (for human breath is magical), so begin to breathe a little more slowly and a little deeper than usual. Focus on your breath, imagine it entering your body through the heart and nourishing your whole being, and then being given out again in blessing via the heart centre. When you feel peaceful and stilled within, raise your left hand a little and cup it. This is your receiving hand, and you may imagine the divine essence pouring into it so that you are enabled to give healing with your right hand; yet it is always the heart that is queen of the process, and the gentle breathing that flows 'through' the heart creates a link with celestial light, the ineffable light of the spirit that is the creative principle of all that is.

With your right hand, begin to softly stroke the cat along the spine from head to tail, all the while breathing in the precious celestial light and receiving its inflow through your cupped left hand. As you breathe out, let the light stream into your right hand, and consciously make a heart-gift of it to the cat, so that through rhythmic breathing you are inhaling the divine light and exhaling it imaginarily into the cat's spine via your caressing hand. Do this for five or ten minutes, once or twice a day, or more often if possible.

You can attune yourself to the spiritual light by means of the visualisation of a six-pointed star. Prepare yourself by following the directions given above, and imagine a star formed from two equilateral triangles, one upright and one inverted, merging together perfectly to become the perfect image of a star, shining with a pure radiance of brilliant gold and white which scintillates but yet is a centre of profound mystical peace, the healing peace of the spirit which one touches when in deep communion with nature. Let the light that you breathe in come from the heart of this spiritual star, and know that your own heart is of its essence, and a part of it.

Chapter Nine

Cats and Angels

When working to heal your cat, be sure not to forget the loving assistance of the angels. They work upon countless spheres in the spiritual realms, directing their love upon the earth plane. They can be called upon when gathering herbs, when preparing them for use, and when administering them, so that all these processes are specially blessed. They can be summoned when your cat is very ill or in pain, to soothe and heal the affliction. There are angels for every quality you need to call upon. Angels work in groups, and these groups network in a higher consciousness to administer aid when it is requested. Therefore, they can be specifically or collectively called upon. You might, for instance, ask the Angel of Healing to help your cat overcome its illness, and then the angel presiding over a certain group would answer your invocation; but you could also call upon the 'angels' to help to restore the cat as its healing progresses, because angels never work alone, but are always part of a dedicated group expressing perfect brotherhood in whatever area of service they work; and so, although you might contact a specific angel in order to attune to the quality you need (the Angel of Peace, the Angel of Protection, etc.) it will always be helpful to remember that an angelic throng will also work on your behalf, and that they will not only be willing, but will actively desire to commune with you, and become your friends.

Having a group of radiant friends who love you unconditionally, will help you unstintingly, and who are always eager to spiritually lift you high above the dull earth plane and surround you with joy, delightful humour (the angels have a wonderful sense of humour!), deep peace and the harmony of angelic life—a wonderful boon to any healer! Your cat will actually be able to help you commune with the angels, as well as receiving the benefit of their healing, because animal souls are in some ways closer to the eternal truths and wisdom than human beings at this point in human evolution.

It is easy to contact the angelic realm. Focus gently on your breath, and breathe a little more slowly and deeply, but not in any way that makes you uncomfortable. Remember that the spiritual spheres, and the angels who inhabit them, are to be found within. Become aware of the six-pointed star within your own heart, a star that has no divisions within it. Give the healing blessing that lies within your own heart out to the world, because as soon as you begin to give of yourself, the angels are instantly with you. Now make your petition to the angels; but remember that your communion will be on the wavelength of love (not sentimentality), and that love is the key to all your dealings with the angels.

When calling upon the angelic spheres on behalf of your cat, it is important to realise that the animal itself will readily respond to angelic influence, without any need on your part to facilitate the process other than the simple methods described by communion and petition. Cats, always more astral than physical, are already close in spirit to the angelic realm.

Don't forget to make a point of calling on the angels when preparing your herbal remedies, as described at the beginning of this chapter, because the angels will amplify the healing virtues of the natural materials you use. You will also feel a gentle but distinct guidance as to which recipe or particular herb to choose, from the range which is useful for the cat's condition.

It is helpful to call on the great Cat Angel, the goddess Bast or Pasht, when making a specific healing request for your cat. Light a white or golden candle, and imagine that you sit at the feet of Bast, manifesting as a huge black cat wearing a precious gold collar bearing the symbol of Horus, and who looks on you with mystical, kind, golden-glowing eyes. Put your request to her, and leave the candle in a safe place to burn down. Make an offering to an animal charity as a sacrifice to Bast. If your means are small, it need not be very much; but it is best that something is given. Bast was the goddess of happiness and pleasure, carnival and laughter, in ancient Egypt, and has strong associations with the mighty archangel who ministers to all animals, on the earthly plane and elsewhere.

Healing always comes to us directly from angelic realms, and these ineffably lovely beings can be called upon when administering any kind of healing, herbal, spiritual, crystal, orthodox, or when using the Bach Flower Remedies. Bear in mind that there is an angel presence within the six-pointed star, and that the star is a symbol for the mystical power in the human heart, the divine sword in the stone of matter. You can use this power to bring wholeness and healing to your cat at the deepest soul level.

Chapter Ten

Charms, Runes and Healing Chants

In herbal tradition it has always been customary to use a charm, rune or chant whilst administering healing and medicine. A charm is a short verse said softly to enhance the healing effects of the herbs, but it can also refer to an object specially prepared for a magical purpose; a rune is always a spoken or written form of incantation; and a chant is more usually a kind of rustic prayer. In my opinion, all three are a kind of prayer, even though, if any are performed to override a person's free will, the supplication is certainly to a negative deity.

The ancient mystery schools taught that energy follows thought, and this is another useful aspect of charms. You are making a channel with your own positive thought for the healing essence to flow through, and so more readily reach your patient; the charm is also a prayer to the spirits of nature, the healing angels and to the Divine Spirit; and so the use of charms, as long as they are not used to break spiritual law, can be considered beneficial. I have always found them so, and in case you would like to bring a touch of traditional magic to your herbal healing, I have included some here for your use. Of course, you can make up your own instead, if you prefer. It is interesting to remember that there are in existence actual photographs showing the results of the blessing given by a priest to a cup of water. After the blessing had been given, a number of distinct white crosses were seen, as if engraved on the water, on the developed photographs. Charms, runes and chants, then, are forms of blessing, and, as the photographs indicate, can actually be digested by your cat!

An old charm to be recited whilst applying herbal treatment for eczema and other skin complaints (possibly salvaged and Christianised from pagan times), runs as follows:

As Christ was a-walking
He saw the Virgin Mary sitting on a cold marble stone.
He said unto her,
'If it is a white ill thing,
Or a red ill thing,
Or a black ill thing,
Or a sticking, crackling, pricking, stabbing,
Bone ill thing, or a sore ill thing,
Or a swelling ill thing, or a rotten ill thing,
Or a cold creeping ill thing, or a smarting ill thing,
Let it fall from thee to the Earth in My name,
And the name of the Father, Son and Holy Spirit,
    Amen.'

A healing rune that can be used generally comes from the Hebrides:

The shield of Michael is over you,
King of the bright angels,
To shield you and to circle you
From your summit to your soul.

Here is a herb-gathering rune from the same source:

I will pluck the —
Under the white sun of Sunday
Under the kindly hand of Mary
And she safeguarding me
In the power of the Trinity.

This little rune is specifically for the gathering of St John's wort:

By the Three on high,
By the Three at hand,
By the Three with no end,
Plantlet of Columba,
I gather you now,
I gather you now.

And for figwort:

I will pluck the figwort
With the fullness of sea and land,
At the flow and not the ebb-tide, [of the moon]
With your hand, Mary mild.
The kindly Columba guiding me,
The good Oran protecting me,
And Brigid of generous women
Blessing me and my gathering.

The Celtic blessing is beautifully soothing for a cat agitated and in pain:

Deep peace of the running wave to you,
Deep peace of the flowing air to you,
Deep peace of the quiet earth to you,
Deep peace of the shining stars to you,
Deep peace of the Son of Peace to you.

Charm to mend broken bones, and to take away the pain:

Blessings on your skull,
With holy secrets it is full,
Let it smile on these bones
Precious as earth's stones.
Let it bless these bones
And hush your groans;
Let it work the spell
To knit these bones and make them well.
Blessings, blessings on your skull,
With holy secrets it is full.

Charms for a burn or a scald:

There came three angels from out of the East
One brought fire and two brought frost;
Out fire, in frost,
In the Name of the Father, Son and Holy Ghost.

Great Mother of All, who brings the rain,
Put out this fire, put out this pain.

I would like to bring this book to a close with the simple
Wisewoman's Blessing:

**Blessings be on your herb-healing and charm-chanting,
and on all the facets of your healing craft.**

Appendices

FOLK NAMES OF PLANTS

Agrimony, liverwort, sticklewort, cockleburr, *Agrimonia eupatoria*

Aloe, *Aloe vera* (W. Indies)

American valerian, lady's slipper, noah's ark, nerveroot, *cypripedium pubescens*

Arrowroot, *Maranta arundinacea* (W. Indies and tropical America)

Ash, *Fraxinus excelsior*

Balm, lemon balm, honey plant, bee balm, cure-all, *Melissa officinalis*

Bayberry, candleberry, wax myrtle, *Myrica cerifera*

Benedict's herb, herb bennet, avens, wood avens, goldy star of the earth, blessed herb, *Geum urbanum*

Bilberry, whortleberry, blaeberry, huckleberry, *Vaccinium myrtillus*

Bistort, snakeweed, dragonwort, *Polygonum bistorta*

Bittersweet, waxwork, *Celastrus scandens* (N. America)

Black cohosh, black snakeroot, bugbane, rattleweed, squawroot, *Cimicifuga racemosa*

Blackcurrant, *Ribes nigrum*

Bladderwrack (*see* Kelp)

Blood root, *Sanguinaria canadensis* (N. America)

Blue flag, iris, snake lily, liver lily, *Iris vulgaris*

Bogbean, buckbean, marsh trefoil, *Menyanthes trifoliata*

Boneset, thoroughwort, Indian sage, *Eupatorium perfoliatum*

Borage, common bugloss, bee-plant, star flower, bee bread, *Borago officinalis*

Buckthorn, *Rhamnus cathartica*

Burdock, thorny burr, beggar's buttons, *Arctium lappa*

Butterbur, bog rhubarb, *Petasites hybridus*

Calamus, sweet flag, sweet sedge, *Acorus calamus*

Calendula (*see* Marigold)

Camomile, common matricary, *Matricaria chamomilla*

Candytuft, *Iberis* spp.

Cascara sagrada, sacred bark, *Rhamnus purshiana* (N. America)

Catnip, catmint, *Nepeta cataria*

Cayenne, bird pepper, guinea pepper, *Capsicum minimum* (S. America)

Centaury, feverwort, *Erythraea centaurium*

Chervil, salad chervil, *Anthriscus cerefolium*

Chickweed, starweed, *Stellaria media*

Chicory, succory, endive, *Cichorium intybus*

Chrysanthemum, *Chrysanthemum cinerariaefolium*, also C. *roseum, Pyrethrum roseum* and *P. carneum*

Cinnamon, *Cinnamomum zeylanicum* (Ceylon)

Cinquefoil (*see* Tormentil)

Cleavers, goosegrass, sticky willie, hayriffe, goosebill, *Galium aparine*

Colombo root, *Jateorrhiza palmata* (E. Africa)

Coltsfoot, the Son before the Father, coughwort, foal's foot, horse hoof, *Tussilago farfara*

Comfrey, knitbone, healing herb, bruisewort, blackwort, wallwort, gum plant *Symphytum officinale*

Common club moss, stag's horn club moss, ground pine, *Lycopodium clavatum*

Coriander, *Coriandrum sativum*

Cornflower, bachelor's button, bluebottle, *Centaurea cyanis*

Corn silk (*see* Indian corn)

Cotton lavender, *Santolina chamaecyparissus*

Couchgrass, twitchgrass, *Elymus repens*

Cowslip, paigle, keys of heaven, fairy cup, butter rose, *Primula veris*

Dandelion, field marigold, blow ball, lion's tooth, cankerwort, wet-a-bed, *Taraxacum officinale*

Dill, *Anethum graveolens*

Elder, *Sambucus nigra*

Elm, *Ulmus campestris*

Eucalyptus, blue gum tree, *Eucalyptus globulus*

Eyebright, *Euphrasia officinalis*

Fennel, hinojo, *Foeniculum vulgare*

Feverfew, featherfoil, *Chrysanthemum parthenium*

Figwort, rosenoble, throatwort, carpenter's square, *Scrophularia nodosa*

Fleabane, prideweed, *Erigeron canadense*

Fumitory, earth smoke, *Fumaria officinalis*

Garlic, *Allium sativum*

Gentian, *Gentiana campestris* and others

Geranium, *Geranium dissectum, G. maculatum*

Ginger, *Zingiber officinale* (W. Indies)

Golden rod, *Solidago virgaurea*

Golden seal, orange root, yellow puccoon, ground raspberry, *Hydrastis canadensis* (N. America)

Greater celandine, swallow wort, *Chelidonium majus*

Ground ivy, Gill-go-over-the-ground, alehoof, haymaids, *Glechoma hederacea*

Groundsel, *Senecio vulgaris*

Guaiacum, *Guaiacum officinale* (S. America)

Gum catechu, *Catechu pallidum* (Malaya)

Gum myrrh, *Commiphora molmol* (N. E. Africa and Arabia)

Hartstongue, *Scolopendrium vulgare*

Hawthorn, may bush, *Crataegus oxycantha*

Heartsease (*see* Pansy)

Heather, ling, *Erica vulgaris*

Hogweed, cow parsnip, *Heracleum sphondylium*

Honeysuckle, *Lonicera pericylmenum*

Horehound, *Marrubium vulgare*

Horseradish, *Cochlearia armoracia*

Horsetail, bottlebrush, shave grass, mare's tail, pewter grass, paddock pipes, *Equisetum arvense*

Hyssop, *Hyssopus officinalis*

Iceland moss, *Cetraria islandica*

Indian corn, ornamental maize, sweet corn, *Zea mays*

Ipecacuanha, *Cephaelis ipecacuanha* (S. America)

Irish moss, *Chondrus crispus*

Job's tears, *Coix lacryma Jobi* (grass, Asia)

Kelp, bladderwrack, cutweed, *Fucus vesiculosus*

Lady's bedstraw, maid's hair, cheese rennet, pettimugget, *Galium verum*

Lady's mantle, lion's foot, *Alchemilla vulgaris*

Lavender, spikenard, *Lavandula officinalis*

Lily-of-the-valley, May lily, *Convallaria majalis*

Lime, *Tilia europoea*

Linseed, flax seed, *Linum usitatissimum*

Liquorice, *Glycyrrhiza glabra*

Lobelia, Indian tobacco plant, pukeweed, *Lobelia inflata* (N. America)

Loosestrife, *Lysimachia vulgaris*

Lungwort, sage of Bethlehem, *Pulmonaria officinalis*

Male fern, *Dryopteris filix-mas*

Mallow, common mallow, blue mallow, high mallow, cheese flower, *Malva sylvestris*

Marigold, calendula, pot marigold, summer's bride, Marybud, holigold, *Calendula officinalis*

Marjoram, *Origanum vulgare*

Marshmallow, sweet weed, wymote, guimauve, *Althaea officinalis*

Meadowsweet, queen-of-the-meadow, *Filipendula ulmaria*

Mint, *Mentha viridis*

Mistletoe, all heal, devil's fuge, bird lime, *Viscum album*

Mouse-ear, hawkweed, *Hieracium pilosella*

Mullein, Aaron's rod, blanket herb, lady's foxglove, *Verbascum thapsus*

Mustard, *Brassica nigra* and *B. alba*

Nasturtium, *Tropaeolum majus*

Oak, tanner's bark, *Quercus robur*

Pansy, heartsease, Johnny jump-up, love-in-idleness, *Viola tricolor*

Parsley, carum, *Petroselinum crispum*

Pennyroyal, *Mentha pulegium*

Peony, piney, *Paeonia officinalis*

Peppermint, brandy mint, *Mentha piperita*

Periwinkle, *Vinca minor*

Peruvian bark, *Cinchona succiruba* (S. America)

Pheasant's eye, false hellebore, Adonis, *Adonis vernalis*

Plantain, ribwort, snake plantain, Jack Straw, slan-lus, waybread, *Plantago lanceolata*

Polypody root, female fern, brake root, rock brake, *Polypodium vulgare*

Poppy, corn rose, *Papaver rhoeas*

Prickly ash, toothache tree, *Zanthoxylum americanum* (N. America)

Pumpkin, *Cucurbita maxima*

Quassia, bitter wood, bitter ash, *Picraena excelsa* (W. Indies)

Queen's delight, *Stillingia sylvatica*

Raspberry, *Rubus idaeus*

Red clover, trefoil, *Trifolium pratense*

Redcurrant, *Ribes rubrum*

Red Jamaica sarsaparilla, *Smilax officinalis*, *S. ornata* (Central America)

Reed, common reed, *Arundo phragmites* and others

Rest-harrow, petty whin, cammock, stay plough, *Ononis spinosa*

Rock rose, *Helianthemum chamaecistus*

Rosemary, moorwort, *Rosmarinus officinalis*

Rue, herb of grace, herbygrass, *Ruta graveolens*

Sage, red sage, *Salvia officinalis*

Sanicle, wood sanicle, black snakeroot, *Sanicula europaea*

Sarsaparilla, bamboo brier, *Smilax aristolochiaefolia* (N. America)

Sassafras, *Sassafras variifolium* (N. America)

Senega, *Polygala senega* (N. America)

Senna, *Cassia angustifolia* and *C. senna* (S. Arabia and India)

Shepherd's purse, witches' pouches, pick-pocket, shepherd's heart, *Capsella bursa-pastoris*

Skullcap, madweed, quaker bonnet, *Scutellaria galericulata*

Skunk cabbage, skunkweed, meadow cabbage, polecatweed, *Symplocarpus foetidus* (N. America)

Slippery elm, moose elm, oohooska, *Ulmus fulva* (N. America)

Small-flowered willowherb, *Epilobium parviflorum*

Sorrel, *Rumex acetosa*

Spearmint, *Mentha viridis*

Speedwell, heath speedwell, fluellen, *Veronica officinalis*

Squash, *Cucurbita* (gourd, N. America)

St John's wort, all-saints-wort, *Hypericum perforatum*

Stinging nettle, *Urtica dioica*

Sweet basil, St Josephwort, *Ocimum basilicum*

Tansy, *Tanacetum vulgare*

Thistle, milk thistle, *Silybum marianum*, also Compositae family

Thyme, *Thymus vulgaris*

Tormentil, cinquefoil, *Potentilla erecta*

Turkey rhubarb, *Rheum palmatum* (China)

Valerian, St George's herb, vandal root, setwall, *Valeriana officinalis*

Vervain, *Verbena officinalis*

Violet, *Viola odorata*

Walnut, *Juglans regia*

Watercress, *Nasturtium officinale*

White rose, *Rosa rugosa alba* and other white garden varities

Wild cherry, Virginian prune, *Prunus serotina* (N. America)

Wild garlic, ramsons, *Allium ursinum*

Wild rose, *Rosa canina, R. gallica* and others

Wild strawberry, *Fragaria vesca*

Wild yam, *Dioscorea villosa* (S. America)

Willow, *Salix alba*

Witch hazel, spotted alder, winter bloom, *Hamamelis virginiana* (N. America)

Wood betony, bishopswort, *Stachys betonica*

Wood sorrel, *Oxalis acetosella*

Woodruff, waldmeister tea, *Asperula odorata*

Wormwood, old woman, *Artemisia absinthium*

Yarrow, milfoil, soldier's woundwort, *Achillea millefolium*

Yellow deadnettle, yellow archangel, *Lamium galeobdolon*

Yellow dock, *Rumex crispus*

BOTANICAL NAMES OF PLANTS

Achillea millefolium, yarrow,
milfoil, soldier's woundwort
Acorus calamus, calamus, sweet
flag, sweet sedge
Adonis vernalis, pheasant's eye,
false hellebore, Adonis
Agimonia eupatoria, agrimony,
liverwort, sticklewort,
cockleburr
Alchemilla vulgaris, lady's mantle,
lion's foot
Allium sativum, garlic
Allium ursinum, wild Garlic,
ramsons
Aloe vera, aloe (W. Indies)
Althaea officinalis, Marshmallow,
sweet weed, wymote, guimauve
Anethum graveolens, dill
Anthriscus cerefolium, chervil,
salad chervil
Arctium lappa, burdock, thorny
burr, beggar's buttons
Artemisia absinthium, wormwood,
old woman
Arundo phragmites reed, common
reed
Asperula odorata, woodruff,
waldmeister tea
Borago officinalis, borage,
common bugloss, bee-plant, star
flower, bee bread
Brassica alba, B. nigra, mustard
Calendula officinalis, marigold,
calendula, pot marigold,
summer's bride, Marybud,
holigold
Capsella bursa-pastoris, shepherd's
purse, witches' pouches,
pick-pocket, shepherd's heart
Capsicum minimum, cayenne, bird
pepper, guinea pepper (S.
America)
Cassia angustifolia, C. senna,
senna (S. Arabia and India)
Catechu pallidum, gum catechu
(Malaya)
Celastrus scandens, bittersweet,
waxwork (N. America)

Centaurea cyanis, cornflower,
bachelor's button, bluebottle
Cephaelis ipecacuahna,
ipecacuanha (S. America)
Cetraria islandica, Iceland moss
Chelidonium majus, great
celandine, swallow wort
Chondrus crispus, Irish moss
*Chrysanthemum cinerariaefolium,
C. roseum*, chrysanthemum
Chrysanthemum parthenium,
feverfew, featherfoil
Cichorium intybus, chicory,
succory, endive
Cimicifuga racemosa, black
cohosh, black snakeroot,
bugbane, rattleweed, squawroot
Cinchona succiruba, Peruvian
bark (S. America)
Cinnamomum zeylanicum,
cinnamon (Ceylon)
Cochlearia armoracia, horseradish
Coix lacryma Jobi, Job's tears
(grass, Asia)
Commiphora molmol, gum myrrh
(N.E. Africa and Arabia)
Convallaria majalis,
lily-of-the-valley, May lily
Coroiandrum sativum, coriander
Crataegus oxycantha, hawthorn,
may bush
Cucurbita, squash (gourd, N.
America)
Cucurbita maxima, pumpkin
Cypripedium pubescens, American
valerian, lady's slipper, Noah's
ark, nerveroot
Dioscorea villosa, wild yam (S.
America)
Dryopteris filix-mas, male fern
Elymus repens, couchgrass,
twitchgrass
Epilobium parviflorum,
small-flowered willowherb
Equisetum arvense horsetail,
bottlebrush, shave grass, mare's
tail, pewter grass, paddock
pipes

Erica vulgaris, heather, ling
Erigeron canadense, fleabane, prideweed
Erythraea centaurium, centaury, feverwort
Eucalyptus globulus, eucalyptus, blue gum tree
Eupatorium perfoliatum, boneset, thoroughwort, Indian sage
Euphrasia officinalis, eyebright
Filipendula ulmaria, meadowsweet, queen-of-the meadow
Foeniculum vulgare, fennel, hinojo
Fragaria vesca, wild strawberry
Fraxinus excelsior, ash
Fucus vesiculosus, kelp, bladderwrack, cutweed
Fumaria officinalis, fumitory, earth smoke
Galium aparine, cleavers, goosegrass, sticky willie, hayriffe, goosebill
Galium verum, lady's bedstraw, maid's hair, cheese rennet, pettimugget
Gentiana campestris, gentian
Geranium dissectum, G. maculatum, geranium
Geum urbanum, Benedict's herb, herb bennet, avens, wood avens, goldy star of the earth, blessed herb
Glechoma hederacea, ground Ivy, Gill-go-over-the-ground, alehoof, haymaids
Glycyrrhiza glabra, liquorice
Guaiacum officinale, guaiacum (S. America)
Hamamelis virginiana, witch hazel, spotted alder, winter bloom (N. America)
Helianthemum chamaecistus, rock rose
Heracleum sphondylium, hog weed, cow parsnip
Hieracium pilosella, mouse-ear, hawkweed
Hydrastis canadensis, golden seal, orange root, yellow puccoon,

ground raspberry (N. America)
Hypericum perforatum, St John's wort, all-saints-wort
Hyssopus officinalis hyssop
Iberis, candytuft
Iris vulgaris, blue flag, iris, snake lily, liver lily
Jateorrhiza palmata, Colombo root (E. Africa)
Juglans regia, walnut
Lamium galeobdolon, yellow deadnettle, yellow archangel
Lavandula officinalis, lavender, spikenard
Linum usitatissimum, linseed, flax seed
Lobelia inflata lobelia, Indian tobacco plant, pukeweed (N. America)
Lonicera periclymenum, honeysuckle
Lycopodium clavatum, common club moss, stag's horn club moss, ground pine
Lysimachia vulgaris, loosestrife
Malva sylvestris, mallow, common mallow, blue mallow, high mallow, cheese flower
Maranta arundinacea, arrowroot (W. Indies and Tropical America)
Marrubium vulgare, horehound
Matricaria chamomilla, camomile, common matricary
Melissa officinalis, balm, lemon balm, honey plant, bee balm, cure-all
Mentha piperita, peppermint, brandy mint
Mentha pulegium, pennyroyal
Mentha viridis, mint, spearmint
Menyanthes trifoliata, bogbean, buckbean, marsh trefoil
Myrica cerifera, bayberry, candleberry, wax myrtle
Nasturtium officinale, watercress
Nepeta cataria, catnip, catmint
Ocimum basilicum, sweet basil, St Josephwort
Ononis spinosa, rest-harrow, petty whin, cammock, stay plough

Origanum vulgare, marjoram
Oxalis acetosella, wood sorrel
Paeonia officinalis, peony, piney
Papaver rhoeas, poppy, corn rose
Petasites hybridus, butterbur, bog rhubarb
Petroselinum crispum, parsley
Picraena excelsa, quassia, bitter wood, bitter ash (W. Indies)
Plantago lanceolata, plantain, ribwort, snake plantain, Jack Straw, slan-lus, waybread
Polygala senega, senega (N. America)
Polygonum bistorta, bistort, snakeweed, dragonwort
Polypodium vulgare, polypody root, female fern, brake root, rock brake
Potentilla erecta, tormentil, cinquefoil
Primula veris, cowslip, paigle, keys of heaven, fairy cup, butter rose
Prunus serotina wild cherry, Virginian prune (N. America)
Pulmonaria officinalis, lungwort, sage of Bethlehem
Pyrethrum carneum, P. roseum, chrysanthemum
Quercus robur, oak, tanner's bark
Rhamnus cathartica, buckthorn
Rhamnus purshiana, cascara sagrada, sacred bark (N. America)
Rheum palmatum, Turkey rhubarb (China)
Ribes rubrum, redcurrant
Ribes nigrum, blackcurrant
Rosa canina, R. gallica, wild rose
Rosa rugosa alba, white rose
Rosmarinus officinalis, rosemary, moorwort
Rubus idaeus, raspberry
Rumex acetosa, sorrel
Rumex crispus, yellow dock
Ruta graveolens, rue, herb of grace, herbygrass
Salix alba, willow

Salvia officinalis, sage, red sage
Sambucus nigra, elder
Sanguinaria canadensis, blood root (N. America)
Sanicula europaea, sanicle, wood sanicle, black snakeroot
Santolina chamaecyparissus, cotton lavender
Sassafras variifolium, sassafras (N. America)
Scolopendrium vulgare, hartstongue
Scrophularia nodosa, figwort, rosenoble, throatwort, carpenter's square
Scutellaria galericulata, skullcap, madweed, quaker bonnet
Senecio vulgaris, groundsel
Silybum marianum, milk thistle
Smilax artistolochiaefolia, sarsaparilla, bamboo brier (N. America)
Smilax officinalis, S. ornata red Jamaica sarsaparilla (Central America)
Solidago virgaurea, golden rod
Stachys betonica, wood betony, bishopswort
Stellaria media, chickweed, starweed
Stillingia sylvatica, queen's delight
Symphytum officinale, comfrey, knitbone, healing herb, bruisewort, blackwort, wallwort, gum plant
Symplocarpus foetidus, skunk cabbage, skunkweed, meadow cabbage, polecatweed (N. America)
Tanacetum vulgare, tansy
Taraxacum officinale, dandelion, field marigold, blow ball, lion's tooth, cankerwort, wet-a-bed
Thymus vulgaris, thyme
Tilia europoea, lime
Trifolium pratense, red clover, trefoil
Tropaeolum majus, nasturtium
Tussilago farfara, coltsfoot, the Son before the Father,

coughwort, foal's foot, horse hoof

Ulmus campestris, elm

Ulmus fulva, slippery elm, moose elm, oohooska (N. America)

Urtica dioica stinging nettle

Vaccinium myrtillus, bilberry, blaeberry, whortleberry, huckleberry

Valeriana officinalis, valerian, St George's herb, vandal root, setwall

Verbascum thapsus, mullein, Aaron's rod, blanket herb, lady's foxglove

Verbena officinalis, vervain

Veronica officinalis, speedwell, heath speedwell, fluellen

Vinca minor, periwinkle

Viola odorata, violet

Viola tricolor, pansy, heartsease, Johnny jump-up, love-in-idleness

Viscum album, mistletoe, all heal, devil's fuge, bird lime

Zanthoxylum americanum, prickly ash, toothache tree (N. America)

Zea mays, Indian corn, ornamental maize, sweet corn

Zingiber officinale, Ginger (W. Indies)

Useful Addresses

The United Kingdom
Bach Remedies:
Dr Edward Bach Centre, Mount Vernon, Bakers Lane, Sotwell, Wallingford, Oxfordshire OX10 0PZ.

Tel: 01491 834678. Fax: 01491 825022
Email: info@bachcentre.com
Website: www.bachcentre.com

Remedies can be ordered by mail from the Bach Centre—Dr Bach's legacy and former home, where he discovered and prepared the bulk of his remedies.

Crystals:
Angel Mail Order, 62 West Bradford Road, Waddington, Clitheroe, Lancashire BB7 3JD.

Email: info@iacht.co.uk
Website: www.iacht.co.uk

Angel supply inexpensive, quality crystals.

Herbal suppliers:
G. Baldwin & Co., 171–173 Walworth Road, London SE17 1RW.

Tel: 0207 703 5550. Fax: 0207 252 6264
Email: sales@baldwins.co.uk
Website: www.baldwins.co.uk

Baldwins are a general mail-order herbalist who will supply small quantities. They are also the only UK suppliers of

Swedish bitters, both ready made and in a DIY kit. Maria Treben's book Health Through God's Pharmacy *is also available through Baldwins.*

Neal's Yard Remedies, 15 Neal's Yard, Covent Garden, London WC2H 9DP.

Tel: 0207 379 7222. Fax: 0207 379 0705

Phyto Products, Park Works, Park Road, Mansfield Woodhouse, Nottinghamshire NG19 8EF.

Tel: 01623 644334. Fax: 01623 657232
Email: info@phyto.co.uk
Website: www.phyto.co.uk

Phyto Products supply herbal tinctures, which are excellent for storage against times of crisis—use five drops of tincture per dose, except for blood root, lobelia, wormwood and rue, when only two drops should be used. The company is headed by a practising medical herbalist.

Potters (Herbal Supplies) Ltd, Leyland Mill Lane, Wigan, Lancashire WN1 2SB.

Tel: 01942 405100. Fax: 01942 820255
Email: info@pottersherbal.co.uk
Website: www.pottersherbal.co.uk

Herbs:
Chase Organics, Riverdene, Molesey Road, Hersham, Surrey KT12 4RG.

Tel: 01932 253666. Fax: 01932 252707
Email:chaseorg@aol.com

Excellent seed and general supplier, specialising in organics. Allied to the Henry Doubleday Research Organisation (HDRA) who receive a percentage of all sales. Mail order catalogue.

Landlife Wildflowers Ltd, National Wildflower Centre, Court Hey Park, Liverpool L16 3NA.

Tel: 0151 737 1819. Fax: 0151 737 1820
Email: info@landlife.u-net.com
Website: www.merseyworld.comlandlife

Landlife is a registered charity taking action for a better environment by creating new opportunities for wildlife. They are currently creating a National Wildflower Centre. Landlife is also working to bring wildlife and wild flowers into the lives of city people—especially children. Both seeds and plants are available by mail order.

Suffolk Herbs, Monks Farm, Pantlings Lane, Coggeshall Road, Kelvedon, Colchester, Essex CO5 9PG.

Tel: 01376 572456. Fax: 01376 571189
Email: suffolkherbs@btinternet.com

Seed and general supplier with many otherwise hard-to-get varieties. Mail order catalogue.

The USA
Suppliers of Herbal Medicines:
Ethical Nutrients, 21020 N. Rand Road, #AB, Lake Zurich, IL 60074-3942.

Gaia Herbs, 62 Old Littleton Road, Harvard, MA 01451.

Herb-Pharm, 347 East Fork Road, Williams, OR 97544.

Herbs Etc., 1340 Rufina Circle, Santa Fe, NM 87501.

Kiehls Pharmacy, 109 Third Avenue, New York, NY 10009.

Nature's Way Products Inc., 10 Mountain Springs Parkway, PO Box 2233, Springville, UT 84663.

Planetary Formulas, PO Box 533, Soquel, CA 95073.

Canada
Herbal Medicine Associations:
Canadian Association of Herbal Practitioners, 921, 17th Avenue Southwest, Calgary, Alta., T2T OA4.

Ontario Herbalists Association, 11 Winthrop Place, Stony Creek, Ont. L8G 3M3.

Suppliers of Herbal Medicines:
Gaia Garden Herbal Apothecary (and mail order), 2672 West Broadway, Vancouver BC, V6K 2G3.

Herboristerie Desjardins Inc., 3383 St Catherine Street East, Montreal, Que., H1W 2C5.

International Herbs Co., 31 St Andrews, Toronto, Ont., M5T 1K7.

Australia
Herbal Medicine Association:
National Herbalists Association of Australia, Suite 305, 3 Smail Street, Broadway, NSW 2007.

Suppliers of Herbal Medicines:
MediHerb Pty Ltd., 124 McEvoy St, Warwick, QLD 4370.

Southern Cross Herbals (and mail order), 66 William Street, Gosford, NSW 2250.

Guide to UK/US Measures

All measurements given in *The Cat Herbal* are **British** (cup measures follow the BSI standard; if using teacups halve the dosage). Please follow the conversion guide below when preparing herbs.

UK Measures

1 pint = 20 fluid ounces = 568ml
1 fluid ounce = 28.4ml
1 litre = 1.76 pints = 3⅓ cups
1 cup = 300ml, 10 fluid ounces (liquid): 200g, 8 ounces (dry)
1 teaspoon = 5ml
1 tablespoon = 15ml
1 pound = 16 ounces = 453.592g
1 ounce = 0.0625 pounds = 28.3495g

UK measures	US equivalent measures
1 pint	3 cups
1 fluid ounce	1.2 fl oz
1 litre	4.5 cups
1 cup	20 tbsp or 1.2 cups
1 teaspoon	1.25 tsp
1 tablespoon	1.5 tbsp
1 pound	1 pound
1 ounce	1 ounce

GENERAL INDEX

INDEX OF AILMENTS